Law Enforcement Strategies for Disrupting Cryptomarkets

Vincent Harinam • Barak Ariel

Law Enforcement Strategies for Disrupting Cryptomarkets

A Practical Guide to Network Structure, Trust Dynamics, and Agent-Based Modelling Approaches

 Springer

Vincent Harinam
Independent Researcher
Mournival Applied Research
Calgary, AB, Canada

Barak Ariel
The Hebrew University of Jerusalem
Jerusalem, Israel

University of Cambridge
Cambridge, UK

ISBN 978-3-031-62823-8   ISBN 978-3-031-62821-4   (eBook)
https://doi.org/10.1007/978-3-031-62821-4

This Springer imprint is published by the registered company Springer Nature Switzerland AG
The registered company address is: Gewerbestrasse 11, 6330 Cham, Switzerland

If disposing of this product, please recycle the paper.

Contents

List of Figures

List of Tables

Chapter 1
Introduction

Introduction

Gone are the days when prospective consumers relied solely on local dealers to procure drugs and other illicit goods and services. The advent of digital encryption and Internet connectivity has facilitated the rise of cryptomarkets. Similar in function to Amazon or eBay, cryptomarkets are illicit online marketplaces hosted on the dark web that facilitate the exchange of illegal goods and services. Much like licit online markets, cryptomarkets allow those who wish to purchase illicit goods and services to do so from the comfort of their own homes, placing their order with a vendor and receiving the product through the postal service. Whether it be marijuana, cocaine, bladed implements or hitmen, these platforms are replete with a variety of illicit wares. Cryptomarkets represent a unique context: They facilitate traditional criminal dynamics and introduce new challenges for law enforcement. Moreover, these platforms present a novel opportunity for researchers to test the accuracy of key theoretical precepts applied to terrestrial markets.

Law enforcement agencies have often lagged behind criminal entities, especially in key areas such as cyber and finance (Curtis & Oxburgh, 2022). There are clear challenges posed by the emergence of cybercrimes, but police (and law enforcement) responses to these challenges have so far been limited. The police, as a social institution, are ill-equipped to manage cryptomarkets. In general, national or elite departments handle these illicit markets—which implies that only specialised law enforcement agents are capable and have the capacity to put a dent in this growing area of criminal business. The challenges to law enforcement are all too clear: International criminals that act outside jurisdictional boundaries, state actors with unlimited resources, technology-savvy organised crime groups, small and under-funded anti-cybercrime units and a lack of fundamental training in digital forensics are just some of the barriers to the effective police response to cybercrime in general and cryptomarkets more specifically (Giommoni et al., 2024). The Silk Road and

© The Author(s), under exclusive license to Springer Nature Switzerland AG 2024   1
V. Harinam, B. Ariel, *Law Enforcement Strategies for Disrupting Cryptomarkets*,
https://doi.org/10.1007/978-3-031-62821-4_1

other darknet platforms earned billions before law enforcement brought them down (Dolliver, 2015). The regulation of initial cryptocurrency coin offerings—an area where fraud is prevalent (Tiwari et al., 2020)—and the regulation of binary options trading in which many innocent investors lost their money due to scams (Lacey et al., 2020) both emerged many years after scammers made billions of dollars off innocent investors. More recently, it was revealed that North Korean hackers allegedly stole hundreds of millions in crypto to fund nuclear programmes (Chiang, 2023), many years after the fact.

This book endeavours to push the cryptomarket literature beyond its present methodological limits by documenting the network structure of a cryptomarket and measuring the efficacy of targeted strategies on the transactional network of a cryptomarket. To this end, a combination of social network analysis and agent-based modelling is employed to build the transactional network structure of a cryptomarket and simulate its disruption through sequential node deletion. The overarching aim of this book is threefold. First, all cryptomarket interventions by law enforcement to date are documented and evaluated, providing a breakdown of their evolution and overall efficacy. Second, social network analysis and agent-based modelling will be presented as useful tools for police practitioners and crime researchers when measuring the impact of disruptive interventions to counter criminal networks. Third, the findings herein are used to inform targeted interventions by law enforcement against cryptomarkets. Past law enforcement strategies targeting cryptomarkets have been ineffective and, in some cases, counterproductive (Soska & Christin, 2015; Decary-Hetu & Giommoni, 2017; Van Buskirk et al., 2017). As such, this book explicitly focuses on adaptive simulations and the efficacy of law enforcement interventions. It aims to offer some insight into how law enforcement might structure their cryptomarket intervention strategies to achieve maximum long-term disruptive impact.

Book Structure and Chapter Overview

This book is divided into six chapters, with Chaps. 1 and 6 serving as the introductory and concluding chapters. Chapter 2 is an up-to-date summary of the extant cryptomarket literature, drawing upon a vast swathe of studies across a decade of research. No research questions are posed or analyses conducted in this chapter. The objective of this chapter is to define cryptomarkets and situate these illicit platforms within the cybercrime and organised crime contexts. A secondary objective is to take stock of the present state of cryptomarket research, tracking major scholarly themes across a decade of research. In short, an extensive overview of key themes within the cryptomarket literature is conducted. This provides a strong foundation for those new to the subject of cryptomarkets while also providing new insights to those who are well acquainted with the topic. Furthermore, one overarching benefit of conducting a state-of-the-art literature review is that substantive gaps in the literature can be identified.

Chapter 3 explores the various actions taken by law enforcement organisations against cryptomarkets as well as their measurable impact on the dark web ecosystem thereafter. This chapter delves into how law enforcement understands and engages in interventions against cryptomarkets, how actors on the dark web adjust their operations against disruptions and the implications of this dynamic on the overall dark web ecosystem in the interim and in the long term. Law enforcement's fragmentation of the dark web ecosystem and the inadvertent improvements to criminal efficiency post-intervention are discussed herein.

Chapter 4 seeks to disentangle trust dynamics in a dark web market, uncovering the processes by which trust is created and maintained and how this ultimately affects the network structure of the market. To this end, a battery of statistical analyses is applied to a cryptomarket transactional network to understand how trust is formed among buyers and vendors and how vendors create a lasting reputation on the platform. In addition, the aim is to understand the determinants of a buyer's decision to purchase on a cryptomarket and why specific vendors are chosen over others. Understanding the structural dynamics and transactional mechanisms between vendors and buyers is a pivotal first step in disrupting the ease of operation of a cryptomarket.

Finally, Chap. 5 examines the theoretical and practical elements of agent-based modelling (ABM) as a methodological and strategic tool to inform interventions against criminal organisations and networks. This chapter begins by explaining the intricacies and aims of agent-based modelling and then examines practical ABM use cases in various domains, with a special focus on law enforcement and criminal justice. This chapter also delves into the intricacies of designing an agent-based model. More specifically, a model which tests the effectiveness of several law enforcement strategies against a criminal network is designed, covering each of the necessary steps in this process. Finally, the results of the constructed agent-based model are examined, with the implications for law enforcement interventions being explained.

Data and Methodological Overview

This analysis in this book relies on a buyer-seller dataset from the Abraxas cryptomarket (Branwen et al., 2015). Apart from the anonymous cryptomarket analysed by Duxbury and Haynie (2017), this is the only marketplace where unique identifiers are available for buyers. As such, it was the only known publicly available dataset which allowed for network analysis and adaptive computer simulation. With assistance from Lukas Norbutas of Utrecht University and Cambridge University's Computer Laboratory, this data was extracted from a public data repository established by independent researcher, Gwern Branwen. This data repository contains scraped webpages from 2013 to 2015. Given the infrequent nature of the scrapes, not all webpages have been collected. Nevertheless, Norbutas (2018) estimates that crawls of Abraxas have successfully collected 92.4% of all listed items on the

Abraxas cryptomarket. This includes information on the vendor name, vendor shipping location, listing title, listing price, listing description, transaction date, buyer unique identifier, buyer rating and buyer feedback. HTML links in the dataset were stitched together in Python to recreate the Abraxas website. This recreated website serves as a copy of the original Abraxas cryptomarket, with information on transactions that were successfully scraped. Furthermore, each webpage in the dataset was manually inspected to identify duplicate transactions based on the feedback provided.

While buyers may leave feedback on their original post, they may also return to alter the message. As such, extracting data from these webpages could yield duplicate transactions if each transaction is not properly inspected. Once all duplicates had been identified and removed, a total of 5434 transactions over a period of 7 months (January to July) in 2015 remained. These were stored in an Excel spreadsheet. While Abraxas was established in December 2014, the first transaction occurred on 15 January 2015. It is important to note that this dataset does not include all recorded transactions on Abraxas. This is due to both the infrequency of the scrapes conducted by Branwen et al. (2015) and the vast number of broken webpages that could not be repaired and accessed. As such, while this dataset includes numbers sufficient for analysis, it does not include the full cohort of transactions on the cryptomarket. This is a clear limitation. Nevertheless, there were 269 unique sellers and 2794 unique buyers in the dataset. Importantly, the Abraxas dataset was previously used by Norbutas (2018) in an examination of the geographical distribution of transactions. For the purposes of this book, a two-mode buyer-seller trade network is reconstructed. These data were used in Chaps. 4 and 5.

This research uses a combination of statistical methods. In Chap. 4, a combination of descriptive network analysis, community detection analysis, statistical modelling and trajectory modelling is utilised. Descriptive statistics were used to summarise market transactions, so as to better understand both the nature and composition of illicit transactions on Abraxas. In contrast, community detection analysis was used to discern the subgroup structure of this transactional criminal network. In addition, three regression models were used to determine the predictors of vendor trustworthiness. Three proxy variables were created to measure vendor trustworthiness: success, popularity and affluence. As trust is manifested in a variety of ways, each of these dependent variables reflects a key element of trust. Finally, this chapter leverages k-means trajectory modelling to examine the developmental pattern of vendor trustworthiness on Abraxas.

Chapter 5 employs sequential node deletion based on six law enforcement strategies: lead k (degree centrality), eccentricity, unique items bought/sold, cumulative reputation score, total purchase price and random targeting. Five outcome variables (number of isolates, number of components, average number of nodes in components, average geodesic distance and number of nodes in the largest component) are used to measure the impact of each targeting strategy. This study sets parameters to govern the purported behaviour of actors when nodes are removed. As such, the transactional network's overall behaviour can be accurately modelled (Bright et al., 2015) using evidence-based calculus.

Conclusion

As with all applied research examining emergent phenomena, this book seeks to provide a more refined understanding of dark web cryptomarkets. More importantly, the following chapters were conceptualised, developed and written with the sole intent of improving present law enforcement strategies which target cryptomarkets. While the results and conclusions drawn from these results are not perfectly generalisable to all cryptomarkets, they aim to provide law enforcement with a better understanding of the dynamics which undergird these markets. More specifically, trust, network structure and the tactical effectiveness of interventions are important considerations in developing more compelling countermeasures against these illicit online marketplaces. For law enforcement to be more effective against cryptomarkets, it is advised that an evidence-based approach be taken.

References

Branwen, G., Christin, N., Décary-Hétu, D., Andersen, R. M., StExo, El Presidente, Anonymous, Lau, D. Sohhlz, Kratunov, D., Cakic, V., Buskirk, V., McKenna, M., & Goode, S. (2015, July 12). *Dark net market archives, 2011–2015*. https://www.gwern.net/DNM-archives

Chiang, S. (2023, September 5). *North Korean hackers have allegedly stolen hundreds of millions in crypto to fund nuclear programs*. CNBC. https://www.cnbc.com/2023/09/06/north-korea-hackers-stole-crypto-to-fund-nuclear-program-trm-chainalysis.html

Curtis, J., & Oxburgh, G. (2022). Understanding cybercrime in 'real world' policing and law enforcement. *The Police Journal, 96*(4), 573–592. https://doi.org/10.1177/0032258X221107584

Décary-Hétu, D., & Giommoni, L. (2017). Do police crackdowns disrupt drug cryptomarkets? A longitudinal analysis of the effects of operation Onymous. *Crime, Law and Social Change, 67*, 55–75.

Dolliver, D. S. (2015). Evaluating drug trafficking on the tor network: Silk road 2, the sequel. *International Journal of Drug Policy, 26*(11), 1113–1123.

Duxbury, S., & Haynie, D. (2017). The network structure of opioid distribution on a darknet cryptomarket. *Journal of Quantitative Criminology, 34*(4), 921–941.

Giommoni, L., Décary-Hétu, D., Berlusconi, G., & Bergeron, A. (2024). Online and offline determinants of drug trafficking across countries via cryptomarkets. In *Crime, law and social change* (pp. 1–25).

Lacey, D., Goode, S., Pawada, J., & Gibson, D. (2020). The application of scam compliance models to investment fraud offending. *Journal of Criminological Research, Policy and Practice, 6*(1), 65–81.

Norbutas, L. (2018). Offline constraints in online drug marketplaces: An exploratory analysis of a cryptomarket trade network. *International Journal of Drug Policy, 56*, 92–100.

Soska, K., & Christin, N. (2015). *Measuring the longitudinal evolution of the online anonymous marketplace ecosystem* [Conference presentation]. 24th USENIX Security Symposium, Washington, D.C.

Tiwari, M., Gepp, A., & Kumar, K. (2020). The future of raising finance-a new opportunity to commit fraud: A review of initial coin offering (ICOs) scams. *Crime, Law and Social Change, 73*, 417–441.

Van Buskirk, J., Bruno, R., Dobbins, T., Breen, C., Burns, L., Naicker, S., & Roxburgh, A. (2017). The recovery of online drug markets following law enforcement and other disruptions. *Drug and Alcohol Dependence, 173*, 159–162.

Chapter 2
Cryptomarkets: History, Structure and Operations

Introduction

The primary objective of this chapter is to synthesise the existing academic literature on cryptomarkets, examining and elucidating various scholarly contributions to this subject. This chapter will serve as a literature review, summarising the findings from peer-reviewed sources and providing a balanced analysis of cryptomarkets grounded in existing research on cybercrime and organised crime as we know them today. This chapter is comprised of five sections. First, the phenomenon of cybercrime is examined, delving into its inception, evolution and organisation. Next, the origins and overall functioning of cryptomarkets are investigated, focusing on the significance of onion routing and cryptocurrencies. The next section analyses the structural characteristics of cryptomarkets. In this analysis, the hierarchical administrative framework of cryptomarkets is examined as well as the mode of governance and the presence of adaptable exchange networks that are deeply ingrained within these markets. Section "Cryptomarket administration" examines the three main aspects of cryptomarket research: the individuals involved, the nations represented and the products made available on these platforms. Section "The who, what and where of cryptomarkets" examines the significance of trust and reputation within cryptomarkets, elucidating the diverse strategies employed by vendors to cultivate trust among buyers. This chapter will establish a solid basis for examining cryptomarket interventions and their subsequent impact on the dark web ecosystem.

© The Author(s), under exclusive license to Springer Nature Switzerland AG 2024
V. Harinam, B. Ariel, *Law Enforcement Strategies for Disrupting Cryptomarkets*,
https://doi.org/10.1007/978-3-031-62821-4_2

What Is Cybercrime and How Organised Is It?

The prevalence and complexity of cybercrime activities have surged over the past decade (Phillips et al., 2022). Fraudsters utilising email systems to deceive unsuspecting individuals with fraudulent services and schemes aimed at quick financial gain have been observed for a while (Grabosky, 2007; see more recently Woods & Walter, 2022). Additionally, Internet chatrooms and message boards have been identified as platforms where sexual solicitation occurs, sometimes contributing to the facilitation of the global sex trade (Kamar et al., 2022; Farley et al., 2013). The utilisation of social media platforms by young individuals to engage in bullying behaviours towards their peers has also been documented (Kee et al., 2022). Furthermore, the advancement of technology has resulted in entirely novel categories of criminal activities (Sinclair et al., 2023). Computer-assisted offences such as distributed denial of service attacks and malicious software have caused significant economic damage. Law enforcement agencies face new challenges in the field of cybercrime daily.

While a universally accepted definition is lacking, it is widely agreed upon by scholars that cybercrime encompasses the use of computer technology or cyberspace to facilitate criminal and deviant activities (Bossler & Holt, 2016, p. 45). Furthermore, Grabosky (2007)—and more recently Goni (2022)—classifies cybercrime based on three conceptual dimensions: the utilisation of computers as a means of committing crimes, the targeting of computers as objects of criminal activity and the involvement of computers as secondary elements in criminal acts. However, this categorisation is lacking in one aspect. Although the classification system establishes conceptual demarcations, it frequently encounters instances of categorical convergence. To this extent, certain cyber-enabled crimes fall into multiple categories in this definition. For instance, botnets are a clandestine assemblage of privately owned computers that have been compromised by malicious software and are operated collectively without the awareness or consent of their owners, typically to disseminate unsolicited spam messages. These are compromised computers that are manipulated from a remote location, so computers serve as both the means and the subject of the offence (Ianelli & Hackworth, 2005). Thus, defining cybercrime is not as straightforward as for other crime categories such as homicide, burglary or drug-related offences.

Another type of categorisation was offered by Wall (2001), who identified four distinct types of cybercrime: cyber-trespass, cyber-deception, cyber-pornography and cyber-violence. Similar to the act of trespassing in a physical context, cyber-trespass refers to the unauthorised access of a computer system without the explicit consent of its owner. Cyber-deception, the second category, pertains to the illicit utilisation of the Internet to acquire information from individuals or organisations. Significantly, the concepts of cyber-trespass and cyber-deception are intrinsically connected to the practice of hacking. Holt and Bossler (2014) stated that hackers create viruses and botnet codes, instigating automated malicious attacks. They may also actively participate in attacks against computer systems and sensitive networks

(p. 22). The authors argued that hackers should be primarily understood within the framework of criminality and deviance. In contrast, Brewer and Goldsmith (2014) sought to establish hackers' moral and legal adaptability by proposing the concept of *digital drift*. According to the authors, technological advancements have allowed individuals to engage in criminal activities and lifestyles both online and offline (p. 113). Hackers do not consistently engage in illegal activities; instead, they alternate between intermittent periods of engaging in cybercriminal behaviour and adhering to legal norms.

According to Wall (2007), the third category, known as cyber-pornography, pertains to the various forms of sexual expression facilitated by computer-mediated communications and the dissemination of sexually explicit materials through online platforms (p. 32). This category is widely regarded as the most contentious among the four. Online pornography does not inherently constitute an illegal endeavour in most countries, although it has more content than it should (Lewczuk et al. 2021; Lim et al., 2016; however, compare Strossen, 2000) and is strictly controlled given its addictive nature (see de Alarcón et al., 2019). Cyber-pornography is a prominent component of the Internet, accounting for a substantial share of online data transmission. Many are also concerned about the accessibility and consumption of pornography by minors (Carnevali et al., 2022; Livingstone & Helsper, 2010). Cyber-enabled child pornography, revenge pornography and sexual exploitation are offences that are appropriately classified within this category and are considered crimes in most jurisdictions around the globe.

Cyber-violence constitutes the fourth category within Wall's (2001) comprehensive typology of cybercrime. This pertains to behaviours enacted by individuals that cause harm to others in both virtual and physical environments. This typically encompasses cyberstalking, online harassment and cyberbullying (Dooley et al., 2009; Evangelio et al., 2022; Tokunaga, 2010; Wolak et al., 2007). However, there is a significant conceptual issue with this category (for a broader discussion, Olweus & Limber, 2018). Specifically, "violence" does not fully encompass the descriptive nature of offences in this category. In a more precise manner, while violence generally encompasses physical actions resulting in bodily harm, online stalking, harassment and bullying do not inherently involve physical acts. These criminal activities occur in the virtual realm and do not entail physical damage inflicted upon the victim—unless the online and offline worlds intersect. Thus, again, the dynamic nature of cybercrime results in the gradual obsolescence of definitions and categorisations as time progresses.

Distinct Features of Cybercrime

The larger discourse regarding the novelty of cybercrime is of the utmost significance. The question at hand is whether the concept can be characterised as "old wine in new bottles" or "new wine in new bottles" (Grabosky & Smith, 2001; Wall, 2007; Yar, 2005). In other words, can cybercrimes be considered terrestrial crimes that have been transformed, or do they represent a distinct manifestation realised through a different modality? Many criminologists argue that a crime is a crime, and the modern modus operandi through which crime is manifested does not necessitate a new set of theories to explain criminal behaviour. Deterrence theory, routine activities theory and opportunity theory can all be used to define deviancy, offline or online. As a result, Grabosky (2007) believed that the nature of crimes committed in cyberspace is similar to that of crimes committed in a physical environment. To clarify, as with its terrestrial counterparts, the occurrence of cybercrime can be understood through the convergence of three essential elements: a vulnerable target, a perpetrator driven by motivations and the absence of an effective guardian. This is the essence of the routine activities theory of crime proposed by Cohen and Felson (1979), which is applied extensively in the area of cybercrime (e.g., Holt & Bossler, 2008; Leukfeldt & Yar, 2016; Williams et al., 2019).

However, Yar (2005, p. 424) presented a counterargument against applying routine activities theory to cybercrime: There is a notable distinction between the organisation of people, objects and activities in the physical world and their arrangement in the virtual world. These elements are typically within the stable and structured spatiotemporal configurations of the physical world, and their organisation becomes less stable in the virtual world. Therefore, applying the principles of routine activities theory to cybercrime is challenging. Multiple features of present-day cybercrime set it apart from street offending; some of these characteristics are offered below.

Transnationality

One distinguishing feature that sets digital criminality apart from criminality in the physical world is the capacity for transnational misconduct. A significant proportion of cybercrimes can occur within a particular jurisdiction despite being instigated in a different jurisdiction. This situation can give rise to substantial complexities when there are variations in laws and priorities across the jurisdictions involved. Suppose an individual from one nation becomes a target of an online investment scam originating in another nation. In that case, it is possible that one, both or neither of the authorities in the respective countries may possess an investigative or punitive interest (for a broader discussion on the globalised nature of cybercrime, see Chen et al., 2023; Lusthaus, 2012; Siregar & Sinaga, 2021), which contributes to the emergence of complex multinational organisations that are based in local areas but have a global reach. Significantly, the utilisation of technology plays a role in restructuring conventional labour divisions within a criminal enterprise that crosses borders. Indeed, artificial intelligence contributes to the automation and reduction of skill requirements in certain illegal activities (for an example in the area of pay-for ransomware services, see Gray et al. 2022), but it also facilitates the acquisition of new skills and enables individuals and groups to engage in criminal enterprises on a global scale (Pease, 1991, p. 24; Savona & Mignone, 2004; Wall, 2007).

Anonymity of Organisations

Another feature that makes cybercrime distinct is the anonymity it can offer to more organised actors. Lusthaus (2018) contended that the nature of cybercrime has transformed from sporadic mischievous acts perpetrated by individuals to a lucrative industry driven by financial gain and reliant on the cloak of anonymity. The historical progression of hacking serves as a clear illustration of this transformation. During the period spanning from the 1950s to the 1980s, the practice of hacking was primarily confined to the realm of scientific investigation, as researchers affiliated with universities and government institutions delved into the malevolent aspects of phreaking. Since the proliferation of desktop computers in the 1990s, individual hacking has evolved into establishing organised trading forums, leading to the emergence of professional groups engaged in coordinated cyberattacks. Consequently, an escalating degree of cooperation, coupled with a rising inclination towards professionalisation, has engendered an economic framework founded upon principles of trust and anonymity (Hunt-Sharman, 2022; Paquet-Clouston & García, 2023; Zeng & Buil-Gil, 2023).

Specialisation and Diversification of Labour

As Lusthaus (2018) observed, contemporary organised cybercrime has a distinct division of labour wherein tasks are assigned to individuals specialised in their execution. Increasing specialisation is associated with a corresponding increase in professionalisation. Participants in the cybercrime supply chain are incentivised to develop and refine their creative abilities by focusing on a particular activity or task. This specialisation enables them to effectively showcase their skills to potential customers and business partners. The presence of many actors and affiliated companies leads to increased opportunities for collaboration and networking. Given these circumstances, monetisation becomes unavoidable. The pursuit of profit and exploitation has surpassed previous motivations that were more inclined towards enjoyment and intellectual stimulation (Grabosky, 2007). The alteration in motivation burdens law enforcement agencies, as they must selectively restrict the activities of evil and resourceful individuals rather than those engaging in recreational pursuits.

Adaptability

The distinctive and persistent attribute that characterises cybercrime in its entirety, whether organised or not, is its inherent adaptability. A cybercrime operation or enterprise is complex and dynamic, lacking simplicity or stagnation. Cybercriminal practices and activities vary in both form and orientation, which are contingent upon the prevailing technological advancements and the requisite level of expertise and familiarity with recent developments (see Elluri et al., 2023; Djenna et al., 2023; Gabrian, 2022).

Cybercrime, Illicit Online Markets, and Cryptomarkets

The progression of digital cryptography and peer-to-peer monetary systems has facilitated the expansion of illicit online marketplaces that have established a presence, particularly within the dark web. Cryptomarkets, also known as online illegal marketplaces, represent a distinct forum that enhances conventional criminal dynamics while presenting a growing challenge to law enforcement agencies. An account of the historical background and operational mechanisms of these unauthorised platforms is provided below.

A Cursory Introduction to Cryptocurrencies

Before considering the delinquent use of cryptocurrencies in illicit online marketplaces, it is important to state that the authors do not object in principle to the use or proliferation of cryptocurrencies. Cryptocurrencies, which are digital currencies built on decentralised blockchain technology, have gained considerable prominence and acceptance over time, giving rise to discussions regarding their advantages and consequences.

Cryptocurrencies represent a significant encryption technology utilised within the realm of cryptomarkets. The electronic currency system facilitates direct and anonymous peer-to-peer transactions without any intervention or supervision from a third-party entity. In contrast to traditional fiat currencies, cryptocurrencies are characterised by a decentralised ledger system that maintains a comprehensive record of all transactions conducted using a particular cryptocurrency (Cox, 2016). This phenomenon is commonly referred to as the *blockchain*. Blockchain technology enables transparent visibility of cryptocurrency holdings in users' digital wallets. A "block" is a sequence of transactions involving the transfer of data or assets between users. Due to the decentralised nature of the blockchain, which entails multiple copies distributed across computers worldwide, transactions conducted using cryptocurrencies are inherently irreversible, immune to freezing and resistant to manipulation by external entities such as financial institutions and governmental bodies.

One of the key arguments supporting the adoption of cryptocurrencies revolves around their capacity to effectively tackle obstacles related to financial inclusion and accessibility (Chung et al., 2023; Ozili, 2022). In many developing nations, a substantial proportion of the population requires increased access to conventional banking systems, primarily due to inadequate infrastructure or documentation. Cryptocurrencies provide a viable solution by facilitating direct transactions between individuals, eliminating the necessity for intermediaries (Vincent & Evans, 2019). Consequently, this technology extends the accessibility of financial services to a wider range of individuals, including those who are typically marginalised (Abdulhakeem & Hu, 2021).

Furthermore, a persuasive rationale for adopting cryptocurrencies is lowering transaction costs (see Caton & Harwick, 2022). Traditional financial systems typically rely on intermediaries like banks, credit card companies and payment processors. However, these intermediaries often impose substantial transaction fees, particularly for cross-border transactions. In contrast, cryptocurrencies eliminate intermediaries and optimise the payment process, resulting in a notable reduction in transaction fees. This reduction can yield advantages for individuals making routine transactions and small businesses and entrepreneurs participating in global commerce (Maese et al., 2016).

Moreover, the decentralised nature of cryptocurrencies fundamentally aligns with libertarian advocates (Coats, 2022; Eyal, 2017). Cryptocurrencies function within a decentralised network of computers, precluding the necessity for a central governing entity such as a central bank. The decentralisation process gives users greater authority over their funds and transactions, decreasing the potential for censorship, manipulation and interference from external entities. In this respect, the appeal of cryptocurrencies is further enhanced by their global reach and ability to facilitate cross-border transactions. Cryptocurrencies can surpass geographical limitations and enable effortless cross-border transactions, thereby eliminating the necessity for currency conversion and the accompanying charges. This can yield substantial consequences for international trade, remittances and global economic interactions, promoting a more interconnected and streamlined global economy. This aspect follows the principles of personal financial sovereignty and autonomy, which have gained significance in the globally interconnected and digitised modern society—against many central banks' wishes (Silva & Silva, 2021).

Perhaps contrary to the popular conception of blockchain technology more broadly and cryptocurrency more specifically, the adoption of cryptocurrencies is motivated by the imperative of security and the need to prevent fraud (for a review, see Levi, 2022). Blockchain technology, which serves as the foundational framework for most cryptocurrencies, utilises cryptographic methods to ensure the security of transactions. Every transaction is documented on an unalterable public ledger, diminishing the probability of fraudulent activities, double-spending and unauthorised modifications. Implementing such a high level of security fosters confidence and reliance among users and can bring about transformative changes in industries beyond finance.

On the other hand, despite being controversial subjects, privacy and anonymity are often promoted as advantageous features associated with specific cryptocurrencies. Cryptocurrencies such as *Monero* and *Zcash* (and—more recently—*Data Ownership Protocol* [DOP]) place a significant emphasis on privacy by implementing sophisticated cryptographic methods to safeguard transaction information and protect the anonymity of users (for a review, see Lee, 2019). This can effectively mitigate apprehensions regarding surveillance and data breaches in the contemporary era of digitalisation, where the significance of privacy has progressively grown (Xue et al., 2022).

There are also direct financial motivations for cryptocurrency. For example, cryptocurrencies can function as a safeguard against inflation and economic instability, particularly in areas that are confronted with hyperinflation or volatile economic conditions (see pros and cons in Phochanachan et al., 2022). While the evidence suggests that the anti-inflation potential of cryptocurrency is not as strong as once believed (Sakurai & Kurosaki, 2023), there is still evidence of the utility of cryptocurrencies. The devaluation of traditional currencies resulting from factors such as excessive printing can prompt individuals to seek alternative means of preserving their assets and storing their wealth.

Another noted financial motivation is that cryptocurrencies have engendered innovation by introducing novel concepts such as smart contracts and decentralised finance (DeFi). Smart contracts are autonomous agreements that function without the need for intermediaries, thereby improving efficiency across multiple domains, including contract administration, real estate and construction transactions (Ye et al., 2022), legal arrangements, finances (Davelis et al., 2022), energy systems (Kirli et al., 2022) and food supply chains (Miller et al., 2023; Natanelov et al., 2022). These platforms facilitate lending, borrowing and trading activities in a manner that is both more accessible and automated.

Illicit Online Markets

Illegal online markets refer to online platforms that facilitate the buying and selling of goods and services using cryptocurrencies as the primary medium of exchange. Grabosky (2007) was among the earliest scholars to recognise the potential ability of emerging technologies to facilitate the widespread distribution of illegal goods and services, despite being unaware of their far-reaching effects. The human inclination to employ exponential technologies to exchange illicit commodities through trucking, bartering and trading is not recent. The inaugural electronic commerce transaction took place in 1972; students from MIT and Stanford University employed ARPANET, a packet-switching network developed in the 1960s that later transformed into the Internet (Lukasik, 2010). Driven by rapid technological advancements, the forces of globalisation and the emergence of market innovations, the accessibility of illicit goods and services online quickly emerged for individuals possessing the necessary expertise (Kritika et al., 2021).

Martin (2014a) showed that illicit online markets have evolved into "hybrid markets" that amalgamate conventional social and economic opportunity frameworks with the novel opportunities facilitated by the Internet. The Internet has facilitated the emergence of novel criminal networking channels and fundamentally altered the conventional dynamics between suppliers, intermediaries and buyers (p. 56). However, the operational history of illegal markets online is relatively limited. Its origins can be traced to 2011, when the inaugural cryptomarket known as Silk Road was established by Ross Ulbricht, an enigmatic individual with a background in physics hailing from Austin, Texas (Martin, 2014a). After Ulbricht's apprehension by the Federal Bureau of Investigation (FBI), this online platform was rendered inoperative in 2013. Several cryptomarkets surfaced in the subsequent months, including Silk Road 2.0 (a direct successor), Agora, Atlantis and Cannabis Road; they assumed prominent positions in this emerging landscape. According to Décary-Hétu and Giommoni (2017), the closure of these markets occurred in 2014 as a result of Operation Onymous, a collaborative effort involving the UK's National Crime Agency (NCA), the FBI and Europol. The markets experienced another period of readjustment in 2015, with AlphaBay emerging as the most successful cryptocurrency market up to that point. In July 2017, Operation Bayonet, a collaborative effort involving the FBI, Drug Enforcement Administration (DEA), Europol and Dutch National Police, successfully executed takedowns of AlphaBay and Hansa. These two cryptomarkets were ranked the first and third largest during that period. Today, some of the most prominent dark web marketplaces include Brian's Crabs Club, Vice City, WeTheNorth, Genesis Market, Kingdom Market, Cocorico and Cypher (see Webz.io, 2023).

Cryptomarkets

What exactly are cryptomarkets? They can be defined as Internet-based platforms where individuals engage in the exchange of goods and services while employing digital encryption techniques to safeguard their identities (Martin, 2014a; see also Dupont et al., 2016; Hutchings & Holt, 2015). A more precise definition formulated by Barratt and Aldridge (2016) encapsulates the primary characteristics of contemporary cryptomarkets: marketplaces that facilitate the exchange of goods and services by hosting multiple sellers or vendors. It should be noted that cryptomarkets do not sell goods or services directly. Online marketplaces of illicit nature primarily operate as intermediary platforms that facilitate connections between buyers and vendors willing to participate in voluntary economic exchanges involving a wide range of illegal goods and services (Christin, 2013). These marketplaces ensure participant anonymity for both vendors and purchasers; their locations on the web are concealed and cryptocurrencies are utilised for payment. Importantly, cryptomarkets aggregate and present customer feedback ratings and comments to enhance participant transparency and trust (p. 78). Thus, cryptomarkets are distinguished by their positioning within the dark web, the utilisation of cryptocurrencies and feedback mechanisms and their facilitation of transactions between buyers and vendors. This area is approached with this definition (see a more recent extension in Barratt et al., 2022; Jardine et al., 2023; Giommoni et al., 2023; Martin, 2023).

   While there is no doubt that cryptomarkets are the driving force behind the trade of illegal goods, they are not without societal benefits. First, these platforms reduce the likelihood of physical violence, which characterises illegal physical transactions, by removing direct face-to-face interactions between the parties (Barratt et al., 2016a, b; Morselli et al., 2007). Cryptocurrencies have the potential to address the risks inherent in face-to-face exchanges of tangible assets by offering secure and transparent transactions, thereby diminishing the probability of disputes escalating into violent confrontations. The intrinsic traceability of cryptocurrency transactions serves as a deterrent against fraudulent activities and scams, cultivating an atmosphere of trust among involved parties and reducing the primary driver of violence in the drug market (Tzanetakis et al., 2016).

Customer fraud is less likely with the financial escrow system built into these platforms. Like with the risk mitigation practices on legitimate electronic commerce platforms such as eBay or Amazon, buyers are assured that the product they purchase is "as advertised" (Tzanetakis, 2019). According to Christin (2013), an escrow service is responsible for safeguarding funds until a transaction is deemed finalised by the buyer, at which time the funds are released to the vendor. For example, assume that Vincent intends to acquire a product from Barak. Instead of engaging in a direct monetary transaction with Barak, Vincent remits payment to the intermediary, Matt, who subsequently instructs Barak to ship the item to Vincent. After Vincent verifies receipt of the item, Matt transfers the funds to Barak, retaining a nominal fee for his services. This payment system enables operators of cryptomarkets to resolve disputes that may arise when a vendor asserts that they have shipped an item and the buyer claims to have not received it.

On the other hand, the anonymity and escrow services built into cryptomarkets present significant obstacles for law enforcement agencies, further complicating their endeavours to identify and apprehend individuals engaged in potentially illicit actions (see review in Aldridge, 2019). Particular attention is given to this issue in Chap. 4.

The Primary Operational Environment of Cryptomarkets: The Darknet

It is crucial to contextualise these digital phenomena within their operating environment to understand cryptomarkets comprehensively. The Internet can be divided into surface, deep and dark webs. The entirety of the content of the ordinary Internet can be accessed through popular search engines like Google or Bing. Websites are included in the search engine's index, making them easily accessible to the public without specific configurations or permissions.

Webpages not included in a search engine's index and, therefore, not readily accessible to users make up the deep and dark web components. Epstein (2014) and, more recently, AlKhatib and Basheer (2019) posited that the deep web comprises approximately 96% of all networked webpages, making it nearly 500 times larger than the surface web. Nevertheless, most deep web content is considered to be within the law's boundaries. The term *deep web* encompasses all digital content available on the Internet that is not accessible through conventional search engines due to a lack of indexing, including webpages that are not readily accessible via traditional search queries and necessitate specific credentials, authentication or specialised software for access. According to Barratt and Aldridge (2016), the types of content that fall under the category of restricted access include content that is only available through paywalled websites, content that can only be accessed through specific company or academic databases, databases that are not directly searchable by Google, websites that lack interlinking with other websites, private websites and forums and substantial amounts of nonpublic content from social networking sites (p. 79). Other instances of content on the deep web include websites safeguarded by passwords, services requiring subscriptions and content accessible only upon payment. Many peer-reviewed academic articles are behind paywalls, making them inaccessible to the broader public (for solutions, see Himmelstein et al., 2018).

The dark web makes up a distinct portion of the deep web. It encompasses websites and other forms of online content that are deliberately concealed and can only be accessed through specialised software, such as the TOR (The Onion Router) network, which is discussed below. The dark web is deliberately concealed from conventional search engines, necessitating the use of anonymising tools such as the TOR browser to enable access (Montieri et al., 2018; Ngo et al., 2023; Saleem et al., 2022). The dark web's provision of anonymity and privacy to users leads to a range of applications, encompassing both lawful endeavours, such as safeguarding freedom of expression in oppressive political environments, and illicit activities, including facilitating illegal marketplaces, forums and other criminal undertakings. For example, the utilisation of dark web platforms is frequently observed among political dissidents and whistle-blowers who aim to circumvent stringent censorship laws and excessive government intervention (Bradbury, 2014; Hardy & Norgaard, 2016). Undoubtedly, the primary intention behind developing the software enabling access to the dark web was to serve this purpose.

Cryptomarkets are located within the dark web. Accessing a cryptomarket necessitates unique configurations, explicit authorisation or a specialised browser (Barrett et al., 2016a, b, p. 50; Moe, 2008). As such, a crucial aspect distinguishing cryptomarkets from other illicit exchange networks and distribution systems is their dependence on encryption technology. According to Décary-Hétu and Giommoni (2017, p. 107), the innovation of cryptomarkets does not stem from the creation of novel stealth technology but rather from the amalgamation of multiple technologies that, when integrated, offer participants an elevated degree of anonymity. In this context, cryptomarkets employ two prominent encryption technologies, TOR and cryptocurrencies, to facilitate effective operations and seamless communication among participants.

TOR, The Onion Router, is a freely available communication service that operates on a circuit-based low-latency model. It enables users to access the Internet while maintaining anonymity and concealing their geographical location (Dingledine et al., 2004; Mathewson & Dingledine, 2004). TOR is a network where individuals can search for and host clandestine websites. This feature proves to be highly advantageous for individuals who seek to establish a cryptomarket and ensure the concealment of their hosting location from law enforcement and other parties who may be adversely affected. TOR network was first introduced in 2002, and its initial development was undertaken by the Center for High Assurance Computer Systems in the United States (Bradbury, 2014). Similar to many software applications developed by governmental entities, TOR was created for the exclusive use of state actors but eventually became accessible to the general public after its public release.

The TOR network employs a technique known as onion routing, wherein a user's IP address is routed through a sequence of randomly selected relay points to obscure the user's original location (Bradbury, 2014, p. 14). The individual initiating a data transmission will identify an access point and opt for a randomised routing trajectory using a set of intermediary nodes to conceal the transmission's source. According to Bradbury (2014), when traffic is directed through this route, it undergoes encryption until it reaches the final relay, from which it is then transmitted to a designated IP address on the public Internet (p. 12). Essentially, onion routing dissociates one's physical location from the network destination accessed (Lewman, 2016, p. 16).

Significantly, two studies have revealed a robust correlation between Bitcoin transactions and acquiring goods and services on TOR and cryptomarkets. In a survey by Janze (2017), a comprehensive analysis was performed using panel data consisting of 296,875 product listings from cryptomarkets alongside Bitcoin blockchain transactions. This investigation revealed an intriguing coevolutionary relationship between Bitcoin and cryptomarkets. It can be reliably inferred that transactions occurring within the Bitcoin blockchain and using transaction obfuscation services can be associated with previous transactions made on cryptomarkets. These findings indicate that the sale of one additional item on darknet markets is associated with a subsequent increase of 0.123 transactions on the blockchain after 6 days. Additionally, Foley et al. (2018) estimated that approximately 46% of Bitcoin transactions, amounting to $76 billion, were associated with illicit activities and that a significant portion of these transactions took place within cryptomarkets.

Using TOR (or alternative networks such as I2P, Zeronet, Freenet and Openbazaar) and cryptocurrencies is essential to engage in cryptomarkets. Consequently, individuals who wish to participate in these markets must possess a certain degree of technical expertise, albeit relatively basic. Individuals should understand the underlying technologies to engage effectively in the cryptomarket (Christin, 2013). In their study of Silk Road, Van Hout and Bingham (2013) conducted qualitative interviews and found that vendors regarded proficiency and familiarity with computer systems to be crucial skills. One participant expressed the belief that individuals who were not computer scientists often relied heavily on faith regarding certain aspects of the field (see also van Hout & Bingham, 2013, p. 54). In addition to possessing technological expertise, participants must also have access to various devices, software applications and informational resources. Barratt and Aldridge (2016) analysed the existing literature about drug procurement within the cryptomarket. They showed that individuals seeking to engage in such activities typically needed several vital components, including access to a computer or comparable electronic device, a specialised anonymising browser, the marketplace's unique URL, a certain amount of cryptocurrency, knowledge of a vendor willing to dispatch the drugs to the desired location and an appropriate address for the delivery of the drug package (Barratt & Aldridge, 2016, p. 4).

According to May and Hough (2004, pp. 550–551), the distinction between open and closed markets can be defined as follows: Open markets are accessible to any buyer without the need for a prior introduction to the seller and have minimal barriers to entry, while closed markets require sellers and buyers to have a pre-existing relationship based on trust or third-party endorsement. In the context of cryptomarkets, individuals with sufficient knowledge of anonymity networks and cryptocurrencies can participate, but the ability to establish rapport with customers and behave appropriately on these platforms is essential for meaningful engagement (Aldridge & Décary-Hétu, 2016b; Christin, 2013; Duxbury & Haynie, 2017).

According to Christin (2013) and Martin (2014b), law enforcement organisations typically possess better organisational experience and expertise in prosecuting illicit exchanges that occur in the physical world (i.e. street drug markets) than those that take place in the virtual world. Using TOR and cryptocurrencies introduces additional complexity that most police investigators are not able to overcome. Moreover, the privacy afforded by cryptomarkets facilitates the establishment of diverse communicative norms that are partially observed in conventional organised crime contexts. This topic will be addressed in Chap. 4.

Thus, cryptomarkets represent a notable advancement in criminal activities. They offer sellers a digital platform to promote and distribute their products to a global market, mitigating concerns about potential legal intervention. Maintaining secrecy and anonymity within terrestrial markets poses a significant challenge due to the involvement of fallible human actors. Furthermore, law enforcement entities possess a level of capability comparable to that of terrestrial criminals, enabling them to penetrate criminal networks effectively and acquire valuable information, all while circumventing the challenges posed by technological obstacles. The assertion is made with seriousness that crime prevention in a physical setting is fraught with many distinct challenges.

Organisational Structure and Governance Within Cryptomarkets

Irrespective of legal status, a business's goals and operational capabilities are frequently determined by its organisational framework. The scholarly discourse on organised crime has extensively engaged in debates regarding illicit organisations' horizontal or vertical structure (for a review, see Bichler et al., 2017; Fiorentini, 1999; von Lampe, 2015). Von Lampe (2016) suggested that the market comprises a network of hierarchical bureaucracies that actively employ micromanagement and vertical integration strategies. The media's portrayal of drug traffickers in the Colombian cities of Medellín and Cali as cartels that limit market competition and control global drug prices further reinforced this view of the drug market (Kenney, 2007, p. 233). Malm and Bichler (2011), however, do not provide support for these suppositions, instead demonstrating the presence of a decentralised organisational structure within drug trafficking organisations, rather than a centralised one. Indeed, organised crime has a stronghold on the drug market, but some markets around the globe are organised in a straightforward hierarchical formation (Liddick, 1999; Denley & Ariel, 2019; Klerks, 2001).

The Hierarchical Model of Cryptomarkets

Some of the existing literature has focused on examining the organisational structure and divisions of labour that are prevalent within illegal online marketplaces, with notable contributions by Martin (2014a, b). First, Martin (2014a) asserted that cryptomarkets exhibit a hierarchical structure. This view has been demonstrated by scholarly works on organised crime, and it coincides with Donald Cressey's (1967) perspective that organised crime, particularly in the American context, can be likened to an octopus, characterised by central leadership represented by the head and numerous interconnected branches symbolised by the tentacles. Cressey's observation has contributed to the development of a specific branch of literature on organised crime that focuses on the vertical structure of criminal organisations. According to von Lampe (2016), hierarchical structures consist of multiple components that execute tasks under the coordination of a shared manager. Vertically structured organisations often exhibit well-defined boundaries, internal divisions and a centralised chain of command (von Lampe, 2016, p. 105). Catino (2014, p. 188) asserted that the fundamental operational entity within the Sicilian mafia is referred to as the "family". This criminal organisation maintains a territorial stronghold from which it exercises control over a specific zone or inhabited region; power is subdivided and position on the hierarchy determines the division of labour. The hierarchical structure entails a foundation comprising individuals referred to as "bottom men" or "soldiers" who execute operational directives, *capodecina* (or capos for short) who are entrusted with the management of a unit of soldiers and a democratically elected "representative" or boss who assumes the role of the family's leader (Catino, 2014; von Lampe, 2016).

Establishing a hierarchical chain of command prevents unauthorised engagement in unlawful activities as approval from the superior authority is required. The Sicilian mafia exhibits a vertical macro-organisational structure. In this system, a collective of representatives selects a district boss who subsequently assumes the role of a member within a provincial commission. This commission, in turn, collaboratively nominates a local representative who serves as the secretary and coordinator for the designated province (Catino, 2014, p. 190). These supra-local and provincial configurations facilitate an increased ability to interact with the state. This claim is supported by the historical evidence of the Sicilian mafia's involvement in acts of violence against the state, according to von Lampe (2016, p. 189).

The organisational hierarchical structure of cryptomarkets is expected to exhibit certain similarities. Based on comprehensive and accessible sources of information, Martin (2014a) identified four distinct user categories within the hierarchical structure of the cryptomarket. The individuals within this category consist of administrators, moderators, vendors and consumers. Following von Lampe's (2016) findings, cryptomarkets show a notable level of transparency in their organisational framework and allocation of tasks, wherein each user category assumes distinct yet interconnected roles and competencies (Martin, 2014a, p. 17). Assigning each category of actor a specific role ensures the smooth operation of the platform. However, this description does not accurately represent the reality of these organisations, as the allocation of tasks and responsibilities among different categories of individuals is not deliberate. Rather, actors naturally assume distinct roles based on their positions within the market's organisational structure.

The operational efficiency of hierarchical cryptomarkets is primarily governed by an administrative unit that assumes control over the organisational structure of the platforms. Administrators' responsibilities include serving as executives, overseeing the operations of their respective platforms and establishing the guidelines that govern user conduct. According to Martin (2014a), administrators bear the responsibility of authorising and suspending individual accounts, supervising undisclosed transactions, establishing new product categories, determining the permissibility of item sales and developing and implementing novel security measures and cyber-defence strategies (p. 18). Undoubtedly, an essential ancillary role is the administration of cryptocurrency transactions. This entails the provision of escrow services, which generate sales commissions from each transaction. According to Christin's (2013) examination of financial patterns within the dark web, sales commissions generally make up 3–8% of the overall transactional expense. Martin (2014a) proposed that administrators assume the role of organisational figureheads, actively interacting with media outlets and scholars (p. 18).

Moderators possess limited administrative privileges, but they are crucial in supporting administrators by managing site operations and providing customer assistance. The primary tasks encompassed in this process include regulating forum discussions, detecting fraudulent activity perpetrated by scammers, resolving complaints and providing assistance to vendors and consumers. Therefore, moderators carry out the routine tasks of managing the cryptomarket to ensure the platform's smooth functioning.

Vendors and buyers occupy the lowest tier within this hierarchical structure. To engage in transactions within a cryptomarket, vendors must remit a registration fee to the designated site administrator, after which they can set up their account and initiate the process of listing products they want to sell to potential buyers. Purchasers must set up a complimentary account on the platform. Upon the conclusion of a transaction between a buyer and a vendor, the buyer is allowed to provide public feedback regarding their encounter with the vendor. This holds significant importance as it aids vendors in establishing their reputation and concurrently serves as an indicator to prospective buyers regarding the vendor's quality. Although vendors and buyers are not officially assigned a formal administrative role, they are crucial in facilitating voluntary economic transactions. In addition, they actively participate in two significant endeavours to foster community cohesion: product testing and amicable discussions on forums. Therefore, these individuals assess experiential commodities and establish and sustain a collegial community within a cryptomarket.

The Nonhierarchical Model of Cryptomarkets

There is disagreement regarding the assertion that cryptomarkets are exclusively hierarchical. Norgaard et al. (2018) conducted a study to examine the factors influencing the structure and hierarchy of networks in physical and dark web drug markets. The researchers discovered that illicit online markets tended to exhibit lower levels of hierarchical organisation than their terrestrial counterparts, which typically displayed more monopolistic tendencies. The authors employed agent-based modelling to compare simulated black-market networks' density and average path length. Agent-based modelling is a widely used approach in which the actions and interactions of discrete entities, referred to as agents, are simulated within a broader system. In this instance, the authors generated computerised simulations of illicit market networks, thereby enabling a systematic examination of the networks' operational dynamics within a regulated setting. The researchers focused on the density and average path length of the simulated networks. Density is a measure that quantifies the level of interconnectedness between agents within a network; it can provide insights into the intensity and quality of relationships and interactions. Conversely, the average path length quantifies the mean number of steps or connections required to transition from one agent to another within the network, thereby offering valuable insights into communication efficiency. This approach allows us to understand the operational dynamics of these networks and the potential influence of their structural attributes on their efficacy through the comparative analysis of multiple scenarios.

Their findings indicated that cryptomarkets, characterised by reduced transaction costs and information asymmetries, exhibit a lower prevalence of hierarchical structures compared to terrestrial markets. The effective functioning of a cryptomarket relies heavily on the presence of a decentralised exchange network connecting vendors and consumers, rather than a hierarchy. Natarajan (2006), Kenney (2007), Bright et al. (2014) and Martin (2014a) underscored the significance of organised economic relationships cultivated through community involvement in product evaluation and discussions held in forums. These activities establish a standardised process for voluntary economic exchanges between buyers and vendors, creating a social structure built upon shared interests. Crucially, the diverse capabilities offered by Internet connectivity have the potential to supplant conventional organised crime structures with decentralised networks (Brenner, 2010). As Martin (2014a) showed, in cryptomarkets, illicit commodities are produced by manufacturers, procured by vendors (who may also function as manufacturers) and delivered to consumers through conventional postal services. Nevertheless, there are structural differences between cryptomarket exchange networks and terrestrial illicit distribution networks. It has been observed that cryptomarkets require a smaller number of nodes to operate effectively (Barratt & Aldridge, 2016; Christin, 2013; Martin, 2014a, p. 55), thus implying that cryptomarkets operate in a decentralised and less hierarchical formation than offline drug markets.

Hybridity

The organisational structure of cryptomarkets can be characterised as a novel amalgamation of a hierarchical administrative unit and a decentralised exchange network. In broad terms, the decentralised exchange network enhances the efficiency of voluntary economic transactions and enhances the robustness of the distributed ledger, while the capable centralised administrative entity oversees these transactions to guarantee the contentment of all involved parties and establish ethical guidelines. This hybridity offers several functional advantages, such as enhanced operational efficiency, improved communication transparency and heightened consumer satisfaction awareness. The combination of various governmental paradigms has contributed to facilitating unauthorised online marketplaces.

Cryptomarkets differ from conventional organised crime groups in that they function as both marketplaces and intermediaries, benefiting from improved communication channels and heightened levels of anonymity. Furthermore, the utilisation of encryption and anonymity in cryptomarkets diminishes the potential for implementing a conventional hierarchical system of governance. Indeed, the literature on organised crime seldom documents instances of hybridity, as illicit entities predominantly exhibit horizontal or vertical structures. Furthermore, integrating organisational characteristics derived from mafias and drug trafficking organisations within a cryptomarket is a unique occurrence.

The combination of stringent governance and liberal market principles is suitable for application within illicit markets. The absence of traditional enforcement mechanisms in underground markets highlights the need for a central authority to oversee market transactions and penalise individuals who fail to fulfil their contractual obligations. However, the dominant position held by administrators of cryptomarkets frequently results in collapse of the platform if they are removed. Conversely, the decentralised network of sellers and buyers facilitates user mobility and enables the platform to regenerate quickly.

Cryptomarket Administration

Illicit online marketplaces are characterised by well-defined rules formulated and enforced by administrators, even though this market has no structural and formalised regulations. Significantly, a limited yet expanding portion of the existing literature on cryptomarkets is focused explicitly on governance (see Moeller, 2022; Tzanetakis, 2019). Due to their unlawful nature, environments that foster criminal activity are frequently perceived as domains characterised by a lack of adherence to legal norms (Sotirakopoulos, 2018). However, even in unlawful environments, rational order is still needed. Goods sold on unauthorised online platforms circumvent the established procedures of government-mandated testing, quality control and safety standardisation that are typically applied to conventional consumer products. Still, noncompliance with these regulations would immediately translate into lost revenues (as customer would not return for more). Nevertheless, it can be argued that cryptomarkets exhibit a high degree of collegiality compared to other illicit organisations (Martin, 2014a, p.18). The convergence of mentalities, technologies, resources and institutions enables cryptomarkets to operate as arenas of informal nodal governance. Below, close attention is paid to the administrators of cryptomarkets.

Alongside the immediate link between the drug dealer and the drug buyer, cryptomarket administrators and the online platform play a crucial role in facilitating monetary exchanges, brokerage services and peer-to-peer communications (Andrei et al., 2023). This may be unsurprising to social criminal network scholars (e.g. Papachristos & Bastomski, 2018), as research has shown that familial and associational bonds facilitate the operation of exchange networks by establishing intrinsic social connections and fostering communication and market harmonisation among participants (Windle, 2021). Indeed, participants in the cryptomarket, including vendors and buyers, do not adhere to the same familial ties observed among Italian mafiosi or Colombian drug traffickers, as highlighted by Décary-Hétu (2016). In contrast, interpersonal relationships are contingent upon shared interests in libertarianism, recreational drug consumption and various subcultural domains (Munksgaard & Demant, 2016). For example, the original Silk Road was established based on the principles of libertarianism (Maddox et al., 2016). However, many participants within cryptomarkets may not adhere to or endorse this particular ideology. Consequently, their loyalty may be directed towards a reliable supplier almost opportunistically (Masson & Bancroft, 2018).

The concentration of authority in the administrators of cryptomarkets fosters what has been referred to as "nodal governance" (see an application in Morselli et al., 2017). Initially proposed by Shearing and Wood (2003), the concept of nodal governance posits that formal government, non-governmental organisations and commercial institutions are lacking, and informal groups arise as alternative pseudo-governing bodies. These informal collectives perform various regulatory tasks, such as enforcing contracts and rules, resolving disputes, ensuring security and engaging in policing activities. Thus, nodal governance is prevalent within criminal organisations. According to Diego Gambetta's analysis (1993), the emergence of the Sicilian mafia can be attributed to Italy's transition from feudalism to capitalism during the nineteenth century. The Italian government could not protect itself from predatory attacks that arose due to the emergence of growing markets. The Gabellotti, which preceded the establishment of the Sicilian mafia, played a role in upholding private property rights and offering ad hoc governance. Scholarly literature has presented evidence contrary to the common assumption that illegal markets lack formal conflict resolution mechanisms and are stateless entities, a stance that has also been opposed by Reuter (1985). Indeed, it is possible for order to emerge naturally through repeated interactions between individuals functioning within an illicit setting. The recurrent engagements give rise to established behaviour patterns and social practices that spread among the participants involved in criminal activities. If actors fail to adhere to these norms and customs in subsequent interactions, they will face punishment from compliant actors. The responses range from public exposure and condemnation to social exclusion.

The lack of an established regulatory authority in cryptomarkets creates a conducive environment for administrators' intervention. Morselli et al. (2007) conducted a study on conflict resolution mechanisms in cryptomarkets and noted the emergence of formal regulations regulating the behaviour of both buyers and vendors. As determined by administrators, these rules are typically categorised into moral/ethical and functional. The sale and distribution of certain items, such as child pornography and firearms, are prohibited by moral and ethical regulations. In addition, operational regulations are in place to prevent thefts and scams that could undermine market efficiency and interpersonal trust. The Silk Road Charter composed by Ross Ulbricht can be regarded as a utopian constitution that guided user interaction (Martin, 2014a, p. 13). According to Martin (2014a), the Silk Road Charter characterised the Silk Road as a "global enterprise" guided by principles such as self-ownership, personal responsibility, user equality, personal integrity and a dedication to individual and communal progress (p. 12).

In addition, cryptomarkets' administrators have a significant impact on the implementation of marketplace regulations and the resolution of conflicts that may arise between buyers and vendors (Martin, 2014a, b). Norgaard et al. (2018) documented the dispute resolution procedures of Hansa, which was the third largest cryptomarket in 2017. Notably, the authors observed that Hansa fostered a climate in which buyers and vendors were encouraged to resolve disputes independently. Nonetheless, the platform would intervene and provide a resolution if private efforts proved unsuccessful. If a dispute were determined to favour the buyer, the administrators at Hansa would compel the vendor to compensate the aggrieved buyer.

In the context of nodal governance, administrators of cryptomarkets assume a significant role akin to that of the state, namely, safeguarding individuals from acts of violence, deception or theft (p. 78). In the study conducted by Van Hout and Bingham (2013), one participant expressed the view that the Silk Road vendors formed a cohesive community, with the administrator known as Dread Pirate Roberts assuming a role similar to that of a president (p. 35). Significantly, the chosen mode of governance adopted by administrators resembles the conceptualisation of an organised crime group, which Varase (2010) defined as groups that engage in unlawful activities to regulate and control the production and distribution of a specific commodity or service (p. 14). According to Martin (2014a), administrators are involved in activities such as establishing novel product categories, authorising or prohibiting item sales and supervising all transactions (p. 18). Cryptomarket administrators exercise complete control over their platform's escrow service, enabling them to closely monitor all official transactions between vendors and buyers. Administrators grant the authorisation to transfer cryptocurrencies to vendors after receiving product delivery confirmation from consumers, acquiring a sales commission during the transaction (Martin, 2014a, p. 31).

Finally, the diverse range of brokerage services provided by cryptomarkets, such as escrow and direct communication, incentivises vendors and buyers to embrace a direct business-to-consumer model (Brown & Smith, 2018; Munksgaard & Martin,

2020). This model effectively reduces the participation of drug traffickers, whole-salers, secondary brokers and other specialised intermediaries. Online distribution networks differ from traditional ones in that they enable the connection between nodes and end consumers without the need for geographic proximity or interper-sonal contact. Unlike conventional distribution networks, which involve specialised nodes for distinct distribution stages such as trafficking and wholesaling, online networks facilitate direct connections between nodes and end consumers. The intro-duction of these platforms for drug distribution has led to several notable outcomes, including enhanced price stability, product purity and customer satisfaction (Zaunseder & Bancroft, 2021).

Similarly, the organisation of the cryptomarket into communities enhances the efficacy of distribution networks, representing a noteworthy advancement in the realm of automation within illicit markets. In contrast to conventional terrestrial markets, which rely on interpersonal connections such as friendships, kinship ties or personal contacts, cryptomarkets facilitate transactions by providing transparent and quantifiable information. The involvement of automation and user participation in these processes enables cryptomarkets to function as a "super broker".

Self-Regulation of Cryptomarket-Based Transactions

As highlighted by Lusthaus (2012), cryptomarkets can be understood as brokerage platforms that facilitate the advertisement of goods by vendors and enable buyers to make purchases. Although administrators possess the authority to prohibit the sale of specific goods and services, such as child pornography, they cannot regulate the supply and demand dynamics of the products that are promoted on their platform. Online markets consist of autonomous groups and individuals who do not possess a unified, coherent objective, excepting monetary gain for vendors and the acquisition of goods for buyers. From an intuitive standpoint, participants in cryptomarkets lack complete information beyond the fact of their involvement in voluntary economic transactions. So how do these markets self-regulate?

Market Administrators

The presence of cryptomarket administrators in the management of cryptocurrency transactions implies that they exercise comprehensive supervision over all engage-ments between vendors and consumers. As the guardians of authority, administra-tors can authorise a currency transfer once they have received verification of product delivery from the consumer (Martin, 2014a, p. 31). As in organised crime syndi-cates, administrators have the authority to impose penalties such as the suspension of offenders' accounts upon individuals who fail to fulfil their contractual commit-ments. As "capable guardians", administrators serve to deter fraudulent activities among marketplace participants (Cohen & Felson, 1979). The presence of inherent conflict reduction mechanisms contributes to the establishment of a relatively well-regulated market. Moreover, administrators must proactively protect vendors and consumers from law enforcement through the development and execution of novel security protocols and cyber defence mechanisms. Similarly, Mafiosi must fulfil the crucial responsibility of safeguarding their clientele from the scrutiny and intervention of law enforcement authorities (Varese, 2010, p. 17).

The administrative unit in cryptomarkets is organised in a hierarchical structure based on nodal governance. This form of governance involves the simultaneous regulation of illicit commodities and the provision of protection. However, it should be noted that the motivations of cryptomarket administrators and individuals interested in organised crime are incomparable. In contrast to Mafiosi, the administrators of cryptomarkets refrain from participating in extortion and instead exhibit benevolent intentions and behaviours (Linder, 2019; Wallbach et al., 2020).

This comparative analysis aims to illustrate specific characteristics of cryptomarkets that resemble those of traditional organised crime groups. It should be noted that cryptomarkets are not inherently associated with organised crime groups, nor is the governance within these markets straightforward or simple. Nevertheless, according to Lusthaus (2012), the fact of providing a safe environment for illegal transactions, limiting entry to individuals engaged in deviant activities and enforcing contracts through third-party involvement does not inherently qualify illicit online marketplaces as organised crime syndicates.

Violence-Free Environment

The ability of participants in cryptomarkets to remain anonymous and geographically dispersed prevents them from causing harm to individuals they consider untrustworthy. The unlikelihood of violence in cryptomarkets stems from the platform's ability to eliminate physical contact and facilitate voluntary economic exchanges. It is, therefore, no surprise that the existing body of literature has demonstrated an inverse correlation between the use of the cryptomarket for drug trades and instances of violence (Aldridge & Décary-Hétu, 2014; Morselli et al., 2017; Van Hout and Bingham, 2013). Mohamed and Fritsvold (2010) showed that vendors operating in cryptomarkets face a lowered risk of experiencing violence compared to traditional "street" dealers. This can be attributed to the fact that the majority of their customers consist of middle-class university students, a population that generally exhibits a strong aversion towards engaging in severe interpersonal violence.

According to Barratt et al. (2016a, b), cryptomarkets exhibit significantly lower levels of threats and violence than terrestrial markets frequented by customers of cryptomarkets (p. 20). Buyers, in general, have reported experiencing safer and more convenient transactions due to the complete avoidance of face-to-face interactions with potentially hazardous sellers (see also Van Hout & Bingham, 2013). Barratt et al. (2016a, b) examined the drug use patterns of 3794 participants from 57 different countries. Their findings revealed that 1.3% of individuals who utilised cryptomarkets reported experiencing threats to personal safety and 1% reported instances of physical violence. In contrast, a study revealed that threats to personal safety and physical violence were encountered by 14% and 6% of individuals who made purchases from acquaintances, 24% and 10% of individuals who made purchases from familiar dealers and 35% and 15% of individuals who made purchases from unfamiliar individuals, respectively.

However, the apparent lack of hostility and minimal instances of aggression in cryptomarkets can also be attributed to vendors' conduct. According to Martin (2014a, p. 40), vendors in cryptomarkets are encouraged to establish a socially constructive public image that is devoid of violence and aligns with the perceived priorities of their customer base. Furthermore, violence in cryptomarkets can be deemed futile due to its lack of strategic significance. According to Aldridge and Décary-Hétu (2014), attaining financial success frequently requires cryptomarket vendors to rely on additional altruistic attributes and distinct skills such as excellent customer service and proficient writing abilities. This contrasts with conventional dealers, who rely on physical intimidation to retain their market dominance.

Conflict Resolution and the Lack Thereof

The absence of violence does not necessarily eliminate the possibility of engaging in malicious activities that could disrupt the functioning of a cryptomarket. Buyers and vendors frequently fall prey to fraudulent activities carried out by fellow participants. According to Morselli et al. (2017), the most prevalent fraudulent activities in online drug markets are vendors falsely claiming to have shipped the drugs and buyers claiming not to have received the drugs. These scams can be linked to inadequate management by administrators: This commonly manifests as a situation of negligence, wherein administrators exhibit a sluggish response in addressing misconduct committed by individuals on their platform. Mismanagement by administrators of cryptomarkets undermines consumer confidence and engenders market instability. Nevertheless, effectively regulating participants' behaviour in a cryptocurrency market is challenging due to the high degree of anonymity and the encryption mechanisms employed within these platforms. Therefore, attaining a formal top-down governance structure in cryptomarkets poses significant challenges (Thomaz et al., 2020).

However, notwithstanding the challenges associated with top-down governance in cryptocurrency markets, it is worth noting that buyers and vendors possess the ability to address and settle conflicts independently. In his work titled *Disorganised Crime*, Peter Reuter (1985) posited that despite lacking a centralised governing authority, illegal drug markets can resolve disputes among participants. Drawing on this concept, Morselli et al. (2017) conducted a study examining various cryptomarket forums. They identified six peer-to-peer conflict resolution strategies typically lacking in offline drug markets: (1) exhibiting a disposition of tolerance and patience in situations of dissatisfaction, (2) refraining from engaging in conflicts and abstaining from intervention, (3) socially excluding or publicly denouncing individuals who engage in undesirable behaviour, (4) issuing threats against individuals who engage in undesirable behaviour, (5) engaging in negotiations to resolve issues privately and (6) seeking the assistance of an impartial third party to mediate the situation. Additionally, Morselli et al. (2017) observed that cryptomarket participants have access to four distinct channels in the event of conflicts. Participants can establish direct communication via integrated messaging systems, utilise the formal support ticket system to inform administrators about conflicts, publicly denounce untrustworthy individuals on forums or adversely affect vendors' reputations by providing negative feedback.

The Who, What and Where of Cryptomarkets

Most of the academic literature on cryptomarkets consists of descriptive or qualitative studies (Baratt & Aldridge, 2016). The descriptive studies in this field have aimed to record and analyse the various categories, nature and volume of illicit commodities and services (Aldridge & Décary-Hétu, 2014; Martin, 2014a). The qualitative studies have endeavoured to discern the attributes and motivations of individuals involved in cryptomarkets by conducting interviews with buyers and vendors. In this regard, existing studies can be effectively classified into three distinct categories based on the topic of inquiry and examination: the nature of the items being sold, the identities of the individuals involved in the sales and the geographical origins and destinations of shipments. It is crucial to clarify that this categorisation needs to be more comprehensive, as numerous studies exist that do not fit within these identified categories, including investigations into trust, conflict resolution and network structure.

Silk Road's motto described the diverse range of illicit substances available on the platform, indicating that if a substance could be consumed through smoking, injection or nasal ingestion, it was highly probable that Silk Road would offer it. Cryptomarkets provide a wide array of illegal goods and services, including drugs, malware, weapons, stolen credit card and banking information, counterfeit money, aeroplane tickets, child pornography, chemical substances and hired assassins (Baratt & Aldridge, 2016; Christin, 2013; Décary-Hétu et al., 2018; Hutchings & Holt, 2015; Martin 2014a). The quantification of transaction volume in cryptomarkets poses challenges. Nonetheless, Aldridge and Décary-Hétu (2016a) devised a viable approach that involves tallying the quantity of buyer feedback messages associated with a particular listing. Although not flawless, this approach offers researchers consistently precise estimations of monthly revenue based on item categories.

The Products and Services Sold in Cryptomarkets

Most research on the products sold in cryptomarkets has focused on controlled substances. Van Buskirk et al. (2016) determined that cannabis, pharmaceuticals, MDMA, cocaine and methamphetamine were the substances most frequently traded within the 16 marketplaces they examined. Additionally, they observed a slight reduction in the prevalence of new psychoactive substances during their study period (p. 20). Lamy et al. (2020) observed the trade of fentanyl, fentanyl analogues and other synthetic opioids revealed that DreamMarket, which holds the distinction of being the most extensive cryptomarket to date, consistently provides a wide range of synthetic opioids at both retail and wholesale rates. Interestingly, China emerged as the primary source country for novel synthetic opioids, whereas 52.6% of all listings for fentanyl-type drugs were attributed to vendors claiming to operate from the United States and Canada.

Cunliffe et al. (2019) analysed digital traces to investigate the extent of nonmedical prescription psychiatric drug usage across 31 cryptomarkets. Their results revealed that diazepam, alprazolam, Adderall, modafinil and methylphenidate are the most commonly utilised sedatives and central nervous system stimulants. The United States and the United Kingdom were the leading providers of these goods, representing 41.4% and 31.1% of total sales, respectively. Interestingly, antidepressants and mood stabilisers did not show significant popularity within the context of cryptomarkets. The authors concluded that the sale of nonmedical prescription psychiatric drugs is primarily driven by those with a high potential for abuse.

Considerable uniformity is observed in the prevalence of drugs across various cryptomarkets. According to Soska and Christin (2015), online sales of cannabis, MDMA (ecstasy) and cocaine-related substances have been significant since 2015, accounting for approximately 70% of total sales. The observed consistency implies that cryptomarkets prefer certain drug types over others. However, there has been a notable increase in the size and extent of smaller niche drug markets on the dark web in recent years. Barrera et al. (2019) conducted a study on the six largest cryptomarkets wherein they determined that the annual lower-bound estimate for tobacco sales amounted to US $194,940. Additionally, the survey by Barratt et al. (2016a, b) is significant for its findings regarding the Global Drug Survey, which involved a sample size of 3794 participants. The results indicate that MDMA/ecstasy (55%), cannabis (43%) and LSD (35%) were the drug categories most frequently acquired through cryptomarkets.

However, a distinct category of research focuses on examining the impact of evolving drug policies on the sales within cryptomarkets and the potential consequences for user well-being, given the expansion of these online marketplaces. Martin et al. (2018) conducted a study employing an interrupted time series analysis to examine the correlation between the rescheduling of hydrocodone products in the United States and the subsequent rise in the availability of illicit prescription opioids in cryptomarkets. The researchers discovered that there was a notable rise in the market share of opioids in cryptomarkets, from 6.7% to 13.7%, after the hydro-codone rescheduling.

Furthermore, a notable shift occurred in the composition of the opioid market, characterised by a substantial surge in the sales of fentanyl. This assertion was substantiated by Lokala et al. (2019), which explored the correlation between the accessibility of opioids in cryptomarkets and the occurrence of unintentional overdoses in Ohio. The study analysed a dataset comprising 72,751 opioid advertisements obtained from DreamMarket and Agora. The researchers discovered a significant time-lagged correlation of 0.84 between cryptomarket advertisements for opioids on the Agora platform and instances of overdoses recorded in the medical records of Montgomery County, Ohio. This study represented an inaugural attempt to examine the associations between the availability of illegal substances in cryptomarkets and epidemiological data in the physical world.

Notwithstanding the escalating prevalence of detrimental drug consumption, it is worth noting that cryptomarkets also have the potential to mitigate the adverse consequences associated with drug use through the dissemination of harm reduction knowledge to purchasers. Previously conducted analyses have clarified consumer preferences regarding transactions in the cryptomarket (Van Buskirk et al., 2016). Unsurprisingly, the quality of the drugs emerged as a significant determinant influencing consumers' inclination to utilise cryptomarkets. Caudevilla et al. (2016) studied laboratory analyses performed on samples submitted by vendors operating within cryptomarkets and discovered that the samples exhibited a higher level of purity and a lower degree of adulteration compared to samples obtained from sources on land.

The Purchasers

A significant portion of the initial literature on cryptomarkets concentrated on two main areas: the analysis of Silk Road data and the examination of user experiences and vendor characteristics through interviews (Maddox et al., 2016). The qualitative research conducted by van Hout and Bingham (2013) investigated the decision-making processes and motivational factors that drive consumers to engage in cryptomarket transactions. Based on the findings of a solitary case study, van Hout and Bingham (2013) argued that the inclusion of diverse controlled substances and the dynamics of cryptomarket reputation systems play significant roles in fostering user engagement. Furthermore, van Hout and Bingham (2013) discovered that individuals were drawn to the Silk Road platform due to curiosity and personal concerns. This was determined by monitoring discussion threads and conducting anonymous online interviews with a sample size of 20 participants. This study represented the inaugural attempt to investigate the demographic composition of individuals involved in cryptomarkets. The findings indicated that a significant proportion of users are Caucasian males aged 18–25 and that they exhibit a preference for substances such as MDMA, ketamine, cannabis and cocaine. The small sample size limits the generalisability of the findings from this study, but the findings are supported by three additional papers (Bancroft & Reid, 2016; Van Buskirk et al., 2016).

Regarding consumer participation, Barratt et al. (2016a, b) conducted a digital ethnography over 2 years (2012–2014). Their study involved a sample of 17 individuals who were buyers on the Silk Road platform. The comprehensive and unstructured interviews shed light on the fact that consumer engagement in cryptomarkets can be likened to a child in a confectionery store in that the abundance of products minimises the inclination to stockpile drugs. This phenomenon contributes to the regulation of drug consumption. The initial phase of euphoria commonly observed in individuals who have successfully procured drugs from a cryptomarket for the first time is gradually replaced by a consistent or declining pattern of drug consumption (Bancroft & Reid, 2016). A study conducted by van Hout and Hearne (2016) explored the viewpoints and perspectives of members of cryptomarket forums regarding new psychoactive substances. The findings revealed that purchasers demonstrated a high level of knowledge on the subject, placing significant importance on harm reduction and exchanging information with vendors before making buying decisions. Van Buskirk et al. (2016) observed that consumers in cryptomarkets generally exhibit greater involvement and engagement within their respective communities. Furthermore, Aldridge and Décary-Hétu (2016b), Décary-Hétu et al. (2018) and Demant et al. (2018) provided evidence indicating a growing trend in cryptomarkets towards facilitating business-to-business transactions and social drug dealing, rather than solely focusing on business-to-consumer transactions.

Geographic Spread

Several studies have demonstrated the potential for the globalisation of the drug trade through the dark web. Investigating the geographical dispersion of cryptomarket activity, Dolliver et al. (2018) revealed that Australia, Canada, Germany, the Netherlands, the United Kingdom and the United States exhibited the highest prevalence of listings and transactions involving heroin, cocaine and prescription drugs. Furthermore, heroin and cocaine are predominantly manufactured in South Asia and South America, two regions that have become significant production hubs. Van Buskirk et al. (2017) further discovered that 61.8% of the identified drug listings and 68% of the overall unique vendors on the Agora market came from the United States, the United Kingdom, Australia, China and the Netherlands. Australia exhibited the highest estimated number of sellers per capita, with a rate of 4.73 sellers per million individuals. This phenomenon can be comprehended intuitively given Australia's geographical isolation and comparatively elevated drug prices, both of which foster a greater inclination towards a domestic market catering to Australian consumers. Australia's involvement in the cryptomarket drug trade is quite distinctive, as argued by several scholarly studies (Phelps & Watt, 2014) that have unveiled a concentrated domestic market in Australia characterised by drug prices that surpass the average.

Broséus et al. (2017) investigated the spatial distribution of drug trafficking in the Evolution marketplace. The findings revealed that countries within Europe and the Anglosphere exhibited disproportionately high sales and numbers of listings on the Evolution platform. The United States accounted for 64% of drug listings and 30% of sales. Significantly, Broséus et al. (2017) also illustrated a certain degree of product specialisation, as evidenced by the fact that certain countries predominantly sourced niche prescription drugs. Such drugs comprised 98% of listings in the Netherlands, 97% in Canada, 96% in Spain and 94% in Sweden. Tsuchiya and Hiramoto (2021) similarly observed a greater prevalence of cryptomarket transactions in Europe, the United States, Canada and Australia than in other countries. However, they noted that transaction frequency differed considerably depending on the day of the week; there was a notable disparity between weekdays (particularly Monday, Tuesday and Wednesday) and weekends (Saturday and Sunday). This finding indicates that individuals utilising cryptomarkets tend to engage in drug transactions on weekdays, specifically from Monday to Wednesday, presumably to acquire substances for personal consumption during the upcoming weekend. This aligns with the findings of Aldridge and Décary-Hétu (2016b), Barratt et al. (2016a, b) and Demant et al. (2018), who argued that drug purchases made on cryptomarkets are primarily for recreational purposes rather than for wholesale transactions.

Demant et al. (2018) analysed product reviews from 15 cryptomarkets to gain insights into buyers' behaviour in these markets. The analysis indicated that, over time, local cryptomarkets emerge, with sellers and buyers living within the same country. An examination of publicly accessible crawls of the cryptomarket Abraxas by Norbutas (2018) revealed a tendency among buyers to engage in transactions with multiple sellers located within the same country while actively avoiding purchases from sellers in foreign countries. Furthermore, Norbutas (2018) found that online drug trade networks, much like their terrestrial counterparts, are significantly influenced by geographic limitations, despite their capacity to facilitate access to extensive international supplies for end-users (p. 96).

The COVID-19 pandemic significantly impacted consumer demand within cryptocurrency markets. Al (2021) analysed 851,199 transactions across 30 cryptomarkets over 10 months of 2020 and revealed a surge in the demand for COVID-19–related personal protective equipment, medications such as hydroxychloroquine and fraudulent dissemination of medical information. Additionally, the researchers observed an increase in COVID-19–related listings on cryptomarkets after the implementation of the Wuhan lockdown and European nations' enforcement of travel restrictions in March 2020. Conversely, a significant decline in listings was noted after restrictions were removed in Western countries.

Thus, cryptomarkets provide a diverse range of illegal commodities and services. The acquisition and trade of these commodities are predominantly carried out by individuals residing in developed nations in the Western hemisphere. These platforms primarily serve as facilitators for the illicit exchange of substances such as cannabis, cocaine, psychedelics and prescription drugs. There is empirical evidence indicating that certain cryptomarkets are witnessing a surge in the distribution of novel and highly hazardous substances such as fentanyl, although several cryptomarkets have implemented a prohibition on the trade of this particular product due to the inherent risks associated with its consumption (Lamy et al., 2020).

Buyer–Seller Relationships

Duxbury and Haynie (2017) analysed the structure of a transactional opioid network that operates on the dark web, looking both at the local and global levels. Using exponential random graph modelling, they illustrated that the opioid network exhibits a high degree of localisation, with the formation of distinct subgroups in which a minority of vendors are responsible for a majority of transactions. However, trust is a more robust indicator for selecting vendors than factors such as product diversity or affordability. Buyers tend to engage in repeat transactions with vendors they trust. On average, buyers on the cryptomarket make approximately 60% of purchases from the same vendor. Thus, social commerce networks within cryptomarkets operate according to the principle of preferential attachment, whereby vendors with high desirability amass a substantial customer base (Duxbury & Haynie, 2018; Diekmann et al., 2014; Stephen & Toubia, 2009). Nadini et al. (2022) observed 31 million Bitcoin transactions across 40 cryptomarkets from 2011 to 2021. Their findings indicated that half of the buyers and vendors engaging in trading activities use user-to-user pairs. These trading pairs exhibit long-term stability, often remaining unaffected by the COVID-19 pandemic and persisting even after the closure of the cryptomarket where the pair was initially established.

Andrei et al. (2023) suggested that the implementation of third-party enforcement mechanisms such as escrow systems decreases the volume of illicit drug transactions conducted in cryptomarkets. This observation implies the necessity for the natural establishment of trust and mutual exchange among users rather than the involvement of trust intermediaries.

The Role of Trust and Reputation in Cryptomarkets

The notions of trust and reputation influence the dynamics of the emerging and swiftly progressing domain of cryptomarkets. Trust can be defined as the level of confidence that individuals and participants place in the dependability, safety and genuineness of different components within the ecosystem of the cryptomarket, including the fundamental blockchain technology and the security protocols implemented for cryptocurrency exchanges. The overall credibility of the market and the level of transparency exhibited by projects and their objectives also play a large role. Trust is established by consistently fulfilling obligations, implementing secure technological protocols and preventing fraudulent activities that may compromise the market's integrity (for a broader discussion, see Gambetta, 2000).

In contrast, reputation refers to the communal perception and evaluation of individuals, projects or entities within the community of the cryptomarket. The outcome is derived from multiple participants' actions and behaviours over time. A favourable reputation can cultivate a perception of trustworthiness and dependability, thereby drawing the attention and involvement of investors, partners and users towards particular projects or platforms. However, a poor reputation that has been negatively affected by fraudulent activities, security breaches or unethical behaviour can result in reduced trust and subsequently decreased participation and market value. The dissemination of individuals' reputations within the cryptomarket ecosystem is facilitated by online communities, social media platforms and informal communication channels, significantly impacting decision-making processes and moulding the collective perception of different participants.

Thus, trust and reputation are closely linked and mutually supportive elements within the cryptomarket. Establishing a robust basis of trust significantly augments the standing of the projects and individuals involved. In the other direction, favourable standing can reinforce trust and foster broader participation. In the ever-evolving landscape of the cryptomarket, the establishment and preservation of trust and cultivation of a favourable reputation are crucial to the enduring viability and expansion of this domain. Still, it seems that betrayal is a prevailing modus operandi in cryptomarkets involving illicit goods. According to Wright and Decker (1994) and Hamill (2011), the act of betraying one's friends, family and associates is a common occurrence within the criminal underworld. The vulnerability of trust within the criminal underworld can be attributed to the unfavourable self-centeredness and inclination to engage in risky behaviour that are often exhibited by individuals involved in illegal activities (Gambetta, 2009, p. 30). Undoubtedly, criminals' various situational limitations, such as the risks of death, arrest and betrayal, can encourage them to consider breaching contractual commitments and fleeing when circumstances necessitate such actions.

How Do People Assign Trust to Others?

The absence of a governing body to enforce contractual obligations exacerbates the situation, unlike in legitimate markets. How can trust be fostered among criminals? Trust is the mechanism that individuals employ to manage and navigate the inherent risks and uncertainties that arise during their interactions with others (von Lampe & Johansen, 2004). Therefore, trust is crucial in facilitating collaboration among criminals when governance is lacking, enabling the successful execution of illicit activities. It is reduced to the specific degree of subjective probability that an individual assigns to the possibility that another individual or group of individuals will carry out a particular action. This assessment is made before any monitoring of the action occurs, even in situations where monitoring is not possible. It is made within a context that impacts the individual's actions (von Lampe & Johansen 2004).

Therefore, it becomes crucial to contemplate the methodology employed in assessing the trustworthiness of one's accomplices in criminal activities. To foster cooperation, a trustee must demonstrate a temporary suspension of their self-centred attitude to the truster (Williamson, 1993, p. 458). The issue of trust deficit within the criminal realm poses significant challenges for individuals who place trust in others. Employing a game theory approach, Gambetta and Bacharach (2001) revealed that a trustee's most advantageous course of action is to cheat or renege when a truster chooses to cooperate or endow trust. However, in repeated interactions, cheating has the most significant negative impact on trustees (Gambetta, 2009). The continuous display of deceitful behaviour by the trustee serves as a deterrent for the truster, ultimately resulting in the loss of any potential prospects for future business endeavours. Given the prevailing uncertainties and ethical laxity, it is possible to comprehend the inherent fragility and scarcity of trust within criminal activities.

A partial response can be found from social network analysis scholars who study how the lack of trust within social and, specifically, criminal networks of different scales affects the nodes (see Buskens, 2002; Carrington, 2011; Kloess & van der Bruggen, 2023). Transactions conducted among cybercriminals do not rely on the concept of "thick trust" (Khodyakov, 2007; see more recently Werbach, 2018) or bonding capital (Lo, 2010). The relationships in question are constructed based on a superficial or shallow trust that can be quickly established or broken due to their reliance on situational factors rather than a profound bond between the individuals involved. After all, it is more difficult to form a trusting relationship with someone acting under a pseudo-name whom you have never met in person and whose primary interest is to sell you cannabis online.

A study on botnet forums provides a case in point. Décary-Hétu and Dupont (2012) discovered that the level of trust placed in a vendor is frequently influenced by straightforward indicators, none of which are linked to trust aspects one would expect in the offline illicit goods trade. Typically, these criteria included the quantity of accolades obtained or the extent of an individual's professional connections. In this instance, trust at a superficial level was established based on individual attributes and prior conduct rather than through shared encounters that fostered a more profound sense of trust. However, a separate study conducted by Dupont et al. (2016) uncovered that the evaluation systems employed in botnet forums exhibit significant bias based on the rater's position in the community. In other words, individuals who recently joined the forum showed a decreased propensity to share negative reviews or evaluations. The predominant source of negative feedback was derived from individuals occupying positions of authority within the forum, namely, staff members and administrators. Notably, a mere 2.4% of the forum's members actively engaged in 75% of "trust exchanges".

Trust plays a pivotal role within cryptomarkets as well. Individuals or entities responsible for establishing cryptomarkets prioritise the development of unity and camaraderie among users with diverse functional backgrounds (Lacson & Jones, 2016). Examining the interactions between vendors and consumers reveals that these relationships tend to be established based on trust and professionalism (van Hout & Bingham, 2013, p. 387). To facilitate the exchange of goods and services, consumers and vendors must establish a mutual sense of trust. This trust is necessary to effectively communicate the quality of products and ensure the appropriate currency is used for the transaction. In this scenario, trust is established by sharing expectations among all parties involved in a voluntary transaction. To a significant degree, users of the cryptomarket openly exchange information regarding the quality of drugs and their value compared to street-level prices through online forums. Dasgupta et al. (2013) revealed that purchasers could accurately estimate the street value of diverted prescription opioids and predict the relative pharmacologic potency of different opioid molecules (p. 178). Undoubtedly, the accessibility of such high-quality information is limited within traditional criminal markets due to the absence of trust and the imperative for secrecy, resulting in the absence of dependable information about experiential goods.

Establishing Trust Behind a Veil of Anonymity

The perpetration of a criminal act frequently relies to a significant degree on the criminal's capacity to conceal their communications. This leads to law enforcement agencies' heightened difficulties in discerning individuals' intentions. Historically, criminals have employed encrypted methods of communication, which typically involved in-person exchanges in crowded establishments or secluded golf courses and long-distance communication facilitated by disposable mobile devices and covert radio frequencies (Gambetta, 2009, p. 155). Presently, however, the utilisation of encryption technology and direct messaging systems by cryptomarkets has effectively mechanised the maintenance of confidentiality and privacy. Cryptocurrencies and anonymity networks exhibit a higher degree of efficacy in confounding law enforcement authorities and, by extension, increasing the users' trust and confidence that the transaction will not lead to an arrest. The utilisation of routing software and cryptocurrencies facilitates the automation of these processes. This assertion is not intended to imply the invincibility of encryption in the cryptomarket, as it is acknowledged that human errors can still occur. However, this effectiveness in concealing information streamlines the communication process within cryptomarkets, allowing users to express their unlawful intentions and preferences openly. This is advantageous for individual advancement and effective exchange of information.

Promotion of Products

Sellers must participate in promotion to interact effectively and actively with potential customers. This involves establishing their identity as a reliable supplier and highlighting the superior quality of their products relative to others. Since numerous illicit commodities and services are experiential, it becomes necessary to establish a distinct trademark that can effectively link a vendor with their respective product. Heroin vendors have historically employed distinctive stamped delivery bags to distribute their products to clientele (Goldstein et al., 1984; Wendel & Curtis, 2000). The stamps served the purpose of establishing the dealer's distinct identity and the heroin product that they distribute. Similarly, vendors in the cryptomarket can personalise their seller pages to set themselves apart from other vendors. This feature is of utmost significance, as it enables them to establish direct connections with buyers. To differentiate themselves from different vendors and develop a direct connection with customers, vendors often adopt distinct usernames, including Joker's Stash's, Brian's Club, Vclub, Yale Lodge and UniCC (for additional vendor names, see Hämäläinen, 2019; Hämäläinen et al., 2021).

Nevertheless, due to the operational nature of dark web markets, the identities associated with vendors are ephemeral, and entities that presently enjoy a sense of security may cease to exist in the future (Wadsworth et al., 2018). Nonetheless, the establishment of reputations plays a crucial role in enabling criminal collaborations; individuals involved in illegal activities frequently lack familiarity or prior interactions with each other, necessitating the development of a foundation upon which trust can be established (Yip et al., 2013, p. 526). Furthermore, in light of the prevailing economic instability and the absence of a system of checks and balances within the realm of criminal activities, the significance of a positive reputation is equally, if not more, pronounced in illicit markets compared to legitimate ones (Przepiorka & Aksoy, 2017). According to Leeson (2005), users must determine in advance whether the individuals they wish to engage in trade with are "cheaters" or "cooperators" (p. 79).

Trust, Reputation and Customer Feedback

In cryptomarkets, vendor reputations are established based on consumers' incentives to offer publicly accessible feedback regarding vendor interactions. Customer feedback encompasses a diverse range of expression methods, which can include elaborate remarks regarding the duration of shipping, the discreet packaging methods and the perceived effectiveness of the illegal substances, as well as a straightforward rating system based on a five-star system (Jung et al., 2022; Kiss & Szigei, 2023). The reputation of a vendor may be widely known within the public domain of a cryptomarket, as it is openly showcased on their seller page (Christin, 2013; Tzanetakis et al., 2016). Vendors in cryptomarkets do not have the ability to modify the feedback that is publicly displayed on their respective pages, regardless of whether it is positive or negative—this serves as yet another barrier between fraudulent vendors and their customers. Therefore, it is impossible for self-serving vendors to artificially inflate their reputations, unless they employ bots and fictitious users (see Szigeti et al., 2023). Furthermore, it can be assumed that these reputations are current, as consumers frequently provide feedback upon receiving the requested product (van Hout & Bingham, 2013). Thus, providing customer feedback on interactions within the cryptomarket establishes trust within an environment inherently characterised by uncertainty.

Reputation and Sales

Przepiorka et al. (2017) found that vendors with higher ratings tended to have a longer presence in the market. This concept is intuitively logical, as a favourable reputation contributes to the sustained existence of a business by fostering loyalty among existing clientele and attracting new customers. Hardy and Norgaard (2016) and Janetos and Tilly (2017) employed data on cannabis listings sourced from Silk Road to examine the correlation between reputation and pricing. A mature vendor with a high rating tends to charge prices that are 20% higher compared to a mature vendor with a low rating. Typically, vendors with more reviews tend to impose higher prices than sellers who have received a relatively limited number of reviews, irrespective of their rating. Sellers with lower rankings opt to exit the market rather than reduce their prices in response to negative feedback. This finding aligns with the research conducted by Batikas and Kretschmer (2018) on the Agora marketplace, which revealed that vendors in cryptomarkets exhibited a higher tendency to exit the market in response to negative feedback received from customers. Moreover, according to Wagner's (2017) study involving a field experiment in a Chilean start-up accelerator, the provision of negative feedback reduces the likelihood of a start-up's continuation and increases the probability of its exit from the market.

A vendor's steady transaction history also decreases the probability of market withdrawal, as a more extensive transaction history is positively associated with sustained market engagement (Cabral & Hortaçsu 2010). In a related vein, online reviews on Yelp have a significant influence on the demand for restaurants (Luca, 2011) and hotels (Hollenbeck, 2017) and in the context of cryptomarkets (Przepiorka et al., 2017).

Additional Marketing Techniques

Feedback does not constitute the sole approach through which vendors can establish trust with buyers. Remarkably, vendors may engage in corporate mimicry to an extent considered outlandish due to their strong desire for a positive reputation. Cryptomarket vendors employ a variety of strategies to enhance their reputations. Christin (2013) asserted that as a minimum requirement, vendors are expected to engage potential customers with a warm and professional demeanour. According to Martin (2014a), the content of posts posted on these forums exhibits a notable disparity from the customary communication approaches attributed to traditional drug dealers. Their messages are expected to resonate positively with consumers who are accustomed to receiving exceptional levels of customer service in various domains of their daily lives.

Vendors may also employ legitimate retail strategies like Bitcoin lotteries and seasonal sales. On 4/20, also known as "International Pot Day", Silk Road held a major celebration wherein Ross Ulbricht eliminated all commission fees for cannabis transactions. More broadly, Ladegaard (2017) conducted a study which found that newly established vendors often employ strategies such as providing low-cost or complimentary samples to attract and retain customers.

Some vendors may utilise conscientious marketing strategies, proclaiming their dedication to selling products that incorporate high-quality ingredients. In certain instances, vendors may also influence consumers by asserting that their products were procured from impoverished agrarian farmers rather than individuals involved in the illicit drug trade (Martin, 2014a, p. 39). Indeed, it has been observed that terrestrial drug vendors evaluate prospective customers, a practice that encourages enduring relationships with clients through credit or discounts (Chalmers & Bradford, 2013; Jacques et al., 2014).

Conclusion

This chapter aimed to synthesise the existing body of literature on the cryptomarket, encompassing the major strands of research up until now. Indeed, the scholarly discourse surrounding cryptomarkets is presently in its nascent stage due to their relatively recent emergence. This chapter drew from some of the classic studies in criminology to understand how this offenders' market operates. However, the degree to which the existing criminological theories apply to cybercrime remains contested, and there is a need for further theoretical work.

References

Abdulhakeem, S. A., & Hu, Q. (2021). Powered by Blockchain technology, DeFi (Decentralized Finance) strives to increase financial inclusion of the unbanked by reshaping the world financial system. *Modern Economy, 12*(1), 1.

Aldridge, J. (2019). Does online anonymity boost illegal market trading? *Media, Culture and Society, 41*(4), 578–583.

Aldridge, J., & Décary-Hétu, D. (2014). *Not an "eBay for drugs": The cryptomarket "silk road" as a paradigm shifting criminal innovation.* SSRN.

Aldridge, J., & Décary-Hétu, D. (2016a). Cryptomarkets and the future of illicit drug markets. In *The internet and drug markets* (pp. 23–30). European Monitoring Centre for Drugs and Drug Addiction.

Aldridge, J., & Décary-Hétu, D. (2016b). Hidden wholesale: The drug diffusing capacity of online drug cryptomarkets. *International Journal of Drug Policy, 35*, 7–15.

AlKhatib, B., & Basheer, R. (2019). Crawling the dark web: A conceptual perspective, challenges and implementation. *Journal of Digital Information Management, 17*(2), 51.

Andrei, F., Barrera, D., Krakowski, K., & Sulis, E. (2023). Trust intermediary in a cryptomarket for illegal drugs. *European Sociological Review.*

Bancroft, A., & Reid, P. (2016). Concepts of illicit drug quality among darknet market users: Purity, embodied experience, craft and chemical knowledge. *International Journal of Drug Policy, 35*, 42–49.

Barratt, M., & Aldridge, J. (2016). Everything you always wanted to know about drug cryptomarkets* (*but were afraid to ask). *International Journal of Drug Policy, 35*, 1–6.

Barratt, M., Ferris, J., & Winstock, A. (2016a). Safer scoring? Cryptomarkets, social supply and drug market violence. *International Journal of Drug Policy, 35*, 24–31.

Barratt, M., Lenton, S., Maddox, A., & Allen, M. (2016b). "What if you live on top of a bakery and you like cakes?"—Drug use and harm trajectories before, during and after the emergence of Silk Road. *International Journal of Drug Policy, 35*, 50–57.

Barratt, M. J., Lamy, F. R., Engel, L., Davies, E., Puljevic, C., Ferris, J. A., & Winstock, A. R. (2022). Exploring Televend, an innovative combination of cryptomarket and messaging app technologies for trading prohibited drugs. *Drug and Alcohol Dependence, 231*, 109243.

Barrera, V., Malm, A., Décary-Hétu, D., & Munksgaard, R. (2019). Size and scope of the tobacco trade on the darkweb. *Global Crime, 20*(1), 26–44.

Batikas, M., & Kretschmer, T. (2018). *Entrepreneurs on the darknet: Reaction to negative feedback*. SSRN. https://ssrn.com/abstract=3238141.

Bichler, G., Malm, A., & Cooper, T. (2017). Drug supply networks: A systematic review of the organizational structure of illicit drug trade. *Crime Science, 6*(1), 1–23.

Bossler, A., & Holt, T. (2016). On the need for policing cybercrime research. *ACJS Today, 41*(1), 14.

Bradbury, D. (2014). Unveiling the dark web. *Network Security, 4*, 14–17.

Brenner, S. (2010). *Cybercrime: Criminal threats from cyberspace*. Praeger.

Brewer, R., & Goldsmith, A. (2014). Digital drift and the criminal interaction order. *Theoretical Criminology, 19*(1), 23–41.

Bright, D. A., Greenhill, C., & Levenkova, N. (2014). Dismantling criminal networks: Can node attributes play a role? In C. Morselli (Ed.), *Crime and networks* (pp. 148–162). Routledge.

Broséus, J., Rhumorbarbe, D., Mireault, C., Ouellette, V., Crispino, F., & Décary-Hétu, D. (2017). Studying illicit drug trafficking on Darknet markets: Structure and organisation from a Canadian perspective. *Forensic Science International, 264*, 7–14.

Brown, R., & Smith, R. G. (2018). Exploring the relationship between organised crime and volume crime. *Trends and Issues in Crime and Criminal Justice, 565*, 1–15.

Buskens, V. (2002). *Social networks and trust* (Vol. 30). Springer Science & Business Media.

Cabral, L., & Hortaçsu, A. (2010). The dynamics of seller reputation: Evidence from eBay. *Journal of Industrial Economics, 58*, 54–78.

Carnevali, D., Cavazzana, L., Grimoldi, L., Magnoni, P., Principi, N., & Pellai, A. (2022). The use of online pornography among minors: Epidemiological analysis of the phenomenon. *Minerva Pediatrics, 74*, 579–585.

Carrington, P. J. (2011). Crime and social network analysis. In *The SAGE handbook of social network analysis* (pp. 236–255).

Catino, M. (2014). How so mafias organize? Conflict and violence in three mafia organizations. *European Journal of Sociology, 55*(2), 177–220.

Caton, J. L., Jr., & Harwick, C. (2022). Cryptocurrency, decentralized finance, and the evolution of money: A transaction costs approach. *Journal of New Finance, 2*(4), 2521–2486.

Caudevilla, F., Ventura, M., Fornís, I., Barratt, M. J., Vidal, C., Iladanosa, C. G., et al. (2016). Results of an international drug testing service for cryptomarket users. *International Journal of Drug Policy, 35*, 38–41.

Chalmers, D., & Bradford, J. (2013). Methamphetamine users' perceptions of exchanging drugs for money: Does trust matter? *Journal of Drug Issues, 43*(3), 256–269.

Chen, S., Hao, M., Ding, F., Jiang, D., Dong, J., Zhang, S., et al. (2023). Exploring the global geography of cybercrime and its driving forces. *Humanities and Social Sciences Communications, 10*(1), 1–10.

Christin, N. (2013, May). Traveling the Silk Road: A measurement analysis of a large anonymous online marketplace. In *Proceedings of the 22nd international conference on World Wide Web* (pp. 213–224). https://doi.org/10.1145/2488388.2488408.

Chung, S., Kim, K., Lee, C. H., & Oh, W. (2023). Interdependence between online peer-to-peer lending and cryptocurrency markets and its effects on financial inclusion. *Production and Operations Management., 32*, 1939.

Coats, W. (2022). A libertarian money. *Journal of Applied Business and Economics, 24*(5), 1–6.

Cohen, L., & Felson, M. (1979). Social change and crime rate trends: A routine activity approach. *American Sociological Review, 44*(4), 588–608.

Cox, J. (2016). Staying in the shadows: The use of bitcoin and encryption in cryptomarkets. In *Internet and drug markets* (pp. 41–47). EMCDDA.

Cressey, D. (1967). Methodological problems in the study of organized crime as a social problem. *AAPSS, 374*(1), 101–112.

Cunliffe, J., Décary-Hêtu, D., & Pollak, T. (2019). Nonmedical prescription psychiatric drug use and the darknet: A cryptomarket analysis. *International Journal of Drug Policy, 73*, 263–272.

Dasgupta, N., Freifeld, C., Brownstein, J., Menone, C., Surratt, H., Poppish, L., Green, J., Lavonas, E., & Dart, R. (2013). Crowdsourcing black market prices for prescription opioids. *Journal of Medical Internet Research, 15*(8), e178.

Davelis, A., Butt, U. J., Pendlebury, G., & Hussein, K. E. (2022). Emerging technologies: Blockchain and smart contracts. In *Blockchain and other emerging technologies for digital business strategies* (pp. 143–169).

de Alarcón, R., de la Iglesia, J. I., Casado, N. M., & Montejo, A. L. (2019). Online porn addiction: What we know and what we don't—A systematic review. *Journal of Clinical Medicine, 8*(1), 91.

Décary-Hétu, D. (2016). Policing cybercrime and cyberterror. *Global Crime, 17*(1), 123–125.

Décary-Hétu, D., & Dupont, B. (2012). The social network of hackers. *Global Crime, 13*(3), 1–16.

Décary-Hétu, D., & Giommoni, L. (2017). Do police crackdowns disrupt drug cryptomarkets? A longitudinal analysis of the effects of Operation Onymous. *Crime, Law, and Social Change, 67*(1), 55–75.

Décary-Hétu, D., Mousseau, V., & Vidal, S. (2018). Six years later: Analyzing online black markets involved in herbal cannabis drug dealing in the United States. *Contemporary Drug Problems, 45*(4), 366–381.

Demant, J., Munksgaard, R., & Houborg, E. (2018). Personal use, social supply or redistribution? Cryptomarket demand on Silk Road 2 and Agora. *Trends in Organized Crime, 21*(1), 42–61.

Denley, J., & Ariel, B. (2019). Whom should we target to prevent? Analysis of organized crime in England using intelligence records. *European Journal of Crime, Criminal Law and Criminal Justice, 27*(1), 13–44.

Diekmann, A., Jann, B., Przepiorka, W., & Wherli, S. (2014). Reputation formation and the evolution of cooperation in anonymous online markets. *American Sociological Review, 79*, 65–85.

Dingledine, R., Mathewson, N., & Syberson, P. (2004). Tor: The second-generation Onion Router. In *13th USENIX security symposium*, San Diego, CA.

Djenna, A., Barka, E., Benchikh, A., & Khadir, K. (2023). Unmasking cybercrime with artificial-intelligence-driven cybersecurity analytics. *Sensors, 23*(14), 6302.

Dolliver, D., Ericson, S., & Love, K. (2018). A geographic analysis of drug trafficking patterns on the TOR Network. *Geographical Review, 108*(1), 45–68.

Dooley, J. J., Pyżalski, J., & Cross, D. (2009). Cyberbullying versus face-to-face bullying: A theoretical and conceptual review. *Zeitschrift für Psychologie/Journal of Psychology, 217*(4), 182–188.

Dupont, B., Côté, A., Savine, C., & Décary-Hétu, D. (2016). The ecology of trust among hackers. *Global Crime, 17*(2), 129–151.

Duxbury, S., & Haynie, D. (2017). The network structure of opioid distribution on a darknet cryptomarket. *Journal of Quantitative Criminology, 34*(4), 921–941.

Duxbury, S., & Haynie, D. (2018). Building them up, breaking them down: Topology, vendor selection patterns, and a digital drug market's robustness to disruption. *Social Networks, 52*, 238–250.

Elluri, L., Mandalapu, V., Vyas, P., & Roy, N. (2023). *Advances in cybercrime prediction: A survey of machine, deep, transfer, and adaptive learning techniques.* ArXiv. arXiv:2304.04819.

Evangelio, C., Rodriguez-Gonzalez, P., Fernandez-Rio, J., & Gonzalez-Villora, S. (2022). Cyberbullying in elementary and middle school students: A systematic review. *Computers and Education, 176*, 104356.

Eyal, I. (2017). Blockchain technology: Transforming libertarian cryptocurrency dreams to finance and banking realities. *Computer, 50*(9), 38–49.

Farley, M., Franzblau, K., & Kennedy, M. (2013). Online prostitution and trafficking. *Albany Law Review, 77*(3), 1039–1094.

Fiorentini, G. (1999). Organized crime and illegal markets. In B. Bouckaert & G. De Geest (Eds.), *Encyclopedia of law and economics* (pp. 434–459).

Foley, S., Karlsen, J., & Putnins, T. (2018). Sex, drugs, and bitcoin: How much illegal activity is financed through cryptocurrencies? *Review of Financial Studies, 32*(5), 1798–1853.

Gabrian, C. A. (2022). How the Russia-Ukraine War may change the cybercrime ecosystem. *Bulletin Of Carol I National Defence University, 11*(4), 43–49.

Gambetta, D. (1993). *The Sicilian Mafia: The business of private protection.* Harvard University Press.

Gambetta, D. (2000). Can we trust trust? In D. Gambetta (Ed.), *Trust: Making and breaking cooperative relations* (pp. 213–237). Department of Sociology, University of Oxford.

Gambetta, D. (2009). *Codes of the underworld: How criminals communicate.* Princeton University Press.

Gambetta, D., & Bacharach, M. (2001). Trust in Signs. In K. Cook (Ed.), *Trust and society* (pp. 148–184). Russell Sage Foundation.

Giommoni, L., Décary-Hétu, D., Berlusconi, G., & Bergeron, A. (2023). Online and offline determinants of drug trafficking across countries via Cryptomarkets. In *Crime, law and social change* (pp. 1–25).

Goldstein, P. J., Lipton, D. S., Preble, E., Sobel, I., Miller, T., Abbott, W., et al. (1984). The marketing of street heroin in New York City. *Journal of Drug Issues, 14*(3), 553–566.

Goni, O. (2022). Cybercrime and its classification. *International Journal of Electronics Engineering and Applications, 10*(1), 1–17.

Grabosky, P. (2007). The internet, technology, and organized crime. *Asian Criminology, 2*, 145–161.

Grabosky, P. N., & Smith, R. (2001). Telecommunication fraud in the digital age: The convergence of technologies. In D. Wall (Ed.), *Crime and the internet* (pp. 29–43). Routledge.

Gray, I. W., Cable, J., Brown, B., Cuiujuclu, V., & McCoy, D. (2022). Money over morals: A business analysis of Conti Ransomware. In *In 2022 APWG symposium on electronic crime research (eCrime)* (pp. 1–12). IEEE.

Hämäläinen, L. (2019). Usernames of illegal drug vendors on a darknet cryptomarket. *Onoma, 50*, 43–68.

Hämäläinen, L., Haasio, A., & Harviainen, J. T. (2021). Usernames on a Finnish online marketplace for illegal drugs. *Names, 69*(3).

Hamill, H. (2011). *The hoods: Crime and punishment in West Belfast.* Princeton University Press.

Hardy, R., & Norgaard, J. (2016). Reputation in the Internet black market: An empirical and theoretical analysis of the Deep Web. *Journal of Institutional Economics, 12*(3), 515–539.

Himmelstein, D. S., Romero, A. R., Levernier, J. G., Munro, T. A., McLaughlin, S. R., Greshake Tzovaras, B., & Greene, C. S. (2018). Sci-Hub provides access to nearly all scholarly literature. *eLife, 7*, e32822.

Hollenbeck, B. (2017). The economic advantages of chain organization. *The Rand Journal of Economics, 48*(4), 1103–1135.

Holt, T. J., & Bossler, A. M. (2008). Examining the applicability of lifestyle-routine activities theory for cybercrime victimization. *Deviant Behavior, 30*(1), 1–25.

Holt, T. J., & Bossler, A. (2014). *Cybercrime.* Oxford University Press.

Hunt-Sharman, J. (2022). Transnational organised cybercrime. *Australasian Policing, 14*(2), 5–7.

Hutchings, A., & Holt, T. J. (2015). A crime script analysis of the online stolen data market. *British Journal of Criminology, 55*(3), 596–614.

Ianelli, N., & Hackworth, A. (2005). *Botnets as a vehicle for online crime.* Carnegie Melon University.

Jacques, S., Allen, A., & Wright, R. (2014). Drug dealers' rational choices on which customers to rip-off. *International Journal of Drug Policy, 25*(2), 251–256.

Janetos, N., & Tilly, J. (2017). *Reputation dynamics in a market for illicit drugs* (Unpublished paper).

Janze, C. (2017). Are cryptocurrencies criminals best friends? Examining the co-evolution of Bitcoin and darknet markets. In *Twenty-third Americas conference on information systems*.

Jardine, E., Cruz, S., & Kissel, H. (2023). Media coverage of darknet market closures: Assessing the impact of coverage on US search and Tor use activity. *Crime, Law and Social Change, 79*(3), 263–289.

Jung, B. R., Choi, K. S., & Lee, C. S. (2022). Dynamics of Dark Web financial marketplaces: An exploratory study of underground fraud and scam business. *International Journal of Cybersecurity Intelligence & Cybercrime, 5*(2), 4–24.

Kamar, E., Maimon, D., Weisburd, D., & Shabat, D. (2022). Parental guardianship and online sexual grooming of teenagers: A honeypot experiment. *Computers in Human Behavior, 137*, 107386.

Kee, D. M. H., Al-Anesi, M. A. L., & Al-Anesi, S. A. L. (2022). Cyberbullying on social media under the influence of COVID-19. *Global Business and Organizational Excellence, 41*(6), 11–22.

Kenney, M. (2007). The architecture of drug trafficking: Network forms of organisation in the Colombian cocaine trade. *Global Crime, 8*(3), 233–259.

Khodyakov, D. (2007). Trust as a process. *Sociology, 41*(1), 115–132.

Kirli, D., Couraud, B., Robu, V., Salgado-Bravo, M., Norbu, S., Andoni, M., et al. (2022). Smart contracts in energy systems: A systematic review of fundamental approaches and implementations. *Renewable and Sustainable Energy Reviews, 158*, 112013.

Kiss, T., & Szigeti, Á. (2023). Ranking trust factors affecting risk perception in illicit drug purchase on the darknet: A large-scale survey study in Hungary. *European Journal on Criminal Policy and Research*, 1–16.

Klerks, P. (2001). The network paradigm applied to criminal organisations: Theoretical nitpicking or a relevant doctrine for investigators? Recent developments in The Netherlands. *Connect, 24*(3), 53–65.

Kloess, J. A., & van der Bruggen, M. (2023). Trust and relationship development among users in Dark Web child sexual exploitation and abuse networks: A literature review from a psychological and criminological perspective. *Trauma, Violence, & Abuse, 24*(3), 1220–1237.

Kritika, K., Himanshi, H., Dubey, R., & Mittal, Y. (2021). Delve into the ambience of anonymity: Deep web. In *Proceedings of 3rd international conference on computing informatics and networks: ICCIN 2020* (pp. 391–400). Springer Singapore.

Lacson, W., & Jones, B. (2016). The 21st century DarkNet market: Lessons from the fall of Silk Road. *International Journal of Cyber Criminology, 10*(1), 40–61.

Ladegaard, I. (2017). We know where you are, what you are doing and we will catch you: Testing deterrence theory in digital drug markets. *The British Journal of Criminology, 58*(2), 414–433.

Lamy, F., Daniulaityte, R., Barratt, M., Lokala, U., Sheth, A., & Carlson, R. (2020). Listed for sale: Analyzing data on fentanyl, fentanyl analogs and other novel synthetic opioids on one cryptomarket. *Drug and Alcohol Dependence, 213*, 1–8.

Lee, J. H. (2019). Rise of anonymous cryptocurrencies: Brief introduction. *IEEE Consumer Electronics Magazine, 8*(5), 20–25.

Leeson, P. T. (2005). Endogenizing Fractionalization. *Journal of Institutional Economics, 1*(1), 75–98.

Leukfeldt, E. R., & Yar, M. (2016). Applying routine activity theory to cybercrime: A theoretical and empirical analysis. *Deviant Behavior, 37*(3), 263–280.

Levi, M. (2022). Frauds in digital society. In W. Housley, R. Fitzgerald, R. Beneito-Montagut, & A. Edwards (Eds.), *The SAGE handbook of digital society* (pp. 480–499).

Lewczuk, K., Nowakowska, I., Lewandowska, K., Potenza, M. N., & Gola, M. (2021). Frequency of use, moral incongruence and religiosity and their relationships with self-perceived addiction to pornography, internet use, social networking and online gaming. *Addiction, 116*(4), 889–899.

Lewman, A. (2016). Tor and links with cryptomarkets. In *Internet and drug markets* (pp. 33–40). EMCDDA.

Liddick, D. (1999). The enterprise "model" of organized crime: Assessing theoretical propositions. *Justice Quarterly, 16*(2), 403–430.

Lim, M. S., Carrotte, E. R., & Hellard, M. E. (2016). The impact of pornography on gender-based violence, sexual health and well-being: What do we know? *Journal of Epidemiology and Community Health, 70*(1), 3–5.

Linder, C. (2019). The entrepreneurial criminal: How trust coordinates illicit drug cryptomarkets. In *Entrepreneurship and development in the 21st century* (pp. 171–189). Emerald Publishing Limited.

Livingstone, S., & Helsper, E. (2010). Balancing opportunities and risks in teenagers' use of the internet: The role of online skills and internet self-efficacy. *New Media and Society, 12*(2), 309–329.

Lo, T. W. (2010). Beyond social capital: Triad organized crime in Hong Kong and China. *The British Journal of Criminology, 50*(5), 851–872.

Lokala, U., Lamy, F., Daniulaityte, R., Sheth, A., Nahhas, R., Roden, J., Yadav, S., & Carlson, R. (2019). Global trends, local harms: Availability of fentanyl-type drugs on the dark web and accidental overdoses in Ohio. *Computational and Mathematical Organization Theory, 25*(1), 48–59.

Luca, M. (2011). *Reviews, reputation, and revenue: The case of yelp.com.* (Working Paper).

Lukasik, S. (2010). Why the ARPANET was built. *IEEE Annals of the History of Computing, 33*(3), 4–21.

Lusthaus, J. (2012). Trust in the world of cybercrime. *Global Crime, 13*(2), 71–94.

Lusthaus, J. (2018). *Industry of anonymity.* Harvard University Press.

Maddox, A., Barratt, M., Allen, M., & Lenton, S. (2016). Constructive activism in the dark web: Cryptomarkets and illicit drugs in the digital "demimonde" information. *Communications Society, 19*, 111–126.

Maese, V. A., Avery, A. W., Naftalis, B. A., Wink, S. P., & Valdez, Y. D. (2016). Cryptocurrency: A primer. *Banking Lj, 133*, 468.

Malm, A., & Bichler, G. (2011). Networks of collaborating criminals: Assessing the structural vulnerability of drug markets. *Journal of Research in Crime and Delinquency, 48*(2), 271–297.

Martin, J. (2014a). *Drugs on the dark net.* Palgrave Macmillan.

Martin, J. (2014b). Lost on the Silk Road: Online drug distribution and the "cryptomarket.". *Criminology & Criminal Justice, 14*(3), 351–367.

Martin, J. (2023). Cryptomarkets and drug market gentrification. In *Digital transformations of illicit drug markets: Reconfiguration and continuity* (pp. 127–139). Emerald Publishing Limited.

Martin, J., Cunliffe, J., Décary-Hétu, D., & Aldridge, J. (2018). Effect of restricting the legal supply of prescription opioids on buying through online illicit marketplaces: Interrupted time series analysis. *BMJ, 361*, 1–27.

Masson, K., & Bancroft, A. (2018). Nice people doing shady things': Drugs and the morality of exchange in the darknet cryptomarkets. *International Journal of Drug Policy, 58*, 78–84.

Mathewson, N., & Dingledine, R. (2004, May). Practical traffic analysis: Extending and resisting statistical disclosure. In *International workshop on privacy enhancing technologies* (pp. 17–34). Springer Berlin Heidelberg.

May, T., & Hough, M. (2004). Drug markets and distribution systems. *Addiction Research & Theory, 12*(6), 549–563.

Miller, T., Cao, S., Foth, M., Boyen, X., & Powell, W. (2023). An asset-backed decentralised finance instrument for food supply chains—A case study from the livestock export industry. *Computers in Industry, 147*, 103863.

Moe, M. E. G. (2008). Quantification of anonymity for mobile ad hoc networks. *Electronic Notes in Theoretical Computer Science, 244*, 1–12.

Moeller, K. (2022). Hybrid governance in online drug distribution. *Contemporary Drug Problems, 49*(4), 491–504.

Mohamed, R., & Fritsvold, E. (2010). Is the college campus a safe haven for drug dealers? *Symbolic Interaction, 34*(2), 309–311.

Montieri, A., Ciuonzo, D., Aceto, G., & Pescapé, A. (2018). Anonymity services Tor, I2P, JonDonym: Classifying in the dark (web). *IEEE Transactions on Dependable and Secure Computing, 17*(3), 662–675.

Morselli, C., Giguere, C., & Petit, K. (2007). The efficiency/security trade-off in criminal networks. *Social Networks, 29*(1), 143–153.

Morselli, C., Décary-Hétu, D., Paquet-Clouston, M., & Aldridge, J. (2017). Conflict management in illicit drug cryptomarkets. *International Criminal Justice Review, 27*(4), 237–254.

Munksgaard, R., & Demant, J. (2016). Mixing politics and crime—The prevalence and decline of political discourse on the cryptomarket. *International Journal of Drug Policy, 35*, 77–83.

Munksgaard, R., & Martin, J. (2020). How and why vendors sell on cryptomarkets. *Trends and Issues in Crime and Criminal Justice, 608*, 1–12.

Nadini, M., Bracci, A., ElBahrawy, A., Gradwell, P., Teytelboym, A., & Baronchelli, A. (2022). Emergence and structure of decentralised trade networks around dark web marketplaces. *Scientific Reports, 12*(1), 1–9.

Natanelov, V., Cao, S., Foth, M., & Dulleck, U. (2022). Blockchain smart contracts for supply chain finance: Mapping the innovation potential in Australia-China beef supply chains. *Journal of Industrial Information Integration, 30*, 100389.

Natarajan, M. (2006). Understanding the structure of a large heroin distribution network: A quantitative analysis of qualitative data. *Journal of Quantitative Criminology, 22*(2), 171–192.

Ngo, F. T., Marcum, C., & Belshaw, S. (2023). The dark web: What is it, how to access it, and why we need to study it. *Journal of Contemporary Criminal Justice, 39*(2), 160–166.

Norbutas, L. (2018). Offline constraints in online drug marketplaces: An exploratory analysis of a cryptomarket trade network. *International Journal of Drug Policy, 56*, 92–100.

Norgaard, J., Walbert, H., & Hardy, R. (2018). Shadow markets and hierarchies: Comparing and modeling networks in the Dark Net. *Journal of Institutional Economics, 14*, 1–23.

Olweus, D., & Limber, S. P. (2018). Some problems with cyberbullying research. *Current Opinion in Psychology, 19*, 139–143.

Ozili, P. K. (2022). CBDC, Fintech and cryptocurrency for financial inclusion and financial stability. *Digital Policy, Regulation and Governance, 25*(1), 40–57.

Papachristos, A. V., & Bastomski, S. (2018). Connected in crime: The enduring effect of neighborhood networks on the spatial patterning of violence. *American Journal of Sociology, 124*(2), 517–568.

Paquet-Clouston, M., & García, S. (2023). On the dynamics behind profit-driven cybercrime: from contextual factors to perceived group structures, and the workforce at the periphery. *Global Crime, 24*(2), 122–144.

Pease, K. (1991). The Kirkholt Project: Preventing burglary on a British public housing estate. *Security Journal, 2*, 73–77.

Phelps, A., & Watt, A. (2014). I shop online—Recreationally! Internet anonymity and Silk Road enabling drug use in Australia. *Digital Investigation, 11*(4), 261–272.

Phillips, K., Davidson, J. C., Farr, R. R., Burkhardt, C., Caneppele, S., & Aiken, M. P. (2022). Conceptualising cybercrime: Definitions, typologies and taxonomies. *Forensic Science, 2*(2), 379–398.

Phochanachan, P., Pirabun, N., Leurcharusmee, S., & Yamaka, W. (2022). Do Bitcoin and traditional financial assets act as an inflation hedge during stable and turbulent markets? Evidence from high cryptocurrency adoption countries. *Axioms, 11*(7), 339.

Przepiorka, W., & Aksoy, O. (2017). *Social order in online markets and the "collapse" of institutions* (Unpublished manuscript). Department of Sociology/ICS, Utrecht University.

Przepiorka, W., Norbutas, L., & Corten, R. (2017). Order without law: Reputation promotes cooperation in a cryptomarket for illegal drugs. *European Sociological Review, 33*(6), 752–764.

Reuter, P. (1985). *Disorganized crime*. MIT Press Cambridge.

Sakurai, Y., & Kurosaki, T. (2023). Have cryptocurrencies become an inflation hedge after the reopening of the US economy? *Research in International Business and Finance, 65*, 101915.

Saleem, J., Islam, R., & Kabir, M. A. (2022). The anonymity of the dark web: A survey. *IEEE Access, 10*, 33628–33660.

Savona, E., & Mignone, M. (2004). The fox and the hunters: How IC technologies change the crime race. In *Crime and technology: New frontiers for regulations, law enforcement and research* (pp. 7–28).

Shearing, C., & Wood, J. (2003). Nodal governance, democracy, and the new "denizens". *Journal of Law and Society, 30*(3), 400–419.

Silva, E. C., & Silva, M. M. D. (2021). Motivations to regulate cryptocurrencies: A systematic literature review of stakeholders and drivers. *International Journal of Blockchains and Cryptocurrencies, 2*(4), 360–388.

Sinclair, R., Bland, M., & Savage, B. (2023). Dating hot spot to fraud hot spot: Targeting the social characteristics of romance fraud victims in England and Wales. *Criminology and Public Policy, 22*, 591.

Siregar, G., & Sinaga, S. (2021). The law globalization in cybercrime prevention. *International Journal of Law Reconstruction, 5*(2), 211–227.

Soska, K., & Christin, N. (2015). Measuring the longitudinal evolution of the online anonymous marketplace ecosystem [Paper presentation]. In *24th USENIX security symposium*, Washington, D.C.

Sotirakopoulos, N. (2018). Cryptomarkets as a libertarian counter-conduct of resistance. *European Journal of Social Theory, 21*(2), 189–206.

Stephen, A., & Toubia, O. (2009). Explaining the power-law degree distribution in a social commerce network. *Social Networks, 31*(4), 262–270.

Strossen, N. (2000). *Defending pornography: Free speech, sex, and the fight for women's rights.* NYU Press.

Szigeti, Á., Frank, R., & Kiss, T. (2023). Trust factors in the social figuration of online drug trafficking: A qualitative content analysis on a darknet market. *Journal of Contemporary Criminal Justice, 39*(2), 167–184.

Thomaz, F., Salge, C., Karahanna, E., & Hulland, J. (2020). Learning from the Dark Web: leveraging conversational agents in the era of hyper-privacy to enhance marketing. *Journal of the Academy of Marketing Science, 48*, 43–63.

Tokunaga, R. S. (2010). Following you home from school: A critical review and synthesis of research on cyberbullying victimization. *Computers in Human Behaviour, 26*(3), 277–287.

Tsuchiya, Y., & Hiramoto, N. (2021). Dark web in the dark: Investigating when transactions take place on cryptomarkets. *Forensic Science International: Digital Investigation, 36*, 1–38.

Tzanetakis, M. (2019). Informal governance on cryptomarkets for illicit drugs. In *Governance beyond the law: The immoral, the illegal, the criminal* (pp. 343–361).

Tzanetakis, M., Kamphausen, G., Werse, B., & von Laufenberg, R. (2016). The transparency paradox. Building trust, resolving disputes and optimising logistics on conventional and online drugs markets. *International Journal of Drug Policy, 35*, 58–68.

Van Buskirk, J., Naicker, S., Roxburgh, A., Bruno, R., & Burns, R. (2016). Who sells what? Country specific differences in substance availability on the Agora cryptomarket. *International Journal of Drug Policy, 35*, 16–23.

Van Buskirk, J., Bruno, R., Dobbins, T., Breen, C., Burns, L., Naicker, S., & Roxburgh, A. (2017). The recovery of online drug markets following law enforcement and other disruptions. *Drug and Alcohol Dependence, 173*, 159–162.

Van Hout, M., & Bingham, T. (2013). Surfing the Silk Road': A study of users' experiences. *International Journal of Drug Policy, 24*, 524–529.

Van Hout, M., & Hearne, E. (2016). New psychoactive substances (NPS) on cryptomarket fora: An exploratory study of characteristics of forum activity between NPS buyers and vendors. *International Journal of Drug Policy, 40*, 102–110.

Varese, F. (2010). *Organized crime: Origins, resources and organization.* Routledge.

Vincent, O., & Evans, O. (2019). Can cryptocurrency, mobile phones, and the internet herald sustainable financial sector development in emerging markets? *Journal of Transnational Management, 24*(3), 259–279.

von Lampe, K. (2015). *Organized crime: Analyzing illegal activities, criminal structures, and extra-legal governance.* Sage Publications.

von Lampe, K. (2016). *Organized crime.* Sage Publications.

von Lampe, K., & Johansen, P. (2004). Organized crime and trust: On the conceptualization and empirical relevance of trust in the context of criminal networks. *Global Crime, 6*(2), 159–184.

Wadsworth, E., Drummond, C., & Deluca, P. (2018). The dynamic environment of cryptomarkets: the lifespan of new psychoactive substances (NPS) and vendors selling NPS. *Brain Sciences, 8*(3), 46.

Wagner, R. (2017). *Does feedback to business-plans impact new ventures? Fundraising in a randomized field experiment.* (Working Paper).

Wall, D. S. (2001). Maintaining order and law on the internet. In D. S. Wall (Ed.), *Crime and the internet* (pp. 167–183). Routledge.

Wall, D. (2007). Policing cybercrimes: Situating the public police in networks of security within cyberspace. *Police Practice and Research, 8*(2), 183–205.

Wallbach, S., Lehner, R., Roethke, K., Elbert, R., & Benlian, A. (2020). Trust-building effects of Blockchain features—An empirical analysis of immutability, traceability and anonymity. *ECIS 2020 RESEARCH PAPERS.*

Webz.io. (2023). *The top 10 dark web marketplaces in 2023.* https://webz.io/dwp/the-top-10-dark-web-marketplaces-in-2023/

Wendel, T., & Curtis, R. (2000). The heraldry of heroin: "Dope stamps" and the dynamics of drug markets in New York City. *Journal of Drug Issues, 30*(2), 225–259.

Werbach, K. (2018). *The blockchain and the new architecture of trust.* MIT Press.

Williams, M. L., Levi, M., Burnap, P., & Gundur, R. V. (2019). Under the corporate radar: Examining insider business cybercrime victimization through an application of routine activities theory. *Deviant Behavior, 40*(9), 1119–1131.

Williamson, O. (1993). Calculativeness, trust, and economic organization. *Journal of Law and Economics, 36*(1), 453–486.

Windle, J. (2021). Horizon scanning of global drug markets. In *Routledge handbook of transnational organized crime* (pp. 215–231).

Wolak, J., Mitchell, K. J., & Finkelhor, D. (2007). Does online harassment constitute bullying? An exploration of online harassment by known peers and online-only contacts. *Journal of Adolescent Health, 41*(6), S51–S58.

Woods, D. W., & Walter, L. (2022). Reviewing estimates of cybercrime victimisation and cyber risk likelihood. In *2022 IEEE European symposium on security and privacy workshops (EuroSandPW)* (pp. 150–162). IEEE.

Wright, R., & Decker, S. (1994). *Burglars on the job: Streetlife and residential break-ins.* Northeastern University Press.

Xue, L., Liu, D., Ni, J., Lin, X., & Shen, X. S. (2022). Enabling regulatory compliance and enforcement in decentralized anonymous payment. *IEEE Transactions on Dependable and Secure Computing, 20*(2), 931–943.

Yar, M. (2005). The novelty of cybercrime. *European Journal of Criminology, 2*, 407–427.

Ye, X., Zeng, N., & König, M. (2022). Systematic literature review on smart contracts in the construction industry: Potentials, benefits, and challenges. *Frontiers of Engineering Management, 9*(2), 196–213.

Yip, M., Webber, C., & Shadbolt, N. (2013). Trust among cybercriminals? Carding forums, uncertainty and implications for policing. *Policing and Society, 23*(4), 516–539.

Zaunseder, A., & Bancroft, A. (2021). Pricing of illicit drugs on darknet markets: A conceptual exploration. *Drugs and Alcohol Today, 21*(2), 135–145.

Zeng, Y., & Buil-Gil, D. (2023). Organizational and organized cybercrime. In *Oxford research encyclopedia of criminology and criminal justice.*

Chapter 3
The Role of Law Enforcement in the Regulation of Cryptomarkets (and the Limited Role of Deterrence)

Introduction

In this chapter, a series of fundamental questions are asked about the role of law enforcement in regulating cryptomarkets: Which law enforcement agencies are responsible? What can be done to prevent these events? What kind of legal framework is necessary to deal with the transgressors? These are challenging questions, and it is doubtable that anyone has all the answers. Nevertheless, this chapter offers details on some successful and less-than-successful attempts to disrupt cryptomarkets. As this chapter will show, there exists a pervasive undercurrent of social stigma directed towards individuals with less hazardous responsibilities within the field of law enforcement (see more recently Ariel 2023 on police officers' ideation of the "Rambo cop" rather than crime prevention, even though the latter is a more effective crime control policy). Due to the relatively low incidence of physical violence and the inherent challenges of identifying and apprehending perpetrators, the enforcement of cybercrime law is not as common as that of law dealing with traditional crimes. Ongoing efforts to combat cryptomarkets thus deviate from standard police work.

Law enforcement entities are certainly aware of the deficits in their approach and efforts, and the need for a systemic shift towards a more robust response to cybercrime and cryptomarkets is a topic of continuous conversation in regulatory bodies (Cohen, 2023; Narain & Moretti, 2022; US Attorney's Office, 2022). It is known that when law enforcement interventions are focused on disrupting certain activities, they do have a detrimental impact on the operational conditions of cryptomarkets, leading to the closure of the prominent firms they target within a relatively brief timeframe (Martin, 2023). The question, however, is whether these crackdowns have a meaningful effect on the cryptomarket ecosystem. To answer it, this chapter will delve into the diverse measures implemented by law enforcement agencies in response to cryptomarkets. This is done by first presenting key cases of crackdowns and then critically assessing the attempts made thus far to disrupt illicit cryptomarkets.

Noteworthy Cryptomarket Takedowns

Operation Onymous

Several noteworthy disruptions have occurred over the years, with prominent "players" taken out by police interventions. These operations are usually conducted on a global scale, with multiple agencies acting in tandem. Perhaps the most famous was the apprehension of the operator of the original Silk Road cryptomarket, Ross Ulbricht—also known as Dread Pirate Roberts—by the FBI on 2 October 2013 (see review of the case and its implications in Lacson & Jones, 2016; also Phelps & Watts, 2014). This led to the total disruption of the Silk Road cryptomarket and the confiscation of more than $33 million worth of Bitcoin. However, after the FBI shut down the initial Silk Road, a subsequent iteration known as Silk Road 2.0 surfaced, allegedly under the management of multiple administrators. In response, the FBI launched Operation Onymous in conjunction with the Department of Homeland Security and Europol to tackle Silk Road 2.0 and other new cryptomarkets. This operation resulted in the closure of numerous cryptomarkets and the arrest of vendors on a global scale. A total of seven prominent cryptomarkets, including Silk Road 2.0, Cloud 9 and Hydra, along with 260 webpages operating on the darknet ".onion" network, were subjected to closure.

As Lacson and Jones (2016) show, Silk Road 2.0 was one of the most significant cryptomarkets to be seized by law enforcement, achieving monthly sales that surpassed an average of $8 million. It boasted a user base of over 150,000 active individuals. The successful execution of the takedown operation necessitated the cooperation of law enforcement agencies spanning 17 nations, leading to the apprehension of a total of 17 individuals. Among those arrested was "Defcon", who served as the administrator of Silk Road 2.0. These individuals assumed the role previously held by Ross Ulbricht in Silk Road 1.0 and intended to establish a more secure and resilient platform for their illicit endeavours. The administrators, including Defcon, were required to navigate a complex network of secrecy and security protocols to safeguard against potential infiltration by law enforcement agencies (Moeller et al., 2017). As noted by Hartel and Van Wegberg (2019), the role of Defcon, like that of other administrators, encompassed the supervision of multiple facets of the site's operations. These responsibilities included overseeing sales transactions, managing vendors and ensuring the efficient functioning of the site's intricate technological infrastructure. The successful functioning of such a website necessitated a wide-ranging comprehension of digital technologies, encryption protocols and the intricate workings of the darknet (Aldridge & Askew, 2017).

Nevertheless, the duration of Silk Road 2.0's existence was relatively brief. Décary-Hétu and Giommoni (2017) observe that Operation Onymous emphasised global endeavours to mitigate illicit activities on the dark web, thereby illustrating the ongoing conflict between criminal organisations exploiting the Internet's anonymity and law enforcement agencies seeking to apprehend and prosecute them. Ultimately, however, law enforcement was able to crack down on Silk Road 2.0 and shut it down.

Operation Bayonet

In 2017, a series of law enforcement initiatives known as Operation Bayonet resulted in cessation of the operations of two prominent drug cryptomarkets, AlphaBay and Hansa. During the seizure, AlphaBay emerged as the preeminent marketplace, boasting an extensive inventory of 369,000 listings and a substantial user base of 400,000 individuals (Zhou et al., 2020).

Following the disruption of AlphaBay, it was anticipated that Hansa would emerge as a prominent marketplace. The strategies used in Operation Bayonet differed from previous interventions: They were intended to damage the trust which undergirds business-to-consumer relations, rather than close the marketplace. The FBI decided to deliberately close AlphaBay without issuing a seizure notice or a public statement, and in doing so they followed a theoretically driven model by disrupting the trust and comfort offenders feel when using these platforms (Duxbury & Haynie, 2018). Indeed, Hansa experienced a significant surge in user activity, with the number of vendors per day increasing eightfold—thus showing clear signs of displacement (Ladegaard, 2019) or, as Van Wegberg and Verburgh (2018, p. 3) refer to it, "migration".

Operation Bayonet originated from two distinct endeavours undertaken by multiple law enforcement agencies. The Dutch police, who had been investigating Hansa since 2016, noted that the principal administrators of the primary site were located in Europe. Drawing inspiration from the operational strategies employed by the FBI during the successful dismantling of the Playpen platform in 2015, law enforcement agents decided to undertake a direct takeover of the Hansa cryptomarket. This approach involved assuming administrative control of the illicit platform, enabling investigators to operate it themselves. It can therefore be inferred that Hansa was under the covert control and operation of the Dutch National Police prior to the shutdown of AlphaBay.

The Dutch authorities, aware of the obfuscation capabilities inherent in Tor, successfully traced a Bitcoin address discovered in an Internet Relay Chat (IRC), a text-based chat system for instant messaging, a conversation involving two individuals suspected to be administrators of Hansa (Abdel, 2021; see more broadly in Gehl, 2018). Through collaboration with a Lithuanian web hosting company which served as the final beneficiary of the Bitcoin transaction, the Dutch authorities successfully identified the physical location of the server hosting Hansa and assumed administrative jurisdiction over the site. Significantly, Van Wegberg and Verburgh (2018) note that the Dutch authorities modified the website's code to extract data about vendors and buyers from encrypted communications; they then changed the Hansa code, which contained the metadata of uploaded product photographs, to accurately determine the specific geographic locations at which product photos of drugs were captured. These reconfigurations yielded crucial investigatory data concerning approximately 420,000 individuals and encompassing no less than 10,000 residential locations (see additional details in Spagnoletti et al., 2021). The information was subsequently employed after the disruption of Hansa to commence a "knock-and-talk" operation at locations that had been obtained during the operation mentioned above (see other applications of the knock-and-talk intervention in Ariel et al. 2019; Denley & Ariel, 2019; and more recently in Denley & Ariel, n.d.). Agencies around the globe conducted home visits to caution individuals against engaging in cryptomarkets in the future. Arrests were made in certain instances, but in most cases a warning approach was used (see Williams & Ariel, 2013, and a more recent application in Bland et al., 2023). The impact of these interventions, however, remains unclear, as cryptomarkets did not subsequently dissipate (see Jardine, 2021; Rawat et al., 2022).

Operation Hyperion

Operation Hyperion is an illustrative instance of a fruitful knock-and-talk endeavour targeting users of illicit online marketplaces. In 2018, authorities initiated contact with individuals utilising cryptomarkets who were suspected of participating in drug-related transactions to discourage them from any potential future transactions. Law enforcement agencies in the United States conducted a year-long investigation targeting multiple vendors. This investigation culminated in 2018 when a Department of Homeland Security operative assumed the role of a money launderer presenting an opportunity to engage in the exchange of US dollars. According to the United States Department of Justice (2020), the operation resulted in the pursuit of approximately 35 vendors operating within the United States, the confiscation of illicit substances and other prohibited items and the appropriation of a sum exceeding $23.6 million in unlawfully obtained digital currency (United States Department of Justice, 2020).

Operation Venetic

Encrypted communication systems have become a double-edged sword in the contemporary age of rapid technological advancement. On the one hand, they protect individuals' privacy and the security of their sensitive information; on the other hand, they provide a haven for the covert operation of criminal networks (Miller &

Bossomaier, 2021). The use of encrypted communication platforms for illicit activities is not a recent phenomenon. For many years, criminals have capitalised on the security these platforms offer to orchestrate a myriad of criminal activities ranging from drug trafficking to terrorism (see Hartel & van Wegberg, 2023; Steel et al., 2020; Weimann, 2016). The modus operandi in these criminal undertakings often involves the use of encrypted channels to facilitate discreet communications that leave no easily traceable evidence, thereby thwarting the efforts of law enforcement agencies to monitor and curb these activities (Teunissen & Napier, 2022).

Over the years, criminal networks have exploited several platforms to secure their communications. For instance, encrypted BlackBerry phones were quite popular among criminal circles (Broadhurst et al., 2018). These devices were customised to disable functionalities like their camera and GPS, enabling them to be used as secure and untraceable communication channels. Over time, these phones became a favoured tool for coordinating illicit activities—until law enforcement cracked the encryption codes, leading to a series of arrests (Bennett, 2012).

In this context, the EncroChat platform serves as a noteworthy case study. EncroChat was initially revered for providing encrypted mobile phones that promised high-level privacy and security. The criminal underworld adopted this tool, utilising its features to coordinate a wide array of illegal activities such as drug transactions and violent crimes. However, this criminal haven was dismantled when law enforcement infiltrated the network, leading to many arrests and criminal charges (on the evidential power and standing of EncroChat evidence, see Griffiths & Jackson, 2022; O'Rourke, 2020). This operation unveiled a substantial volume of information concerning criminal activities. It became a testimony to the constant tussle between criminal networks trying to stay one step ahead and law enforcement agencies adapting to new technological advancements to crack down on illicit activities. As noted by the National Crime Agency in the United Kingdom (NCA, 2020), "entire organised crime groups [were] dismantled during Operation Venetic with 746 arrests, and £54 million criminal cash, 77 firearms and over two tonnes of drugs seized".

Do These Disruption Activities "Work" to Destabilise Cryptomarkets (And Why Not)?

How effective are crackdowns on darknet cryptomarkets? The answer is not straightforward. The efficacy of law enforcement efforts targeting darknet cryptomarkets is a topic of considerable scholarly discussion within the fields of criminology and cybersecurity. Bradley's (2019) doctoral dissertation examines the resilience of the darknet market ecosystem in the face of law enforcement interventions and constitutes a comprehensive review of this topic. Booij et al. (2021) researched vendors' careers, while Norbutas et al. (2020) examined the transferability of reputation among anonymous actors in cryptomarkets. The impact of darknet market seizures on opioid availability has been the subject of recent research conducted by Broadhurst et al. (2021), offering an in-depth analysis of this phenomenon. Furthermore, the scholarly investigation by Dearden and Tucker (2023) presents a notable examination of darknet operations, specifically focusing on using cryptocurrency and the Bitcoin blockchain. The list goes on, but it is clear from this body of research that throughout contemporary history the implementation of cryptomarket crackdowns has resulted in a notable yet transient disturbance in the functioning of these clandestine marketplaces, thereby highlighting their enduring and flexible nature.

A case in point is the increase in transactions with alternative vendors once a particular vendor is shut down. Soska and Christin (2020) analysed 2 years of transactional data. They found that following the shutdown of the Silk Road market the number of dealers on Black Market Reloaded and Sheep underwent significant increases of 200 and 400%, respectively, within 6 weeks. Furthermore, Bhaskar et al. (2019) analysed more than 1.5 million drug sales and observed a notable increase in sales listings on the Sheep market, which grew from 4358 on 17 October 2013 to 8457 by 30 October 2013. In April 2014, the collective number of drug listings on Silk Road 2.0, Agora and Evolution reached 32,000, a 128% increase compared to the original Silk Road platform. It can thus be inferred that the closure of these platforms did not deter buyers or sellers from online drug trading. This is evident from the swift emergence of new platforms to replace those which were taken down, resulting in the continuous growth of the online drug market. Let us take a closer look at the factors underlying this phenomenon.

The Cat-and-Mouse Analogy

Historically, law enforcement agencies have exhibited a relatively sluggish response to the rise of novel cyber threats (Faubert et al., 2021; Koziarski & Lee, 2020). However, in recent years, law enforcement agencies have undertaken multiple endeavours to control, if not dismantle, illegal cryptomarkets (Décary-Hétu & Giommoni, 2017). In general, an effective enforcement effort entails the collaboration of law enforcement entities across different nations to identify and dismantle servers, apprehend significant individuals and confiscate assets linked to such platforms. These actions can effectively disrupt the continuity of unlawful transactions, temporarily decreasing the accessibility of illicit commodities and services within the darknet. Furthermore, these efforts display the law enforcement agencies' ability and readiness to breach the apparent anonymity provided by such platforms, potentially deterring individuals contemplating involvement in illicit activities through the darknet.

However, law enforcement is primarily responsible for dealing with existing vendors, not preventing new ones from entering the market (see Denley & Ariel, 2019). Within the ever-changing realm of cryptomarkets, the interaction between law enforcement agencies and market participants frequently mirrors an ongoing and elusive pursuit. The cat-and-mouse analogy employed in this context represents the persistent pursuit and evasive tactics characteristic of these interactions (see Bancroft & Scott Reid, 2017). Similar to how a mouse quickly adjusts to the predatory techniques employed by a cat, using agility and skill to evade capture, operators within cryptomarkets have demonstrated an impressive ability to adapt to law enforcement strategies. The adaptation phenomenon (discussed more robustly below) frequently presents itself as technological progress, encryption techniques or alternative trading strategies, all devised to evade newly implemented regulations and detection systems. The ability to quickly adjust to new law enforcement strategies enables cryptomarkets to persist and thrive, often in increasingly intricate and evasive manifestations. The continuous and swift progression of technological advancements in this field perpetuates this cycle, consistently presenting novel tools and avenues for evasion.

Conversely, the feline metaphorically symbolises law enforcement agencies encountering the formidable challenge of adapting to the continuously evolving tactics employed by cryptomarkets. The difficulty they face is further complicated by administrative limitations, legal parameters and the need for global collaboration to monitor and apprehend individuals engaged in activities of a worldwide nature. Furthermore, the mouse must cultivate a high level of proficiency to comprehend and manoeuvre through the intricate technological environment within which these markets exist. The feline tends to lag in specific scenarios and must persistently formulate new strategies and adjust its tactics to capture the elusive rodent.

Moreover, it is imperative to recognise the fluid and ever-changing nature of this "game", which frequently undergoes persistent evolution in both power dynamics and strategic approaches. The dynamic between law enforcement and cryptomarkets transcends a simplistic binary opposition of predator and prey; instead, it is a multifaceted, intricate and dynamic interaction that reflects a broader conflict between regulatory efforts and attempts at circumvention, as well as the tension between the rule of law and the emergence of disorder. Hence, the cat-and-mouse analogy conveys a narrative of adaptation, innovation and the unwavering quest for supremacy within a context defined by swift technological progress and worldwide influence. The narrative encompasses a multifaceted storyline in which both entities engage in a perpetual process of learning, adapting and evolving in response to one another's actions. This ongoing interaction forms a dynamic dance that consistently influences the structure and characteristics of the cryptomarket landscape. For example, it seems that the Sky ECC platform emerged as a successor to EncroChat, promising even more secure channels of communication. Sagittae (2023) became a hub for criminal activities before law enforcement agencies infiltrated the network, unravelling the criminal nexus operating under its guise. This further cements the notion that a continual cat-and-mouse game is being played between criminal networks exploiting technological advancements and law enforcement agencies adapting to these changes to maintain law and order.

Advancing Encryption Technologies in the Hands of Organised Criminals

Analysis of trends in technological development from a broader cryptomarket perspective indicates that various popular platforms with encryption features, like Telegram and WhatsApp, can be misused by criminal entities exchanging illegal goods and services for payment, often in the form of cryptocurrency (Stoykova, 2023). While these platforms primarily facilitate lawful communication, their encryption features have sometimes been hijacked by criminals to establish secure communication channels, making the job of law enforcement agencies even more challenging. The ability of offenders to use these advanced encryption technologies is a significant challenge for law enforcement agencies worldwide. Monitoring and infiltration of encrypted platforms necessitates the development of sophisticated techniques, including cyber espionage and the cultivation of informants (Oerlemans & van Toor, 2022). It is a relentless race against time in which new encryption technologies are constantly being developed, with law enforcement agencies striving tirelessly to find methods to bypass these protections. This situation calls for a collaborative effort among countries and agencies and necessitates the development of techno-legal frameworks to govern the use of encrypted communication platforms and prevent their exploitation for criminal endeavours (Kabra & Gori, 2023).

Superrational and Highly Motivated Actors

We see how highly active vendors in the cryptomarket ecosystem embody the intersection of criminal innovation and technological expertise, functioning within a digital realm that consistently undergoes transformation and adjustment to advancements in technology and law enforcement tactics. The assumption is that these entities constantly seek ways to avoid disruption. The activities undertaken by vendors depict sombre yet intricately structured and advanced processes, wherein illicit activities converge with business acumen within the context of the modern digital era. Therefore, as illustrated by Shortis et al. (2020), the takedown of advanced offenders poses significant challenges for law enforcement agencies, policymakers and researchers endeavouring to comprehend and mitigate illicit markets. The underlying assumption is that highly motivated, savvy criminal entrepreneurs are behind these operations, which is why cracking down on them is not easy and why law enforcement is axiomatically one step behind these criminal minds (see more broadly in Martin, 2023).

Furthermore, within a relatively short period of 2–3 months following the noteworthy crackdowns detailed above—the takedown of Silk Road, Operation Onymous, Operation Bayonet, Operation Hyperion and Operation Venetic—both vendor activity and consumer confidence rebounded to their previous levels, leading to a restoration of equilibrium in the overall dark web ecosystem. After the closure of the Silk Road, individuals involved in the platform exhibited a greater inclination to employ enhanced methods of communication and encryption to ensure heightened security. This finding is particularly significant as it indicates that the strategies and technologies employed by users of cryptomarkets are enhanced with each instance of law enforcement intervention resulting in market closure. These examples of migration underscore a considerable problem and beg the question: What is the point of enforcement if the market not only recovers immediately after interventions but potentially even becomes more efficient? What else, that is not counterproductive, can be done to exert pressure on these criminal elements?

Criminals' Adaptation to Law Enforcement Tactics

Consideration of the efficacy of enforcement measures suggests that they are occasionally compromised by the rapid adaptation and evolution of the platforms they target. As alluded to earlier, new markets are frequently observed to emerge in the aftermath of takedowns of prominent cryptomarkets, and these new markets frequently integrate insights derived from exposure of the weaknesses that precipitated the demise of the preceding market (Duxbury & Haynie, 2018). These iterations might incorporate heightened security protocols, advanced anonymisation techniques or decentralised frameworks that exhibit greater resilience against law enforcement interventions. The concept of crime displacement holds significant importance in the discourse surrounding crime analysis and prevention: Criminal activities are relocated rather than diminished as criminal entities exhibit adaptability in response to law enforcement strategies, thereby modifying multiple facets of their illegal activities such as the selection of venues, timing and modus operandi (Jansen & van Lenthe, 2016; Hui et al., 2017; Moitra, 2005).

Furthermore, there are clear signs of adaptation. As Martin et al. (2020) observed, although a crackdown may result in temporary disruption, its long-term effects on the entire ecosystem will be uncertain. New participants quickly emerge to replace their predecessors, often employing more advanced and secure methods (Chawki, 2022; Décary-Hétu et al., 2016). Caulkins and Kleiman (2018) argued that crackdowns may inadvertently result in the proliferation of criminal activities on a larger scale. After a substantial law enforcement operation, individuals and merchants associated with the closed marketplace might disperse to alternative established platforms or set up new ones, thereby expanding the reach of their activities throughout the darknet. This dispersion has the potential to complicate future law enforcement actions, which may encounter increasingly significant challenges.

Globalisation and Crime

One reason for the challenges encountered by law enforcement in dealing with cybercrime is that "jobs" involving a regional vendor who intends to sell illicit goods outside their territory are common and difficult to interrupt. The server may sit in one country, the operations in another, and the clients may be residents of yet another country—while, at the same time, the products are physically situated in multiple locations around the world. Indeed, for some products, the cryptomarket distribution network exhibits a localised nature, whereby vendors and buyers from the same countries tend to engage in transactions with each other, rather than cross-border transactions that are more expensive and riskier due to the additional checks made by customs officers. This may often be the case (Martin, 2023), but the pattern of transactions does not always follow this format. Law enforcement becomes more difficult in cases where the two parties in an exchange do not reside in the same jurisdiction. Some examples are shared below.

The Problem of Displacement

So far, it has been shown how the literature points to clear signs of digital spatial displacement, with criminal activities transitioning from one platform to another rather than ceasing altogether (Ladegard, 2019; Wada et al., 2012). After the takedown of the original Silk Road market, a considerable number of users transitioned to alternative online marketplaces in response to its closure (Demant et al., 2018). Similarly, when the FBI closed AlphaBay without providing a formal seizure notice or issuing a public statement, the Hansa market witnessed a substantial upsurge in user engagement, as evidenced by an eightfold increase in the daily number of vendors—a clear manifestation of displacement (Ladegaard, 2019).

The concept of digital displacement arises as a noteworthy factor when criminal activities are migrated from one geographic location to another in response to law enforcement interventions. For example, in the unlicensed e-pharmacy industry, website takedowns were often ineffective, as the online pharmacies could displace other compromised hosts (Leontiadis & Hutchings, 2015); when local Chinese regulators began cracking down on counterfeit cigarettes, Shen et al. (2010, p. 294) observed that:

> Counterfeit cigarette manufacturing and trading originated from the southern coastal provinces of mainland China, Fujian and Guangdong, which borders Hong Kong and Macao. Yunxiao (Fujian province) and Chaoshan and Guangzhou (Guangdong province) are notorious for producing counterfeit cigarettes. However, in recent years, due to the centrally coordinated operations persistently carried out to curb cigarette counterfeiting in these areas, several counterfeiting businesses have been displaced to inland China.

Spatial Displacement

When law enforcement activities are intensified in a specific area, criminals may seek out alternative locations where the likelihood of being detected is perceived to be lower (in the context of territorial policing, see Ariel & Partridge, 2017), relocating their illicit activities to other regions or jurisdictions with less rigorous law enforcement interventions. This spatial migration exemplifies the dynamic and flexible nature of criminal networks and individuals, highlighting a fundamental obstacle to law enforcement endeavours that seek to suppress them: Globalisation has made physical migration much more accessible. This underscores the importance of adopting a holistic, regionally focused strategy to mitigate crime, whereby multiple jurisdictions collaborate and synchronise their efforts to reduce the risk of spatial displacement—a solution proposed in more detail below.

Modus Operandi Displacement

The capacity for adaptability also encompasses the ability to modify the modus operandi, which has been recognised for some time in the cybercrime community (Smith et al., 2003). Criminals can change their tactics as a reaction to law enforcement strategies, displacing their methods to evade detection and capture. As an illustration, a criminal organisation engaged in selling *distributed denial of service* (DDoS) attacks for hire may adapt its tactics in response to heightened security measures implemented in their targeted victims by employing other types of attacks that are not based on DDoS approaches to exploiting vulnerabilities in digital security systems (Brunt et al., 2017; Vu et al., 2023). These patterns exemplify behavioural displacement, necessitating a persistent need for adaptation and innovation to prevent crime.

Increasing Criminal Efficiency Through Decentralisation as a Result of Crackdowns

Based on the existing body of evidence, it may be posited that the closure of the Silk Road resulted in a more significant challenge in policing, rather than simplifying, the task. This iatrogenic effect can be easily observed in the emergence of numerous other cryptomarkets after the dismantling of the Silk Road. According to Martin (2023), the increased decentralisation of cryptomarket trading is one of the factors contributing to this phenomenon, particularly in comparison to when the Silk Road was at its height. In the latter part of January 2014, the sales volumes observed on multiple and initially smaller cryptomarkets surpassed the documented figures for Silk Road. This surge in sales and expansion into new markets has been widely regarded as compelling evidence of the phenomenon known as the "hydra effect". Undoubtedly, the elimination of a single cryptomarket leads to the emergence of numerous alternative platforms.

Anonymity

Finally, it is important to be reminded that, within the domain of cybercrime, anonymity and the expansive nature of the digital realm present significant obstacles to the efficacy of deterrence measures. The transnational character of cybercrime means that it is challenging to guarantee offenders' prompt and definitive apprehension. Furthermore, it is common for cybercriminals to conduct their activities in regions where cyber legislation is inadequate, thus taking advantage of the loopholes and inconsistencies in global legal systems. This ultimately undermines the potential efficacy of deterrence tactics because anonymity in cryptomarkets frequently empowers individuals to engage in criminal activities, as they perceive the likelihood of apprehension to be minimal.

Additionally, the transnational characteristic of cybercrime introduces a heightened level of intricacy in terms of the enforcement of laws and the apprehension of perpetrators, thereby potentially diminishing the perceived level of certainty regarding punishment. Hence, to optimise the efficacy of deterrence theory for addressing cybercrime, it is imperative to adopt a comprehensive strategy that augments detection capabilities and promotes international collaboration.

Do Crackdowns Deter and Prevent Cryptomarkets?

According to Bhaskar et al. (2019, 230), there is a lack of evidence that shutdowns have deterrent effects. This conclusion is not the exception to the norm; in fact, many studies in criminology, across different types of criminal behaviours (both online and offline), struggle to ubiquitously support deterrence theory as a method of preventing or controlling crime (Ariel, 2012; Ariel et al., 2017, 2018). To address the effectiveness of deterrence theory in cryptomarkets, attention must first be turned to the concept of deterrence more broadly (though more attention will be paid to cybercrime).

The foundation of deterrence theory in criminology lies in the notion that the occurrence of criminal acts can be averted by creating a perception among potential offenders that the costs or penalties associated with an act outweigh the potential gains (Nagin, 2013). Derived from classical criminological theory, which dates to early scriptures in different cultures (see review in Roth, 2014), deterrence theory relies on a fundamental human consideration: Individuals prefer to avoid pain and have a proclivity towards rewards. Punishment is an outcome that rational people will tend to avoid, so it is assumed that an effective threat will prevent them from pursuing behaviours that will result in such a cost. In many ways, this fundamental axiom is the cornerstone of nearly all legal systems: The state threatens prospective offenders through legal action (including punitive consequences) to deter them from committing crimes (Pratt et al., 2017).

Specific Versus General Deterrence

Deterrence can be categorised into two distinct classifications: specific deterrence and general deterrence (see generally in Stafford & Warr, 1993). Specific deterrence centres on discouraging individual offenders from engaging in *additional* future criminal activities by instilling a fear of potential punishment. General deterrence, on the other hand, aims to discourage the general population from participating in criminal behaviour by creating a sense of fear of potential punishment through penalising *others* (Loughran et al., 2015).

The concept of specific deterrence is predicated upon the underlying belief that individuals who have experienced punitive repercussions for their criminal behaviours will exhibit reduced propensity to subsequently partake in similar activities. The objective is to implement a punitive measure of sufficient magnitude to deter individuals from engaging in the same offence again (Gibbs, 1968). As shown in Piquero and Paternoster (1998), if you drive over the speed limit, are caught by a speed camera and receive a ticket, you will be deterred from speeding—at least on the road segment where the speed camera is positioned (whether receiving a ticket will change your driving behaviour altogether is not clear). In the realm of cybercrime, a punished hacker may be dissuaded from partaking in similar illicit activities in subsequent instances due to their firsthand encounter with punitive measures (Geers, 2010; Maimon et al., 2021).

In contrast, general deterrence aims to influence prospective offenders who observe the punitive consequences imposed on others. Again, the underlying principle of this framework assumes that individuals are rational agents who strive to optimise their gains while minimising their expenses (Apel & Nagin, 2011). For example, when the criminal justice system initiates legal proceedings and imposes a lengthy incarceration period on a cryptomarket vendor such as Silk Road, it (presumably) communicates a deterrent message to prospective vendors of illicit goods online by highlighting the significant repercussions associated with such behaviour. This serves to dissuade them from participating in comparable illicit activities.

Deterrence within the domain of cybercrime is also achieved through the enforcement of stringent legal frameworks that impose penalties for actions such as selling drugs and weapons on cryptomarkets. Globally, governments and organisations are collaborating to increase the likelihood of apprehending cyber offenders by bolstering their cyber surveillance capabilities and facilitating the exchange of information about cyber threats and individuals involved in criminal activities in the digital realm (Hui et al., 2017). In addition, initiatives aimed at enhancing public knowledge regarding the gravity of the consequences of cybercrimes also contribute to the promotion of a broader deterrent impact, which may cause prospective offenders to reassess their inclination to participate in illicit behaviours owing to the substantial risks involved (Hong & Neilson, 2020).

Certainty, Severity and Celerity of Punishment

The efficacy of deterrence theory can be subjected to critical analysis by considering three distinct yet interconnected factors: the certainty of apprehension and punishment, the severity of punishment and the celerity of apprehension. These elements are crucial for ensuring the effective deterrence of criminal behaviour, especially in terms of cybercrime (Nagin, 2013; see also review by Von Hirsch et al., 1999).

The initial component, the certainty of apprehension or punishment, posits that the perceived probability of being detected and subsequently penalised is a powerful deterrent for prospective offenders. In cyberspace, certainty can be strengthened by implementing advanced cyber surveillance networks, establishing proficient cybersecurity forces and fostering international collaboration to track and apprehend individuals engaged in cybercrime—all these factors can lead people to believe that there is an elevated chance of apprehension. For example, the advancement and implementation of sophisticated artificial intelligence systems capable of identifying atypical patterns and behaviours within a network can enhance confidence that individuals involved in illicit activities will be apprehended. Another example involves the use of advanced technologies to compromise the anonymity that is assumed when using cryptocurrency, virtual private networks (VPNs) or the Tor network. Furthermore, the cultivation of international partnerships aimed at addressing the worldwide scope of cybercrime has the potential to increase the likelihood of penalties being imposed and consequently to bolster the impact of the deterrent.

The second factor, namely, the severity of punishment, suggests that the potential consequences of committing a crime should be sufficiently punitive to deter individuals from participating in such behaviour. To achieve efficacy within the realm of cybercrime, legislative measures should establish penalties proportionate to the severity of the offence committed, thereby functioning as a strong deterrent for prospective wrongdoers.

For instance, implementing substantial monetary penalties, extended incarceration or the confiscation of assets may be perceived as practical means of discouragement. Governments and international organisations can engage in collaborative efforts aimed at establishing legal frameworks which promote consistency in the severity of penalties across national boundaries. This can serve as a preventive measure to deter the potential creation of safe havens for cybercriminals.

Finally, celerity of apprehension suggests that the speed with which punishment is administered following the commission of a crime is crucial in deterring individuals from engaging in criminal behaviour. The timeliness of responses by law enforcement agencies can indicate their efficiency and preparedness, thus acting as a deterrent to potential offenders. This may encompass the expeditious identification of cyber transgressions, prompt inquiries and timely judicial procedures within cyberspace. Implementing dedicated cybercrime units within law enforcement organisations and equipping them with the requisite resources and knowledge can accelerate the apprehension and prosecution of offenders, thereby augmenting promptness as an element of deterrence.

Does Deterrence Theory "Work"?

The question of whether deterrence theory "works" is a complicated one and depends on many factors, including but not limited to what was meant by works, on whom it works and the degree to which it can be assumed that that behaviour is affected by the threat of sanction. Overall, however, it can be said that while deterrence theory serves as a fundamental framework for the comprehension and tackling of criminal conduct, its efficacy in diminishing crime, particularly cybercrime, is subject to significant constraints (see examples in Apel & Nagin, 2011; D'arcy & Herath, 2011; Loughran et al., 2015; Nagin, 2013).

Despite the theoretical underpinnings of deterrence theory and its incorporation into numerous criminal justice systems, it has encountered criticism regarding its efficacy in reducing crime rates. As previously noted, the fundamental premise of deterrence theory posits that individuals are rational agents who engage in a cost-benefit analysis before participating in criminal behaviour. The rational choice model, however, has faced criticism for its perceived oversimplification. Numerous criminal acts are perpetrated spontaneously, with actors often influenced by circumstances that hinder rational decision-making (Pratt et al., 2017). Hence, it can be argued that the applicability of a systematic decision-making process may be limited in various scenarios, thereby rendering deterrence measures less effective.

For deterrence to be efficacious, the components of certainty, severity and celerity of punishment must be appropriately coordinated. Nevertheless, it is frequently observed that these elements lack cohesion in practice (Nagin, 2013). The criminal justice system frequently experiences delays which diminish the expeditiousness of punishment, a crucial factor for achieving deterrence. Moreover, the capture of individuals is not consistently ensured due to diverse systemic and logistical limitations. Therefore, it is possible that individuals with criminal intent may not perceive the level of risk associated with apprehension and subsequent punishment as sufficiently substantial, thereby diminishing the deterrent impact.

In addition to examining the severity of punishment, another fundamental aspect of deterrence theory has been subjected to critical analysis. Numerous empirical investigations have demonstrated that the implementation of increasingly severe punishments does not invariably result in a commensurate reduction in crime rates. Indeed, it is worth noting that the implementation of unduly severe sanctions can occasionally yield unintended consequences, such as a rise in criminal behaviour or the cultivation of a societal environment characterised by defiance and non-adherence (Sherman, 1993).

Furthermore, it is frequently observed that deterrence strategies fail to effectively tackle the fundamental socio-economic determinants that give rise to criminal conduct, including but not limited to poverty, educational deficiencies and restricted avenues for social and economic advancement. Deterrence theory's exclusive emphasis on punitive measures may fail to acknowledge the significance of preventive measures and rehabilitation endeavours that address the underlying factors contributing to criminal behaviour (see discussion in Bland et al., 2023).

General deterrence does not seem to "work" when dismantling cryptomarkets either. The consequence of Operation Onymous was the swift emergence of Silk Road 3.0, a new online platform, shortly after the shutdown of Silk Road 2.0. Thus, instead of causing prospective vendors to think twice before setting up illegal operations, the removal of one platform immediately gave way to new vendors who opportunistically leveraged the aftermath of the crackdown by rebranding themselves with a new name and logo in order to entice users from the platform that had just been shut down. As previously noted, a considerable number of users who had previously been active on Silk Road 2.0 chose to transition to Evolution and Agora, some of the largest cryptomarkets to date. Indeed, Evolution experienced a 26% growth in its total listings following Operation Onymous. Middle Earth Marketplace implemented a robust marketing strategy by temporarily waiving its membership fee, leading to a notable surge of 44% in the number of drug listings (Hiramoto & Tsuchiya, 2023; Demant et al., 2018).

Specific deterrence has a limited effect and frequently backfires when applied to individuals who are subject to formal social controls. The status of the 17 individuals apprehended during Operation Onymous as site administrators remains uncertain (Décary-Hétu & Giommoni, 2017): The administrators of the cryptomarket subsequently recommenced their activities with other recently established cryptomarkets.

Crackdowns Lead to Defragmentation and Greater Criminal Efficiency

As has been argued, the efficacy of law enforcement interventions targeting cryptomarkets has proven inadequate, potentially yielding adverse outcomes. Following the closure of markets, sales volumes typically reverted to comparable levels observed before the closure. Additionally, new markets emerged as substitutes for those which were discontinued. As mentioned above, this observation is supported by El Bahrawy et al. (2020), who analysed 24 distinct instances of cryptomarket closures spanning from 2011 to 2019, examining 133 million Bitcoin transactions involving 38 million users. This analysis aimed to ascertain users' inclination to transition to alternative marketplaces after the closure of a marketplace. The total value of transactions conducted through the cryptocurrency addresses examined in the research surpassed $4.2 billion. It was observed that around 66.1% (+/− 16.1%) of individuals involved in a cryptomarket had transitioned from a closed market to the largest subsequently accessible marketplace. Furthermore, the migration of users occurred rapidly, as evidenced by the prompt recovery of trading volumes among migrating users after the closure. To a certain degree, the leading two destination marketplaces observed a rise in their trading volume share, commencing 2 days after closure and reaching saturation approximately 6 days later with a share of 27%. This share is more than twice the amount observed at the time of closure. In contrast, the second most popular destination experienced a notable increase in its market share from 5% to 8.7%.

It is crucial to acknowledge that the fragmentation observed can be attributed, at least in part, to the decentralised exchange networks employed by cryptomarkets. According to Martin (2023), in the event of a cryptomarket shutdown, the user community demonstrates resilience by either migrating to alternative platforms or, as exemplified by the case of Silk Road 1.0, promptly establishing and repopulating a substitute website (p. 23). This combination of mobility and durability results in a highly resilient illicit entity that is challenging to eradicate. While there may be moral objections to tolerating the continuous operation of organised crime, it can be argued that dismantling a criminal monopoly can exacerbate the crime issue, leading to its rapid proliferation.

Therefore, although individual cryptomarkets may seem fragile, the resilience of the overall ecosystem can be attributed to the coordinated migration of users. Closures, whether the result of police intervention or an exit scam, have a transient impact on trading volume.

Crossover Between Cryptomarkets and Street Markets

It is crucial for law enforcement agencies to consider the impact of cryptomarket shutdowns on terrestrial criminal markets. Zambiasi (2022) conducted a study to assess the potential influence of cryptomarket shutdowns on the volume of illicit drug transactions in public spaces and the incidence of criminal activities typically associated with street-level drug distribution. Significantly, the researcher analysed the incidence of criminal activity during the periods leading up to and following the closure of cryptomarkets. This analysis utilised a regression continuity design, which allowed for consideration of exogenous temporal fluctuations in the accessibility of online drug markets in conjunction with high-frequency data. In brief, Zambiasi (2022) reveals that the closure of cryptomarkets tends to lead to a temporary surge in drug trafficking, especially marijuana-related offences, which experience an approximate 5% rise.

However, this heightened level of criminal activity tends to normalise and return to pre-shutdown levels within 18 days. The study did not find cryptomarket closure to have a significant influence on the occurrence of thefts, assaults, homicides and prostitution. The findings of the study also indicate that individuals who engage in cryptomarket activities exhibit distinct characteristics compared to those involved in traditional street drug trade operations.

So, What Can Be Done?

Improve the Monitoring of Cryptocurrency Transactions

Despite the intrinsic pseudonymity attributed to cryptocurrencies, it is crucial to acknowledge that every transaction is diligently recorded and archived on the blockchain. Meiklejohn et al. (2013) argue that the adoption of this technology gives law enforcement agencies the opportunity to trace the sources of transactions and addresses, which can be linked to particular identities.

Given that transfers of cryptocurrency can be traced, the first thing to do is enhance capacity to monitor the blockchain. One approach to monitoring transactions involves using sophisticated software tools to analyse blockchain data. Hileman and Rauchs (2017) reviewed the capabilities of software tools such as Chainalysis, Elliptic and CipherTrace, which can help law enforcement agencies establish connections between different addresses and transactions within the blockchain. Since then, more sophisticated apparatuses have been developed and continue to enter the market (e.g. Bistarelli et al., 2019). These tools possess the capacity to reveal patterns that are suggestive of illicit conduct.

However, the increasing prevalence of privacy-enhancing technologies, such as mixers or tumblers, and privacy-centric cryptocurrencies like Monero (https://www.getmonero.org), Zcash (https://z.cash) or DOP (https://dop.org) poses significant challenges for law enforcement agencies. Utilisation of these technologies introduces intricacies in tracing transactions and establishing their associations with particular identities. Another example is utilisation of Bitcoin clustering, a methodology that consolidates multiple addresses under the jurisdiction of a solitary user; although users can create new addresses for each transaction, it is possible to establish connections between multiple addresses and a single user by analysing patterns and transactional relationships among these addresses (Harrigan & Fretter, 2016).

Nevertheless, in light of the prevailing obstacles, it is crucial to underscore the importance of international cooperation and information sharing among law enforcement entities and the industry to monitor cryptocurrency transactions proficiently. The global nature of cryptocurrencies and darknet markets means that effective enforcement requires cross-border collaboration, as Europol (2020) often highlights.

Appropriate Legal Regulatory Frameworks

While this book does not delve into the legal aspects of cryptocurrency, it is essential to highlight that legal frameworks and regulations must be implemented to address the potential misuse of cryptocurrencies for illicit activities. Many countries around the world are presently implementing strategies to establish regulatory structures for cryptocurrencies. However, the development of genuinely effective regulations faces significant challenges (Houben & Snyers, 2018).

There is considerable variation in cryptocurrencies' legal status across different nations. Cryptocurrencies have been acknowledged as lawful means of payment in specific jurisdictions, while in other jurisdictions they are categorised as commodities or securities (Zetzsche et al., 2018). The disparity in legal status between jurisdictions poses challenges for law enforcement agencies in their efforts to investigate and prosecute criminal cases. To address this matter, nations must engage in collaborative efforts to attain a state of consistency in their respective legal definitions and regulatory frameworks concerning cryptocurrencies.

Moreover, it has been observed that present regulations often lack sufficient consideration for the pseudonymous attributes intrinsic to cryptocurrencies (Houben & Snyers, 2018). Regulatory frameworks must consider the unique characteristics of cryptocurrencies and include provisions that effectively tackle these characteristics. To provide an example, it is conceivable that regulatory requirements could compel cryptocurrency exchanges to implement identity verification procedures for their users, similar to the "Know Your Customer" (KYC) protocols utilised by traditional financial institutions (Gruber, 2020).

The implementation and enforcement of suitable legal and regulatory frameworks plays a crucial role in monitoring transaction activities and tackling the utilisation of cryptocurrency in illicit drug markets. Much as the banking industry is the gateway that enforces the rules and flags concerning transactions in the fiat market (i.e. the ordinary cash market), cryptocurrency regulation should involve the imposition of licencing and registration requirements on cryptocurrency exchanges (see Shortis et al., 2020).

However, while there is some movement in this direction, it remains challenging to monitor cryptocurrency transactions due to an underdeveloped regulatory framework in most countries. Cryptocurrencies—unlike traditional financial systems—lack a centralised authority, which complicates the creation of a consistent regulatory framework. The absence of regulation has facilitated illegal activities, including money laundering and the financing of terrorism through the use of cryptocurrency. Anti-Money Laundering/Counter-Financing of Terrorism (AML/CFT) regulations for cryptocurrency transactions should be explicitly implemented (Zetzsche et al., 2018). By enacting regulatory measures, countries can potentially reduce the illicit use of cryptocurrencies in drug-related transactions. To a degree, the enforcement of registration and licencing prerequisites can significantly contribute to preserving a cryptocurrency market that is solely populated by bona fide and law-abiding enterprises. Through the implementation of routine audits and the exercise of oversight, regulatory bodies possess the capacity to determine the degree to which these entities adhere to pertinent laws and regulations (Böhme et al., 2015). The AML regulations mandate that cryptocurrency brokers and exchanges must conduct customer due diligence, report transactions that are considered suspicious and maintain records of transactions, among other stipulations.

The efficacy of implementing legislation that explicitly criminalises the use of cryptocurrencies for illicit activities, such as drug-related transactions, has been demonstrated. Legislation of this kind may incorporate a range of provisions that involve significant penalties, including monetary fines and custodial sentences, thereby serving as a preventive mechanism against potential offenders (Takács et al., 2020).

At the same time, regulations on cryptocurrency which are too stringent may backfire. It is imperative to uphold a balanced equilibrium in enforcing these regulations to avoid hindering the advancement of innovation in cryptocurrency. Zetzsche et al. (2018) argue that many regulations divert cryptocurrency transactions into covert channels, compounding the difficulties law enforcement agencies encounter in overseeing and governing these transactions.

International Multi-stakeholder Monitoring

The importance of international collaboration and the alignment of regulations should not be underestimated, given that cryptocurrencies transcend national borders due to their decentralised nature. Regulatory arbitrage can arise due to the implantation of divergent regulatory strategies by different nations. In the given context, individuals engaged in criminal activities exploit jurisdictions where less rigorous regulations are in place (Crosby et al., 2016).

However, several challenges impede the attainment of effective international collaboration. These challenges include disparities in legal frameworks, variations in privacy legislation and the complex nature of mutual legal assistance treaties (MLATs). It is therefore crucial to enhance and streamline global collaborative frameworks to enable swift and efficient responses to criminal activities linked to cryptocurrencies (Choo, 2015). The enhancement of investigative capabilities through extensive technical training, advanced technological tools and cooperative endeavours at an international level can provide significant support for law enforcement agencies in their efforts to combat the use of cryptocurrencies in illicit drug markets.

International cooperation and collaboration are essential for the achievement of successful investigations. Criminal activities related to cryptocurrencies often involve multiple jurisdictions, primarily due to the transnational nature of cryptocurrency transactions (Soska & Christin, 2020). Establishing and enhancing communication and cooperation channels between diverse agencies and jurisdictions facilitates a coordinated and collaborative response.

It is noted that the successful collaboration between law enforcement agencies from various countries, including the United States, Thailand, the Netherlands, Lithuania, Canada, the United Kingdom and France, in the dismantling of the AlphaBay and Hansa darknet markets in 2017 serves as a notable example of practical international cooperation (Europol, 2017). The operation resulted in the apprehension of several individuals and the seizure of significant amounts of illegal drugs, forged identification documents and digital currency.

In a world where countries are interconnected through the Internet and cryptocurrency, combating drug trafficking is a challenging task that is beyond the capabilities of any single government. Drug traffickers frequently operate in multiple regions, necessitating cooperation between different countries. Cryptocurrencies introduce complexity to the issue by enabling easily concealable transactions on a worldwide scale (Aldridge & Décary-Hétu, 2014). For this and other reasons, global cooperation among law enforcement authorities is crucial to properly tackle this issue. International law enforcement groups like Interpol and Europol facilitate cooperation between nations (Dupont et al., 2016). International cooperation can be promoted by establishing consistent channels for the exchange of information and intelligence, encouraging collaborative efforts in joint operations and facilitating the harmonisation of legal and procedural frameworks. Nations must work together to create widely recognised standards and norms for the regulation of cryptocurrencies. By using proven international accords like the United Nations Convention against Illicit Traffic in Narcotic Drugs and Psychotropic Substances, a solid foundation can be provided for efforts to combat financial crimes (UNODC, 2020).

Furthermore, nations must collaborate to establish universally accepted standards and norms for the governance of cryptocurrencies. Well-established international agreements, such as the United Nations Convention against Illicit Traffic in Narcotic Drugs and Psychotropic Substances, can serve as a fundamental framework for initiatives to tackle financial crimes (UNODC, 2020).

Entities such as the Financial Action Task Force are of utmost significance within this specific framework. The Financial Action Task Force provides internationally recognised guidelines for effectively addressing the challenges associated with money laundering and the financing of terrorism. The scope of these guidelines can be broadened to include the unauthorised utilisation of cryptocurrencies within the domain of drug trafficking, as the Financial Action Task Force has outlined (FATF, 2020).

Ultimately, the involvement of nongovernmental entities, including cryptocurrency exchanges, wallet providers and blockchain analysis firms, has great potential to contribute to these efforts. According to Zevenbergen (2020), these entities can provide law enforcement agencies with substantial data and expertise, assisting and accelerating their investigative procedures.

The proliferation of globalisation, in conjunction with the largely unregulated nature of the Internet, has led to a significant increase in the cross-border character of drug trafficking and money laundering; these offences are increasingly prevalent manifestations of transnational illicit conduct. Moreover, the complex attributes of cryptocurrencies, which are characterised by decentralisation and global accessibility, introduce an additional level of intricacy, allowing a singular transaction to involve multiple parties in disparate jurisdictions (UNODC, 2021). In this context, international cooperation is both beneficial and essential.

International cooperation can be manifested in a range of ways. At the bilateral level, potential measures may include reciprocal sharing of intelligence and information, the transfer of individuals suspected of engaging in criminal activities, the provision of mutual legal assistance in investigative proceedings and collaborative endeavours through joint operations. As an example, the collaborative efforts of law enforcement agencies from seven nations, including the FBI, dismantled the darknet marketplace AlphaBay in 2020 (FBI, 2020). International organisations and forums, such as Interpol, Europol, the United Nations Office on Drugs and Crime (UNODC) and the Financial Action Task Force (FATF), play a central role in multilateral cooperation. According to Interpol (2020), these organisations promote cooperation, set international standards and offer member nations technical assistance and opportunities to enhance their capabilities.

These entities have also been involved in analysing patterns, developing recommendations and facilitating collaboration in the cryptocurrency sphere. For instance, the Financial Action Task Force has issued explicit guidance on implementing its standards for virtual assets and virtual asset service providers (FATF, 2019). UNODC has recently conducted extensive research and implemented comprehensive training programmes focused on the use of cryptocurrencies in the context of drug trafficking (UNODC, 2021). However, the establishment of international cooperation faces numerous challenges. International differences can reduce the potential for collaboration in terms of legal structures, capabilities and preferences. Brunnermeier et al. (2019) underscored how significant an obstacle the lack of standardised cryptocurrency regulations is. It is thus essential to consistently advocate for improved harmonisation and collaboration in this field.

Analysing illicit activities related to cryptocurrencies requires a significant degree of technical expertise. Law enforcement agencies must possess the knowledge and tools to effectively track transactions within the blockchain, determine user identities and gather evidentiary material. The scarcity of resources and expertise in the field presents a notable obstacle, especially for organisations operating in developing nations (UNODC, 2014).

Enhancing Proficiency in the Conduct of Investigations

Despite the inherent challenges associated with monitoring cryptocurrency transactions and implementing regulatory measures, law enforcement agencies can enhance their investigative capabilities to address this issue more efficiently. This involves improving technical skills, making use of advanced technological tools and fostering collaboration among diverse organisations and legal jurisdictions.

Above all, law enforcement agencies must prioritise providing technical training to their personnel. This training is necessary to ensure that personnel thoroughly understand the intricate nature of cryptocurrency transactions (Choo, 2015). This entails understanding the blockchain technology that underlies cryptocurrencies, developing the ability to trace cryptocurrency transactions and recognising patterns indicative of engagement in illicit activities (Tapscott & Tapscott, 2016). Acquiring specialised training in the use of blockchain explorers can enhance investigators' ability to trace the source of transactions effectively. Incorporating advanced technological tools can significantly enhance the operational capabilities of law enforcement organisations. Various tools have been developed to examine blockchain transactions and identify patterns that may indicate participation in illegal activities (Reid & Harrigan, 2013a, b). Law enforcement agencies can use these tools to monitor transactions, determine the identities of any individuals implicated and gather evidence for legal proceedings. Highlighted below are some of these instruments.

Blockchain Analysis

Blockchain analysis is the monitoring of cryptocurrency transactions to trace the movement of funds and pinpoint the individuals involved in questionable transactions. Financial organisations and regulators can identify suspicious activity by examining blockchain data to detect trends such as significant money transfers, repeated transactions involving the same address and dealings with recognised criminal organisations. Furthermore, blockchain analysis can help uncover concealed wallets and bypass transaction mixing services designed to obscure the origin of funds.

Research indicates that blockchain analysis is a highly effective method of monitoring cryptocurrency transactions (Dearden & Tucker, 2023; Dorogyy & Kolisnichenko, 2023; Pelker et al., 2021). Analysing blockchain data requires substantial technical proficiency and specialised software. Financial organisations and regulators must allocate funding for thorough blockchain research using advanced technologies to identify and prevent financial crimes. More importantly, there is a need for a strategic appetite to incorporate blockchain analysis, which is an area of expertise presently reserved by special agencies like the National Crime Agency, the FBI and the CIA.

Behavioural Analysis and Surveillance

Behavioural analysis in the context of cryptocurrencies and illegal markets is rapidly evolving, as criminals adopt new technologies and methods to conceal their activities. Analysts and law enforcement agencies are continuously developing new techniques and tools to detect and counteract the illicit use of digital currencies. Behaviour-based monitoring is used to identify potentially fraudulent activities within cryptocurrency transactions. This technique entails scrutinising the behaviour of cryptocurrency users to detect any abnormal patterns of activity. Studying the movement of cryptocurrency in illegal markets involves analysing transaction patterns, user behaviours and interactions among illicit actors in the digital currency realm to help identify, track and comprehend the dynamics of illicit cryptocurrency use. For example, if a person begins to conduct a large number of transactions or unexpectedly sends cryptocurrency to unusual locations, this may suggest suspicious conduct (Ballis & Verousis, 2022). Behaviour-based monitoring can effectively detect new and emerging dangers in cryptocurrency markets, and by consistently observing user behaviour and recognising activity patterns, financial organisations and regulators can swiftly identify emerging dangers and create robust risk management policies.

One prevalent method of surveillance involves transaction pattern analysis, in which experts examine the patterns of cryptocurrency transactions to identify any questionable actions. Transactions which rapidly pass through several accounts, referred to as "chain hopping", may suggest efforts to launder money. Dividing transactions into numerous small sums, known as "smurfing", may indicate illegal activity (www.chainalysis.com/blog/cryptocurrency-crime-2020-report/).

Wallet analysis helps identify cryptocurrency wallets commonly used for criminal activities, such as those which are linked to darknet marketplaces or receive payments of suspect origin. It is critical to understand the ecology of the darknet market ecology. Studying the movement of money in and out of these markets helps investigators understand the security protocols they use to avoid discovery.

Ransomware and cybercrime monitoring are also vital elements of the behavioural analysis of cryptomarkets because payment in cryptocurrency is frequently requested in ransomware campaigns. Behavioural analysis can help trace these payments, identify the wallets used by hackers and perhaps connect them to broader networks of criminal actors. Social network analysis can then be used to study the connections and interactions among various participants in a cryptomarket to discern groups and prominent individuals involved in illegal activities, such as money launderers and drug traffickers (FBI, 2020).

Finally, heuristic-based identification entails the development of criteria or heuristics based on established patterns of criminal activity, for example, by linking a cryptocurrency address directly to a known unlawful service. Machine learning models (discussed below) can be used to examine transaction data and detect intricate patterns that suggest criminal activities, utilising past data to forecast which transactions may be linked to unlawful behaviours. Blockchain forensics firms focus on examining the blockchain to detect illicit activities, for example, by tracing the source and destination of payments and identifying the usage of mixers and tumblers for money laundering (Blockchain Analysis, 2022).

Nevertheless, behaviour-based monitoring of cryptomarkets is subject to significant challenges that hinder the tracking and analysis of illicit operations. These issues stem from the unique features of cryptocurrencies and the tactics employed by criminals to avoid being detected. The anonymity and pseudonymity characteristics of cryptocurrencies like Monero and Zcash obstruct transparency by concealing transaction details from the public. Cryptocurrencies such as Bitcoin and Ethereum use pseudonymous systems, making it difficult to correlate transactions directly to real-world identities and posing a significant difficulty for monitoring efforts (Meiklejohn et al., 2013).

More importantly, decentralisation eliminates the need for a central authority to oversee transactions; from a law enforcement point of view, this necessitates a collaborative effort across different regions to monitor and regulate unlawful activity effectively. Dealing with jurisdictional difficulties and establishing international cooperation is made more difficult by the fact that Bitcoin can quickly be moved across international borders. The unevenness of regulatory systems and enforcement capacities among different nations makes it difficult to oversee and reduce the use of cryptocurrencies in illicit markets at a global scale (FATF, 2019). Criminals are quick to adopt new technologies and methods to evade detection and will use multiple markets located around the globe. They frequently use mixing or tumbling services to obscure the sources and destinations of illegal payments. These services combine cryptocurrency from several origins, making it much more difficult to trace transactions to their original source. This rapid evolution requires constant adaptation of monitoring tools and techniques, which constitutes a significant burden for researchers and law enforcement agencies (van Wegberg et al., 2018).

Another significant challenge is the volume and complexity of the data involved. Conducting behavioural analysis on cryptocurrency transactions requires sophisticated tools capable of parsing and analysing vast amounts of data to identify patterns indicative of illicit activity. However, the sheer scale of the data and the complexity of transaction networks can overwhelm these tools, making it difficult to extract meaningful insights without substantial computational resources and expertise (Möser et al., 2018a, b). The technical knowledge, computational resources and time needed for efficient behaviour-based monitoring is considerable, especially for smaller organisations or countries with limited technical capabilities. Tackling these challenges will require a comprehensive strategy involving technological advancements, the establishment of standardised regulatory structures and ongoing cooperation among governments, financial entities and technology firms to enhance the efficiency of behaviour-based surveillance in the constantly changing realm of cryptocurrency transactions (Aldridge & Décary-Hétu, 2014).

Lastly, ethical and privacy concerns are associated with the behavioural analysis of cryptocurrency transactions. The balance between monitoring illicit activity and respecting individual privacy rights is delicate. There is a risk that overly aggressive monitoring could infringe on privacy, leading to resistance from the cryptocurrency community and potentially stifling innovation in this space (Reid & Harrigan, 2013a, b). Legitimate users may display atypical behaviour that does not suggest any unlawful actions. It is thus essential to find a balance between identifying suspicious behaviour and avoiding false alarms. Financial institutions and regulators should utilise analytics and machine learning algorithms to analyse user behaviour and detect genuine hazards while reducing the risk of false alarms—a topic discussed below.

Artificial Intelligence and Machine Learning

Machine learning and AI are now commonly employed in the monitoring of cryptocurrency transactions to identify and deter financial crimes. These technologies can be used to analyse large volumes of data and discover patterns of suspicious behaviour that would be challenging or impossible for humans to identify unaided. Historical data can be used to train machine learning algorithms to detect patterns of suspicious behaviour and automatically highlight transactions that fit specific criteria. For instance, a machine learning system can be trained to identify transactions exceeding a specific monetary value, transactions occurring between particular nations or transactions involving recognised criminal organisations. Once a transaction is identified as suspicious, a human analyst can assess it to decide whether it merits additional investigation (Lee et al., 2020; Lorenz et al., 2020).

Moreover, AI can analyse unstructured data from sources like social media and online forums to detect possible instances of money laundering or financing of terrorism. An AI system can also detect suspicious conduct, such as a user discussing a significant transaction with a recognised criminal organisation on a Bitcoin forum, and subject it to closer scrutiny (Pocher et al., 2023).

Nevertheless, AI applications are not infallible and will require ongoing enhancement and advancement to outpace new and evolving threats. Moreover, it is possible that criminals will utilise new technologies to obscure their actions, compounding the difficulty of identifying and stopping financial crimes. To optimise the use of machine learning and AI-based technologies, financial institutions and regulators must invest in the technology and experience necessary to analyse large amounts of data effectively. They must constantly improve their algorithms and machine learning models to stay ahead of new and emerging risks in the cryptocurrency industry (see recently in Alotibi et al., 2022).

Risk-Based Monitoring

Risk-based monitoring is increasingly recognised as a viable and effective method for overseeing cryptocurrency transactions, particularly in AML and CFT. This approach allows firms to allocate their monitoring resources more efficiently by focusing on the transactions with the highest risk. The introduction of risk-based monitoring in the cryptocurrency space is a response to the unique challenges posed by the digital nature of these assets, including the anonymity of users, the speed of transactions and the global reach of the blockchain network.

The Financial Action Task Force has played a pivotal role in shaping the regulatory framework for risk-based monitoring of cryptocurrencies by issuing guidance that requires cryptocurrency service providers to implement measures for the detection and mitigation of money laundering and terrorist financing (ComplyAdvantage, n.d.-a). These measures include conducting due diligence on customers, continuously monitoring transactions for suspicious activity and reporting anomalies to the relevant authorities (Sumsub, 2024). In practice, this means that cryptocurrency firms must assess the risk profile of their customers and monitor transactions in real time, employing advanced analytical tools to detect patterns indicative of illicit activity (GetFocal, 2024).

The challenges of implementing risk-based monitoring in the cryptocurrency sector are not trivial. They include the technical difficulty of analysing transactions on a decentralised network, the need for sophisticated tools to identify suspicious patterns and the regulatory complexity of operating in a global market with diverse legal frameworks. Despite these challenges, risk-based monitoring is considered essential for the integrity of the financial system and the prevention of financial crimes facilitated by cryptocurrencies (ComplyAdvantage, n.d.-b).

Technological tools can be utilised to facilitate the execution of these investigations. Meiklejohn et al. (2013) assert that blockchain analysis software facilitates the tracing of transactions, identification of interconnected address clusters and potential estimation of the geographical locations of users. The tools mentioned above demonstrate an ongoing process of development and improvement in response to emerging challenges such as the increasing utilisation of privacy-focused cryptocurrencies like Monero (Moser et al., 2018a, b).

In a similar vein, the application of advanced statistical methodologies, machine learning algorithms and AI has the potential to enhance the functionality of these tools (Jang & Lee, 2018). These technologies can identify patterns and anomalies in transaction data which may indicate illicit activities. Cryptocurrencies are therefore of considerable importance in the fight against drug trafficking, as traffickers financially depend on these digital currencies.

However, it is essential to acknowledge that the tools and skills described above, although valuable, are insufficient when considered in isolation. As expounded upon in the preceding chapters, appropriate legal frameworks, robust international collaboration and the active involvement of stakeholders from the private sector must accompany the measures mentioned above.

Engagement with the Private Sector and Exchanges in Collaborative Efforts

The effectiveness of law enforcement agencies in tackling drug markets linked to cryptocurrencies relies on the cooperation of the private sector, specifically cryptocurrency exchanges. As laid out in the recommendations made by the Financial Action Task Force (FATF, 2019), these digital platforms serve as intermediaries for the purchase, sale and exchange of cryptocurrencies, affording them access to substantial quantities of user data and transactional details. Unless exchanges take an active role in monitoring and disclosing data, illicit cryptomarkets will continue to flourish.

One procedure that seems clearly necessary to us is adherence to know-your-customer (KYC) and anti-money laundering (AML) protocols. In many "Level 1" exchanges—large and recognised market makers such as Binance or Coinbase—these are compulsory in various legal jurisdictions. Such measures involve collecting identifiable user information, monitoring users' transactions to identify any suspicious activity and reporting such activity to the relevant authorities (Möser et al., 2018a, b).

However, the effectiveness of these measures depends on the degree to which the exchanges comply with regulations and their ability to identify potentially illegal activities. To promote collaboration, agencies have proactively assigned dedicated liaison officers or established points of contact with these exchanges (Ridley, 2020). The effective completion of this undertaking requires not only compliance teams that adhere to the existing rules but also significant technical expertise and a thorough understanding of the strategies employed by individuals involved in drug trafficking when utilising cryptocurrencies (Irwin & Slay, 2017). Therefore, law enforcement agencies must cultivate robust collaborative partnerships with the exchanges. This may involve regular distribution of information, collaborative investigations and even joint efforts to improve skills and capabilities.

Alternatively, regulators could take a deterrent route and punish exchanges for noncompliance. Binance, one of the largest exchanges, is presently involved in a legal dispute with the US Securities and Exchange Commission (SEC). The SEC has accused Binance CEO Changpeng Zhao and its US division of multiple infractions, such as misrepresenting trading volumes, abusing client funds, failing to limit

US customers and providing false information about market surveillance procedures to investors. The SEC also accused Binance of enabling the trading of crypto tokens that might be considered unregistered securities. This lawsuit is a component of a larger SEC initiative to oversee the cryptocurrency industry and is essential to establishing the SEC's jurisdiction over cryptocurrencies.

In addition to cryptocurrency exchanges, other private sector entities can also play a critical role in addressing the issue of drug trafficking facilitated by cryptocurrencies. Such entities include companies specialising in blockchain analysis, cybersecurity firms, banks and traditional financial institutions. These businesses can help detect, monitor and reduce illicit activities linked to digital currency. For example, Chainalysis (www.chainalysis.com) is a prominent company in the field of blockchain analysis, focusing on offering blockchain data and analysis services to government agencies, exchanges and financial institutions in 70 countries. Tools like Chainalysis Reactor (www.chainalysis.com/chainalysis-reactor) allow investigators to track illegal cryptocurrency transactions on the blockchain, pinpoint where cryptocurrency is being laundered and analyse the networks participating in these operations. The company's actions have led to notable achievements in law enforcement, including the confiscation of $1 billion linked to the Silk Road market, the closure of the Hydra marketplace and the dismantling of WelcomeToVideo (McCord et al., 2022). Merkle Science (www.merklescience.com) is another significant player in this field, offering tools for blockchain forensics and the tracking of crypto assets and crimes. These technologies are essential for the investigation of various illegal activities such as fraud, money laundering and illicit cryptocurrency transactions. They help law enforcement agencies, regulatory bodies and financial institutions track the movement of funds, identify illicit tendencies and improve transparency in the cryptocurrency market by examining blockchain transaction data. The examples given above demonstrate the varied and essential functions of private sector entities in the fight against drug trafficking and other illegal activities enabled by cryptocurrencies. These companies make a substantial contribution to the safety and integrity of the financial ecosystem by utilising innovative technologies and working closely with law enforcement.

Conclusion

The use of encrypted communications by criminals presents a multifaceted challenge, in which technological advancements are intricately interwoven with legal and ethical considerations. As societies globally navigate this complex terrain, the focus must remain on the development of strategies to effectively combat criminal networks without undermining the core values of privacy and security that encrypted platforms were initially designed to protect. This remains a focal point of discussion and policy formulation in the contemporary digital age, illustrating the complexities of maintaining security in a world that is increasingly reliant on digital communication platforms.

However, this battle against criminal networks using encrypted platforms also brings important ethical and legal considerations to the fore. While combating criminal activities remains a priority, it is equally imperative to ensure that the privacy and security of lawful users is not compromised. Thus, a delicate balance needs to be struck between curtailing criminal activities and safeguarding the individual's right to privacy. This necessitates a nuanced approach which encourages the development of strong encryption technologies to protect individual privacy and security in the digital realm, albeit with mechanisms to prevent their misuse by criminal entities.

It can be argued that the impact of crackdowns on darknet cryptomarkets is undeniably significant: Crackdowns disrupt criminal networks and diminish the accessibility of illicit goods and services. However, the overall efficacy of these measures is somewhat tempered by the enduring resilience and adaptability exhibited by the criminal networks they target. In order to optimise the enduring consequences of these measures, it is imperative to integrate them with endeavours aimed at mitigating the fundamental demand for illicit commodities and services. This should be accompanied by sustained allocation of resources towards the technological and collaborative approaches necessary to effectively counteract cybercrime.

In general, a comprehensive understanding of crime displacement which considers both spatial and modus operandi displacement will produce a more comprehensive and integrated strategy for crime prevention. This statement recognises the complex and adaptable characteristics of criminal behaviours, highlighting the need for law enforcement organisations to formulate flexible and dynamic approaches in order to effectively deter crime rather than simply displacing it, with the ultimate goal of achieving substantial decreases in criminal activity. This methodology, based on thorough examination and adjustment, is intended to enhance the efficiency and adaptability of crime prevention tactics. Its objective is not solely to react to criminal activities but also to proactively anticipate and mitigate the evolving strategies employed by offenders.

References

Abdel, S. Y. (2021). Case study: Dark web markets. In *Dark web investigation* (pp. 237–247).

Aldridge, J., & Askew, R. (2017). Delivery dilemmas: How drug crypto market users identify and seek to reduce their risk of detection by law enforcement. *International Journal of Drug Policy, 41*, 101–109.

Aldridge, J., & Décary-Hétu, D. (2014). Not an 'Ebay for drugs': The Crypto market 'Silk Road' as a paradigm shifting criminal innovation. *SSRN Electronic Journal*. https://doi.org/10.2139/ssrn.2436643

Alotibi, J., Almutanni, B., Alsubait, T., Alhakami, H., & Baz, A. (2022). Money laundering detection using machine learning and deep learning. *International Journal of Advanced Computer Science and Applications, 13*(10).

Apel, R., & Nagin, D. S. (2011). General deterrence: A review of recent evidence. *Crime and Public Policy, 4*, 411–436.

Ariel, B. (2012). Deterrence and moral persuasion effects on corporate tax compliance: findings from a randomized controlled trial. *Criminology, 50*(1), 27–69.

Ariel, B., & Partridge, H. (2017). Predictable policing: Measuring the crime control benefits of hotspots policing at bus stops. *Journal of Quantitative Criminology, 33*, 809–833.

Ariel, B., Bland, M., & Sutherland, A. (2017). 'Lowering the threshold of effective deterrence'—Testing the effect of private security agents in public spaces on crime: A randomized controlled trial in a mass transit system. *PLoS One, 12*(12), e0187392.

Ariel, B., Sutherland, A., Henstock, D., Young, J., & Sosinski, G. (2018). The deterrence spectrum: Explaining why police body-worn cameras 'work' or 'backfire' in aggressive police–public encounters. *Policing: A Journal of Policy and Practice, 12*(1), 6–26.

Ariel, B., Englefield, A., & Denley, J. (2019). I heard it through the grapevine: A randomized controlled trial on the direct and vicarious effects of preventative specific deterrence initiatives in criminal networks. *Journal of Criminal Law and Criminology, 109*, 819.

Ballis, A., & Verousis, T. (2022). Behavioural finance and cryptocurrencies. *Review of Behavioral Finance, 14*(4), 545–562.

Bancroft, A., & Scott Reid, P. (2017). Challenging the techno-politics of anonymity: The case of crypto market users. *Information, Communication and Society, 20*(4), 497–512.

Bennett, D. (2012). The challenges facing computer forensics investigators in obtaining information from mobile devices for use in criminal investigations. *Information Security Journal: A Global Perspective, 21*(3), 159–168.

Bhaskar, V., Linacre, R., & Machin, S. (2019). The economic functioning of online drugs markets. *Journal of Economic Behavior and Organization, 159*, 426–441.

Bistarelli, S., Mercanti, I., & Santini, F. (2019). A suite of tools for the forensic analysis of bitcoin transactions: Preliminary report. In *Euro-Par 2018: parallel processing workshops: Euro-Par 2018 international workshops, Turin, Italy, August 27–28, 2018, Revised Selected Papers 24* (pp. 329–341). Springer International Publishing.

Bland, M., Ariel, B., & Kumar, S. (2023). Criminal records versus rehabilitation and expungement: A randomised controlled trial. *Journal of Experimental Criminology*, 1–25.

Böhme, R., Christin, N., Edelman, B., & Moore, T. (2015). Bitcoin: Economics, technology, and governance. *Journal of Economic Perspectives, 29*(2), 213–238. https://doi.org/10.1257/jep.29.2.213

Booij, T. M., Verburgh, T., Falconieri, F., & van Wegberg, R. S. (2021, September). Get rich or keep Tryin' Trajectories in dark net market vendor careers. In *2021 IEEE European symposium on security and privacy workshops (EuroSandPW)* (pp. 202–212). IEEE.

Bradley, C. (2019). *On the resilience of the Dark Net Market ecosystem to law enforcement intervention* (Doctoral dissertation). University College London.

Broadhurst, R., Masters, A., Smith, R. G., & Brown, R. (2018). The state of organised crime research in Australia. *Organised Crime Research in Australia, 2018*, 1.

Broadhurst, R., Ball, M., Jiang, C., Wang, J., & Trivedi, H. (2021). *Impact of darknet market seizures on opioid availability* (Research Report No. 18). Australian Institute of Criminology. https://www.aic.gov.au/publications/rr/rr18

Brunnermeier, M. K., James, H., & Landau, J. P. (2019). The digitalization of money. *Brookings Papers on Economic Activity, 2019*(Fall), 77–137.

Brunt, R., Pandey, P., & McCoy, D. (2017). Booted: An analysis of a payment intervention on a ddos-for-hire service. In *Workshop on the economics of information security* (pp. 6–26).

Caulkins, J. P., & Kleiman, M. (2018). Lessons to be drawn from US drug control policies. *European Journal on Criminal Policy and Research, 24*, 125–144.

Chawki, M. (2022). The Dark Web and the future of illicit drug markets. *Journal of Transportation Security, 15*(3–4), 173–191.

Choo, K. K. R. (2015). Cryptocurrency and virtual currency: Corruption and money laundering/terrorism financing risks? *Computer Law and Security Review, 31*(4), 484–492.

Cohen, L. (2023, May 24). *No way to police all cryptocurrency fraud, CFTC commissioner says.* Reuters. https://www.reuters.com/technology/no-way-to-police-all-cryptocurrency-fraud-cftc-commissioner-says-2023-05-23/

ComplyAdvantage. (n.d.-a). *5 best practices for cryptocurrency compliance*. Retrieved from complyadvantage.com

ComplyAdvantage. (n.d.-b). *Cryptocurrency transaction monitoring: What you need to know*. Retrieved from complyadvantage.com

Crosby, M., Nachiappan, P., Verma, S., & Kalyanaraman, V. (2016). Blockchain technology: Beyond Bitcoin. *Applied Innovation, 2*, 6–10.

D'arcy, J., & Herath, T. (2011). A review and analysis of deterrence theory in the IS security literature: Making sense of the disparate findings. *European Journal of Information Systems, 20*(6), 643–658.

Dearden, T. E., & Tucker, S. E. (2023). Follow the money: Analyzing darknet activity using cryptocurrency and the bitcoin blockchain. *Journal of Contemporary Criminal Justice, 39*(2), 257–275.

Décary-Hétu, D., & Giommoni, L. (2017). Do police crackdowns disrupt drug cryptomarkets? A longitudinal analysis of the effects of Operation Onymous. *Crime, Law and Social Change, 67*, 55–75.

Décary-Hétu, D., Paquet-Clouston, M., & Aldridge, J. (2016). Going international? Risk taking by crypto market drug vendors. *International Journal of Drug Policy, 35*, 69–76.

Demant, J., Munksgaard, R., & Houborg, E. (2018). Personal use, social supply or redistribution? Crypto market demand on Silk Road 2 and Agora. *Trends in Organized Crime, 21*, 42–61.

Denley, J., & Ariel, B. (2019). Whom should we target to prevent? Analysis of organized crime in England using intelligence records. *European Journal of Crime, Criminal Law and Criminal Justice, 27*(1), 13–44.

Denley, J., & Ariel, B. (n.d.). A *'Sticks and carrots' approach to serious and organised crime: A cluster randomised controlled trial*.

Dorogyy, Y., & Kolisnichenko, V. (2023). Blockchain transaction analysis: A comprehensive review of applications, tasks and methods. *System Research and Information Technologies, 4*, 37–53.

Dupont, B., Côté, A. M., Savine, C., & Décary-Hétu, D. (2016). The ecology of trust among hackers. *Global Crime, 17*(2), 129–151. https://doi.org/10.1080/17440572.2016.1157482

Duxbury, S. W., & Haynie, D. L. (2018). Building them up, breaking them down: Topology, vendor selection patterns, and a digital drug market's robustness to disruption. *Social Networks, 52*, 238–250.

El Bahrawy, A., Alessandretti, L., Rusnac, L., Goldsmith, D., Teytelboym, A., & Baronchelli, A. (2020). Collective dynamics of dark web marketplaces. *Scientific Reports, 10*, 188–201.

Europol. (2017). *The world's biggest marketplace selling internet-paralysing cyber attacks has been taken down*. Europol. https://www.europol.europa.eu/newsroom/news/world's-biggest-marketplace-selling-internet-paralysing-cyber-attacks-taken-down

Europol. (2020). *Internet organised crime threat assessment 2020*. https://www.europol.europa.eu/activities-services/main-reports/internet-organised-crime-threat-assessment-iocta-2020

FATF. (2019). *Guidance for a risk-based approach to virtual assets and virtual asset service providers*. Financial Action Task Force. https://www.fatf-gafi.org/media/fatf/documents/recommendations/RBA-VA-VASPs.pdf

FATF. (2020). *Virtual assets red flag indicators of money laundering and terrorist financing*. Financial Action Task Force. https://www.fatf-gafi.org/publications/fatfgeneral/documents/virtual-assets-red-flag-indicators.html

Faubert, C., Décary-Hétu, D., Malm, A., Ratcliffe, J., & Dupont, B. (2021). Law enforcement and disruption of offline and online activities: A review of contemporary challenges. In *Cybercrime in context: The human factor in victimisation, offending, and policing* (pp. 351–370).

FBI. (2020). *AlphaBay, the largest online 'dark market,' shut down*. Federal Bureau of Investigation. https://www.fbi.gov/news/stories/alphabay-takedown-071317

Geers, K. (2010). The challenge of cyber attack deterrence. *Computer Law and Security Review, 26*(3), 298–303.

Gehl, R. W. (2018). *Weaving the Dark Web: legitimacy on freenet, Tor, and I2P*. MIT Press.

GetFocal. (2024). *Cryptocurrency transaction monitoring: Best practices in 2024*. Retrieved from getfocal.ai

Gibbs, J. P. (1968). Crime, punishment, and deterrence. In *The Southwestern social science quarterly* (pp. 515–530).

Griffiths, C., & Jackson, A. (2022). Intercepted communications as evidence: The admissibility of material obtained from the encrypted messaging service EncroChat: R v A, B, D and C [2021] EWCA Crim 128. *The Journal of Criminal Law, 86*(4), 271–276.

Gruber, S. (2020). The future of cryptocurrencies: Bitcoin and beyond. *Nature, 588*(7836), 33–36. https://doi.org/10.1038/d41586-020-02921-6

Harrigan, M., & Fretter, C. (2016). The unreasonable effectiveness of address clustering. In *2016 IEEE European symposium on security and privacy workshops* (EuroSandPW) (pp. 1–7). IEEE. https://doi.org/10.1109/EuroSPW.2016.38

Hartel, P., & Van Wegberg, R. (2019). 11 crime and online anonymous markets. In *International and transnational crime and justice* (p. 67).

Hartel, P., & van Wegberg, R. (2023). Going dark? Analysing the impact of end-to-end encryption on the outcome of Dutch criminal court cases. *Crime Science, 12*(1), 1–8.

Hileman, G., & Rauchs, M. (2017). *Global blockchain benchmarking study* (September 22, 2017). Available at SSRN: https://ssrn.com/abstract=3040224 or https://doi.org/10.2139/ssrn.3040224

Hiramoto, N., & Tsuchiya, Y. (2023). Are illicit drugs a driving force for crypto market leadership? *Journal of Drug Issues, 53*(3), 451–474.

Hong, Y., & Neilson, W. (2020). Cybercrime and punishment. *The Journal of Legal Studies, 49*(2), 431–466.

Houben, R., & Snyers, A. (2018). *Cryptocurrencies and blockchain: Legal context and implications for financial crime, money laundering and tax evasion*. European Parliament. http://www.europarl.europa.eu/RegData/etudes/STUD/2018/619025/IPOL_STU(2018)619025_EN.pdf

Hui, K. L., Kim, S. H., & Wang, Q. H. (2017). Cybercrime deterrence and international legislation. *MIS Quarterly, 41*(2), 497–524.

Interpol. (2020). *Cybercrime*. International Criminal Police Organization. https://www.interpol.int/Crimes/Cybercrime

Irwin, A. S., & Slay, J. (2017). Detection and recovery of anti-forensic (VOIP) calls. *Journal of Forensic and Legal Medicine, 50*, 81–90. https://doi.org/10.1016/j.jflm.2017.07.005

Jang, H., & Lee, J. (2018). Anonymity and patterns in the darknet cryptocurrency market. *Information Systems Frontiers, 20*(3), 513–529. https://doi.org/10.1007/s10796-016-9661-8

Jansen, F., & van Lenthe, J. (2016). Adaptation 12 strategies of cybercriminals to interventions from public and private sectors. In *Cybercrime through an interdisciplinary lens* (p. 210).

Jardine, E. (2021). Policing the cybercrime script of darknet drug markets: Methods of effective law enforcement intervention. *American Journal of Criminal Justice, 46*, 980–1005.

Kabra, S., & Gori, S. (2023). Drug trafficking on cryptomarkets and the role of organized crime groups. *Journal of Economic Criminology, 2*, 100026.

Koziarski, J., & Lee, J. R. (2020). Connecting evidence-based policing and cybercrime. *Policing: An International Journal, 43*(1), 198–211.

Lacson, W., & Jones, B. (2016). The 21st century darknet market: Lessons from the fall of Silk Road. *International Journal of Cyber Criminology, 10*(1), 40.

Ladegaard, I. (2019). Crime displacement in digital drug markets. *International Journal of Drug Policy, 63*, 113–121.

Leontiadis, N., & Hutchings, A. (2015). Scripting the crime commission process in the illicit online prescription drug trade. *Journal of Cybersecurity, 1*(1), 81–92.

Lorenz, J., Silva, M. I., Aparício, D., Ascensão, J. T., & Bizarro, P. (2020, October). Machine learning methods to detect money laundering in the bitcoin blockchain in the presence of label scarcity. In *Proceedings of the First ACM international conference on AI in Finance* (pp. 1–8).

Loughran, T. A., Paternoster, R., & Weiss, D. B. (2015). Deterrence. In *The handbook of criminological theory* (pp. 50–74).

Maimon, D., Howell, C. J., & Burruss, G. W. (2021). Restrictive deterrence and the scope of hackers' reoffending: Findings from two randomized field trials. *Computers in Human Behavior, 125*, 106943.

Martin, J. (2023). Cryptomarkets and drug market gentrification. In *Digital transformations of illicit drug markets: Reconfiguration and continuity* (pp. 127–139). Emerald Publishing Limited.

Martin, J., Munksgaard, R., Coomber, R., Demant, J., & Barratt, M. J. (2020). Selling drugs on darkweb cryptomarkets: Differentiated pathways, risks and rewards. *The British Journal of Criminology, 60*(3), 559–578.

McCord, A., Birch, P., & Davison, A. (2022). Technology enabled crime: Examining the role of cryptocurrency. *Kriminologie-Das Online-Journal|Criminology-The Online Journal, 4*, 428–451.

Meiklejohn, S., Pomarole, M., Jordan, G., Levchenko, K., McCoy, D., Voelker, G. M., & Savage, S. (2013). A fistful of bitcoins: Characterising payments among men with no names. In *Proceedings of the 2013 conference on Internet measurement* (pp. 127–140). https://doi.org/10.1145/2504730.2504747

Miller, S., & Bossomaier, T. (2021). Privacy, encryption and counter-terrorism. In *Counter-terrorism, ethics and technology: Emerging challenges at the frontiers of counter-terrorism* (pp. 139–154).

Moeller, K., Munksgaard, R., & Demant, J. (2017). Flow my FE the vendor said: Exploring violent and fraudulent resource exchanges on cryptomarkets for illicit drugs. *American Behavioral Scientist, 61*(11), 1427–1450.

Moitra, S. D. (2005). Developing policies for cybercrime: Some empirical issues. *European Journal of Crime, Criminal Law and Criminal Justice, 13*, 435.

Möser, M., Böhme, R., & Breuker, D. (2018a). An inquiry into money laundering tools in the Bitcoin ecosystem. In *eCrime Researchers Summit* (pp. 1–14).

Möser, M., Soska, K., Heilman, E., Lee, K., Heffan, I., Srivastava, A., Hogan, K., Hennessey, J., Miller, A., Narayanan, A., & Christin, N. (2018b). An empirical analysis of traceability in the monero blockchain. *Proceedings on Privacy Enhancing Technologies, 2018*(3), 143–163. https://doi.org/10.1515/popets-2018-0025

Nagin, D. S. (2013). Deterrence in the twenty-first century. *Crime and Justice, 42*(1), 199–263.

Narain, A., & Moretti, M (2022). *Regulating Crypto*. International Monetary Fund. https://www.imf.org/en/Publications/fandd/issues/2022/09/Regulating-crypto-Narain-Moretti

NCA. (2020). *NCA and police smash thousands of criminal conspiracies after infiltration of encrypted communication platform in UK's biggest ever law enforcement operation*. National Crime Agency. https://www.nationalcrimeagency.gov.uk/news/operation-venetic

Norbutas, L., Ruiter, S., & Corten, R. (2020). Reputation transferability across contexts: Maintaining cooperation among anonymous crypto market actors when moving between markets. *International Journal of Drug Policy, 76*, 102635.

O'Rourke, C. (2020). Is this the end for 'encro' phones? *Computer Fraud and Security, 2020*(11), 8–10.

Oerlemans, J. J., & van Toor, D. A. G. (2022). Legal aspects of the EncroChat operation: A human rights perspective. *European Journal of Crime, Criminal Law and Criminal Justice, 30*(3–4), 309–328.

Pelker, C. A., Brown, C. B., & Tucker, R. M. (2021). Using blockchain analysis from investigation to trial. *Department of Justice Federal Law and Practice, 69*, 59.

Phelps, A., & Watt, A. (2014). I shop online–recreationally! Internet anonymity and Silk Road enabling drug use in Australia. *Digital Investigation, 11*(4), 261–272.

Piquero, A., & Paternoster, R. (1998). An application of Stafford and Warr's reconceptualization of deterrence to drinking and driving. *Journal of Research in Crime and Delinquency, 35*(1), 3–39.

Pocher, N., Zichichi, M., Merizzi, F., Shafiq, M. Z., & Ferretti, S. (2023). Detecting anomalous cryptocurrency transactions: An AML/CFT application of machine learning-based forensics. *Electronic Markets, 33*(1), 37.

Pratt, T. C., Cullen, F. T., Blevins, K. R., Daigle, L. E., & Madensen, T. D. (2017). The empirical status of deterrence theory: A meta-analysis. In *Taking stock* (pp. 367–395). Routledge.

Rawat, R., Mahor, V., Chouhan, M., Pachlasiya, K., Telang, S., & Garg, B. (2022). Systematic literature review (SLR) on social media and the digital transformation of drug trafficking on darkweb. In *International conference on network security and blockchain technology* (pp. 181–205). Springer.

Reid, F., & Harrigan, M. (2013a). *An analysis of anonymity in the bitcoin system* (pp. 197–223). Springer.

Reid, F., & Harrigan, M. (2013b). An analysis of anonymity in the Bitcoin system. In A. Yanai (Ed.), *Privacy, security, risk and Trust (PASSAT), 2012 international conference on and 2012 international conference on social computing (SocialCom)* (pp. 1318–1326). IEEE. https://doi.org/10.1109/SocialCom-PASSAT.2012.84

Ridley, G. (2020). The Role of banks in the cryptocurrency market. *Banking and Finance Review, 12*(1), 27–40. https://doi.org/10.24113/bfr.v12i1.196

Roth, M. P. (2014). *An eye for an eye: A global history of crime and punishment*. Reaktion Books.

Sagittae, G. (2023). On the lawfulness of the EncroChat and Sky ECC-operations. *New Journal of European Criminal Law, 14*, 273–293.

Shen, A., Antonopoulos, G. A., & Von Lampe, K. (2010). 'The dragon breathes smoke' cigarette counterfeiting in the People's Republic of China. *The British Journal of Criminology, 50*(2), 239–258.

Sherman, L. W. (1993). Defiance, deterrence, and irrelevance: A theory of the criminal sanction. *Journal of Research in Crime and Delinquency, 30*(4), 445–473.

Shortis, P., Aldridge, J., & Monica, J. (2020). Drug cryptomarket futures: Structure, function and evolution in response to law enforcement actions. In *Research handbook on international drug policy* (pp. 355–380). Edward Elgar Publishing.

Smith, R. G., Worthington, G., & Wolanin, N. (2003). E-crime solutions and crime displacement. *Australian Institute of criminology: Trends and issues in crime and criminal justice No. 243*. https://www.aic.gov.au/sites/default/files/2020-05/tandi243.pdf

Soska, K., & Christin, N. (2020). Measuring the longitudinal evolution of the online anonymous marketplace ecosystem. *Communications of the ACM, 63*(10), 100–109. https://doi.org/10.1145/3382702

Spagnoletti, P., Ceci, F., & Bygstad, B. (2021). Online black-markets: An investigation of a digital infrastructure in the dark. In *Information systems frontiers* (pp. 1–16).

Stafford, M. C., & Warr, M. (1993). A reconceptualization of general and specific deterrence. *Journal of Research in Crime and Delinquency, 30*(2), 123–135.

Steel, C. M., Newman, E., O'Rourke, S., & Quayle, E. (2020). An integrative review of historical technology and countermeasure usage trends in online child sexual exploitation material offenders. *Forensic Science International: Digital Investigation, 33*, 300971.

Stoykova, R. (2023). Encrochat: The hacker with a warrant and fair trials? *Forensic Science International: Digital Investigation, 46*, 301602.

Sumsub. (2024). *Crypto transaction monitoring guide 2024*. Retrieved from surnsub.com.

Takács, C., Emőd, I., & Bartók, J. (2020). The legal framework of virtual currencies. *Journal of Legal Theory, 20*(1), 61–72.

Tapscott, D., & Tapscott, A. (2016). *Blockchain revolution: How the technology behind bitcoin is changing money, business, and the world*. Penguin.

Teunissen, C., & Napier, S. (2022). Child sexual abuse material and end-to-end encryption on social media platforms: An overview. *Trends and Issues in Crime and Criminal Justice, 653*, 1–19.

U.S. Attorney's Office. (2022). *U.S. Attorney announces historic $3.36 billion cryptocurrency seizure and conviction in connection with silk road dark web fraud*. https://www.justice.gov/usao-sdny/pr/us-attorney-announces-historic-336-billion-cryptocurrency-seizure-and-conviction

U.S. Department of Justice. (2020). *Cryptocurrency: An enforcement framework*. U.S. Department of Justice. https://www.justice.gov/ag/page/file/1326061/download

UNODC. (2014). *The use of the internet for terrorist purposes*. United Nations Office on Drugs and Crime. https://www.unodc.org/documents/frontpage/Use_of_Internet_for_Terrorist_ Purposes.pdf

UNODC. (2020). *Cryptocurrencies: Risks and opportunities for the convention against corruption*. United Nations Office on Drugs and Crime. https://www.unodc.org/documents/corruption/IssuesPapers/Issues_Paper_on_Cryptocurrencies_E.pdf

UNODC. (2021). *World drug report 2021*. United Nations Office on Drugs and Crime. https://www.unodc.org/res/wdr2021/field/WDR21_Booklet_1.pdf

Van Wegberg, R., & Verburgh, T. (2018, May). Lost in the dream? measuring the effects of operation bayonet on vendors migrating to dream market. In *Proceedings of the evolution of the darknet workshop* (Vol. 9).

Van Wegberg, R., Oerlemans, J. J., & van Deventer, O. (2018). Bitcoin money laundering: Mixed results? An explorative study on money laundering of cybercrime proceeds using bitcoin. *Journal of Financial Crime, 25*(2), 419–435.

Von Hirsch, A., & Cambridge University Institute of Criminology Colloquium. (1999). *Criminal deterrence and sentence severity: An analysis of recent research* (p. 1). Hart Publishing.

Vu, A. V., Hutchings, A., & Anderson, R. (2023). No easy way out: The effectiveness of deplatforming an extremist forum to suppress hate and harassment. *arXiv preprint arXiv:2304.07037*.

Wada, F., Longe, O., & Danquah, P. (2012). Action speaks louder than words–understanding cyber criminal behavior using criminological theories. *Journal of Internet Banking and Commerce, 17*(1), 1–12.

Weimann, G. (2016). Terrorist migration to the dark web. *Perspectives on Terrorism, 10*(3), 40–44.

Williams, A. E., & Ariel, B. (2013). The bristol integrated offender management scheme: A pseudo-experimental test of desistance theory. *Policing: A Journal of Policy and Practice, 7*(2), 123–134.

Zambiasi, D. (2022). Drugs on the web, crime in the streets. The impact of shutdowns of dark net marketplaces on street crime. *Journal of Economic Behavior & Organization, 202*, 274–306.

Zetzsche, D. A., Buckley, R. P., Arner, D. W., & Föhr, L. (2018). *The ICO gold rush: It is a scam, a bubble, and a super challenge for regulators*. University of Luxembourg Law Working Paper No. 11/2017.

Zevenbergen, B. (2020). Cryptocurrency exchanges: Nodes of coordination for law enforcement. *Policy and Internet, 12*(4), 425–445. https://doi.org/10.1002/poi3.245

Zhou, G., Zhuge, J., Fan, Y., Du, K., & Lu, S. (2020). A market in dream: The rapid development of anonymous cybercrime. *Mobile Networks and Applications, 25*, 259–270.

Chapter 4
Network Structure and Trust Formation in Cryptomarkets Based on Reputation

Introduction

A significant knowledge gap exists regarding the factors influencing a buyer's choice of vendor within the cryptomarket. The buyer's choice is of particular interest in contexts of information asymmetry, as highlighted by Akerlof (1970). Akerlof (1970) posits that the likelihood of market failure escalates when purchasers encounter difficulties in examining products prior to purchase. The result is the emergence of a market characterised as a "lemon market", in which the absence of accurate and trustworthy information regarding the quality of a product or service being sold leads to a cost being incurred in every transaction conducted within the market (Herley & Florencio, 2010). In addition, given the recognised significance of trust within cryptomarkets, it is reasonable to consider the specific circumstances in which transactions take place. This chapter attempts to address four primary research questions. First, what is the underlying network architecture of Abraxas? Second, how might the structure and composition of the buyers' and vendors' communities on the Abraxas network be described? Third, which market-level metrics and vendor characteristics can be used to predict the trustworthiness of a vendor, specifically in terms of their success (completed transactions), popularity (unique buyers) and affluence (revenue)? Finally, what is the developmental trajectory of vendors' market success, popularity and affluence on Abraxas?

The primary objective of this chapter is to analyse the intricate dynamics of trust within a dark web market. It aims to uncover the mechanisms involved in establishing and sustaining trust and explore the subsequent impact on the market's network structure. A better understanding of these components offers crucial insights for the design of law enforcement interventions.

To illustrate the issue of trust and network formation in a cryptomarket community, Abraxas, a cryptomarket active from 2014 to 2015, is used as the operative example. A conceptual (and often methodological) replication of previous research

V. Harinam, B. Ariel, *Law Enforcement Strategies for Disrupting Cryptomarkets*,
https://doi.org/10.1007/978-3-031-62821-4_4

conducted by Duxbury and Haynie (2017) and Norbutas (2018) is proposed. However, this chapter supplements their approach by looking at market-level indicators that effectively predict the selection of vendors, along with the trajectory of vendor performance over time. As will be shown, these analyses provide a deeper understanding of the influence of trust between buyers and vendors on the configuration of cryptomarkets.

This study applies social network analysis (SNA) to construct and analyse the transactional network, drawing upon the works of Papachristos (2009, 2014) and Duxbury and Haynie (2017). In recent years, a growing body of research has used SNA to gain insights into the operational dynamics of different clandestine networks (Holt et al., 2012; Kenney, 2007; Morselli, 2009; Malm & Bichler, 2011; Natarajan, 2006; Wood, 2017). This literature has shown SNA to be a valuable tool for studying criminal communities such as the cryptomarket environment. (This study will provide information on this analytical approach below. For now, it is simply noted that descriptive network analysis, community detection analysis and statistical and trajectory modelling enable a comprehensive investigation into the trust and network structure development within the Abraxas cryptomarket.) The analyses conducted in this chapter will guide the development and evaluation of simulation models discussed in subsequent chapters.

Trust and Criminal Networks

As shown in the previous chapters, the progress made in digital communication has given unparalleled rise to fresh avenues for criminal activities and deviant behaviour. One particular and fascinating area of tectonic change is how criminals work with other criminals. For example, the issue of proximity between offenders has transformed dramatically, given the nature of computer-facilitated crimes. Those with bad intentions can trade illicit goods and services by evading detection in ways considered impossible just 20 years ago; cybercriminals can exploit technological progress to facilitate collaborative engagement in criminal activities. They can collaborate in ways that no longer require one to assemble in a specific physical setting. They can now build criminal networks and cooperate remotely, adding layers of anonymity and self-protection that challenge law enforcement.

This study wishes to pay close attention to the issue of trust and how it is formed in cryptomarkets. Some level of trust—whether entirely momentary, selective, opportunistic or non-collegial—is required between two or more parties acting together. One must be assured that others will not cheat. One must also avoid dealing with a law enforcement officer, a competitor or someone who does not share a common cause. Therefore, trust remains an integral element of human behaviour, even among criminals. What does trust mean in these circumstances? How is trust affected when people cannot measure the trustworthiness of someone who is perhaps thousands of miles away? What psychosocial and environmental cues are markers of trust between people involved in delinquent acts? How do buyers choose trustworthy vendors out of the hundreds, if not thousands, of drugs, arms or malicious software dealers on the dark web? How can a vendor perform basic know-your-client (KYC) procedures to ascertain that the buyer is not an undercover law enforcement agent?

Historically, Silk Road was not significantly different from Amazon, as the platform provided the necessary conditions to facilitate trust between vendors and buyers of illegal goods and services. As noted in Chap. 2, cryptomarkets can be understood as brokerage platforms that serve as intermediaries between vendors with the necessary capabilities and buyers willing to engage in transactions. Due to their relative success and ongoing expansion, these platforms replicate legitimate platforms' organisational structure, operational procedures and financial risk management capabilities, like eBay and Amazon. At the same time, cryptomarkets still raise clear concerns for all parties about the participants involved and their interrelationships. The dynamics of these transactional relationships and the subsequent impact on the overall configuration of the criminal network are unclear.

From psychological and sociological perspectives, understanding how the network operates and how trust is formed between parties is crucial. Understanding the network architecture of a cryptomarket can offer valuable insights into its inherent weaknesses. By mapping the cryptomarket and capitalising on the fundamental fact that people are often risk-averse and will do anything to avoid apprehension, there are practical ramifications for law enforcement agencies seeking to impede the operational efficiency of these unlawful entities (Bright et al., 2017).

It was noted earlier how law enforcement attempted to break the trust between buyers and sellers when AlphaBay and Hansa were taken down. Instead of issuing a formal notification that the website was down, the FBI and other agencies were able to disrupt both cryptomarkets and cause confusion and mistrust between the parties involved, who assumed technical difficulties, dishonesty (some buyers thought the vendors had disappeared with their cryptocurrency without delivering the goods) or both. Either way, the motivation was indeed to disrupt the fabric of the relationship between parties that already suffered from limited trust. Yet, as has been documented, this operation did not crack down on the entire ecosystem, which soon bounced back and has been operating since with even more enthusiasm.

The Criminal Underworld and Trust

Chapter 2 introduced the concept of trust in the context of cryptomarkets, but this chapter wishes to delve deeper into this concept, given its weight in network formation—and co-offending more broadly. Trust is crucial as an operational tool within criminal enterprises and associations. However, trusting others who are, by definition, "bad people" by their criminality poses significant challenges. How is one to trust someone that breaks the law? If previous markers of trustworthiness exist—via prior association, family ties, being part of the same organised crime group, etc.—then forming trust can be more straightforward (Baker & Piquero, 2010; Fader,

2016; von Lampe, 2016). Yet in the criminal world, when networks of two (or more) individuals are formed, co-offending is often based on short-term associations (Englefield & Ariel, 2017; Morselli et al., 2011; Sarnecki, 2001). Trust is, therefore, more fickle when offenders try to collaborate.

Trust, or rational reliance on others (Pettit, 2004), is fragile. Multiple factors contribute to its formation. Situational constraints, such as the possibility of harm, arrest or betrayal, frequently motivate criminals to disregard their previously expressed or perceived obligations (Serva et al., 2005). Furthermore, in criminal environments, there is typically a lack of a central governing body that can enforce contractual obligations and penalise those who refuse to comply, as is commonly observed in legitimate contexts (Smith & Papachristos, 2016). While it is true that specific criminal organisations, such as the Italian mafia or the Japanese Yakuza, do exert a degree of governance over the entities under their control, this phenomenon is relatively uncommon within the realm of criminal activity (Gambetta, 2000; Catino, 2014; von Lampe, 2016). However, trust can be viewed as a mechanism of coordination, facilitating collaboration among individuals involved in illicit activities, enabling them to work together towards a shared goal (Free & Murphy, 2015; Jaspers, 2017).

Therefore, trust among criminals is not too dissimilar to how normative networks are formed: Trust pertains to the reliance or confidence placed by individuals or entities in the integrity, credibility and dependability of others involved in criminal activities (Lantz & Ruback, 2017). Yet the definition of trust among offenders does have unique features. Gambetta (2000) suggests that trust can be defined as a specific degree of subjective probability that an individual assigns to the likelihood of another individual or group of individuals carrying out a particular action. This assessment is made before any observation of the action or even in situations where monitoring may not be possible, and it is made within a context that impacts the individual's actions (p. 217). This seems particularly pertinent to us: It appears that in an age when people who commit crimes can "check" with whom they partner before the initial contact with their co-offenders, then the reputation of an individual, their social media presence or how their associates perceive them form the foundation of trust between people. People thus "screen out" certain co-offenders—at least in criminal circumstances that require pre-planning rather than spur-of-a-moment criminal behaviours (Ashton & Bussu, 2022; Weerman, 2003).

Furthermore, trust serves as a mechanism through which individuals can effectively manage and navigate the inherent risks and uncertainties that arise in their interactions with others (von Lampe & Johansen, 2004, p. 103). Trust can be defined as an anticipation of the actions of another agent that is pertinent to the decision-making process (Dumouchel, 2005, p. 421). According to these scholars, trust encompasses the assumption of potential future uncertainty. Therefore, it is incumbent upon the individual to determine the inclinations and preferences of the individuals they aim to interact with to the best of their ability. This entails assessing the potential conduct of their soon-to-be collaborators within a specific scenario. Yet, in these circumstances, trust is less about the ability of the person we wish to trust to perform well (which would be an expectation of a certain level of capability);

instead, placing trust in another individual necessitates a rational evaluation of the likelihood that this person may betray or fail to fulfil their obligation (Gambetta, 1988).

For this reason, it becomes immediately apparent why establishing trust in the criminal realm poses a challenge. The co-offender, like oneself, is an individual with self-interested motives, who must suppress their desires (Williamson, 1993). According to Gambetta and Bacharach (2001), employing a game theory framework, it is evident that the most advantageous result is obtained by cheating (reneging) when a person chooses to cooperate (endow trust). However, repeating this result across multiple iterations would result in an exceptionally negative outcome for the person. Cheating is the most advantageous move in a one-off collaboration, but trust is more cost-effective in repeated games. The continuous display of deceitful behaviour by the individuals in question would serve as a deterrent for the person who trusts them, leading to a loss of potential collaborative efforts and prospects for the party charged with cheating. In this context, trust encompasses the ability to discern whether the individuals with whom one interacts are genuinely committed to collaboration or are merely pretending to cooperate while pursuing alternative objectives. The existing lack of trust is exacerbated by the need to establish a substantial level of trust to sustain enduring criminal partnerships. Therefore, partnerships will exhibit sudden and irregular patterns if trust cannot be consistently upheld.

However, trust is not the only factor in establishing co-offending partnerships. Establishing trust is not necessary in situations characterised by a negative-sum outcome, where both parties face potential losses. Gambetta (2000) asserts that cooperation can "come about independently of trust" (p. 213). In such circumstances, agents will behave based on their shared self-interest, as a failure to do so could potentially lead to the imposition of sanctions on all participating agents. Thus, it is unnecessary for an agent to explicitly place trust in another agent or make assumptions about future risks, as it is evident that the opposing agent is acting in alignment with one's interests. Nevertheless, establishing such a framework relies on two essential components: firstly, the assumption that all individuals possess knowledge of their interests and, secondly, the belief that all individuals can verify that their interests are in harmony with the interests of other individuals. While determining the first element can be relatively straightforward, as it involves identifying one's desired outcomes, establishing the second element can present challenges, as an agent may not always be able to discern the desired outcomes of other agents accurately. Thus, trust is not absent in these specific circumstances but takes on a distinct manifestation. While an agent may harbour doubts regarding the trustworthiness of a potential partner, they can still place reliance on the partner's underlying motivations.

The existing body of research (Gambetta, 2000; von Lampe & Johansen, 2004; Gambetta, 2009) has insisted on the lack of trust within criminal networks of different scales. However, it is essential to note that these findings primarily concern illegal activities occurring in conventional, terrestrial markets. It is reasonable to assert that trust dynamics may vary within cyberspace. Multiple academic studies (Holt & Lampke, 2010) have provided evidence suggesting the existence of market-driven dynamics within illicit online markets. Illegal online exchanges are perceived and approached as voluntary economic transactions rather than simply illicit trans-actions. Décary-Hétu and Dupont (2013) conducted a study on a botnet forum. They discovered that trust in a vendor was frequently determined by straightforward indi-cators, such as the number of awards received, the duration of forum participation and the size of one's network. In this scenario, trust at a superficial level was estab-lished based on individual attributes and conduct rather than on shared experiences that foster a profound sense of trust.

Estimating the Role of Trust and Network Structure in Cryptomarkets Through the Concept of Reputation

Trust and Reputation

Although it cannot be denied that duplicity and deception exist on these platforms, van Hout and Bingham (2013a) contend that successful connections among partici-pants in cryptomarkets require trust and professionalism that likely surpass those that characterise terrestrial illicit markets (p. 387). The primary reason for this phe-nomenon can be attributed to the method of information dissemination within cryp-tomarkets in the form of product, vendor and transaction reputation. In this regard, vendors openly disclose information regarding the quality of their products and services, while buyers contribute publicly accessible feedback regarding their inter-actions with these vendors. Therefore, the quality of a product or service and a seller's reliability can be more readily determined in cryptomarkets compared to traditional offline markets.

Establishing vendor reputations depends on the frequency of transactions con-ducted with buyers, who subsequently evaluate their experiences with individual vendors. The evaluation process relies primarily on a numerical rating system rang-ing from 0 to 5 stars. Additionally, written feedback is solicited to provide more comprehensive information regarding the transaction. As far as can be determined, it is not within the vendor's capacity to modify the feedback publicly displayed on their cryptomarket page, regardless of whether it is positive or negative. Therefore, much like legitimate online markets, reputations cannot be artificially enhanced by vendors with self-serving intentions, as they are naturally formed through interac-tions with buyers.

According to Tzanetakis et al. (2016), providing customer feedback within cryp-tomarkets establishes trust within an environment that inherently lacks trust. The illegal drug trade frequently lacks guarantees regarding the actions and intentions of potential trading counterparts. To a certain degree, a vendor's reputation is consid-ered common knowledge on these platforms, as potential buyers can easily consult it by visiting a vendor's page and reviewing the vendor's overall reputation score, along with the feedback provided by previous buyers.

However, does reputation affect the market and its dynamics? Hardy and Norgaard (2016) employed data on cannabis listings sourced from Silk Road to examine the correlation between reputation and pricing. Their analysis demonstrates that reputation is an effective mechanism for self-enforcement, thereby facilitating transactions (p. 32). This implies that vendor reputation plays a significant role as a formal institution in establishing a stable trading environment, particularly among individuals who may not be perceived as inherently honest. Similarly, Janetos and Tilly (2017) found that mature cryptomarket vendors who receive high ratings tend to charge prices that are 20% higher compared to mature vendors with low ratings. This means that reputation is directly linked to the product price and can be monetised by "good" market players: Vendors with a more significant number of reviews tend to impose higher prices than sellers with a limited number of reviews, irrespective of their rating.

Batikas and Kretschmer (2018) studied data from the Agora marketplace. They found that sellers with lower rankings tended to leave the market rather than reduce their prices in response to negative feedback. This suggests that vendors in cryptomarkets are more inclined to discontinue their operations in response to negative feedback. Thus, feedback affects not only the price and the volume of transactions but also presence in the market: lLw scores tend to take out unreputable actors.

In their study, Duxbury and Haynie (2017) analysed the network structure of a transactional opioid network on the dark web, focusing on local and global aspects. The study revealed that the transactional network within the cryptomarket exhibited a diffuse and highly localised structure, wherein numerous buyers engaged in transactions with a limited number of vendors. The transactional network comprised multiple subgroups centred around well-established and successful vendors. The localised subgroups exhibited similar sizes. These findings led Duxbury and Haynie (2017) to conclude that the trustworthiness of vendors is more significant in the selection of vendors than product diversity or affordability. That is, buyers tend to engage in repeat transactions with vendors they trust (p. 23).

Felonious Few and Trust

The notion of the "felonious few" is not limited to cryptomarkets but has broader applicability across many networks and systems. The term "felonious few" essentially denotes a limited number of nodes (or players) inside a network that possesses a disproportionately elevated level of influence, connections or relevance compared to their counterparts. This concept resembles the Pareto principle, also known as the 80/20 rule, which posits that 80% of the effects may be attributed to 20% of the causes. Within cryptomarkets, the term "felonious few" may denote a select group of influential vendors, platforms or brokers who exercise control over a substantial number of market operations. It is argued that, to some degree, this concept is directly linked to trust.

Trust is frequently established based on reputation and historical records, particularly in dynamic and possibly hazardous contexts such as cryptomarkets. The limited number of influential participants in cryptomarkets—i.e. the "felonious few"—typically shows their standing through a gradual reputation-building process. Newly registered users and those who have previously used the platform demonstrate a greater propensity to interact with these established vendors or platforms due to their proven history of successful transactions, positive evaluations and readily available feedback. As the concept of trust encompasses the reduction of uncertainty, alongside reduced search costs, interacting with the powerful few reduces the time and effort users must allocate to ensuring the trustworthiness of vendors or platforms. When a particular group establishes market dominance and maintains a continuous track record, customers tend to trust this group over lesser-known competitors. Consequently, these dominating vendors experience a surge in the reviews, feedback and transactions they receive. Enhanced visibility can improve their reputation, so establishing a feedback loop in which trust attracts a more extensive user base and the increased number of users further reinforces that trust.

Norbutas (2018) provided empirical evidence of this. His study on the Abraxas cryptomarket's transactional network identified low network density: A limited number of vendors were responsible for most transactions. This "power few" feature strongly characterises cryptomarkets more broadly, and it seems to be shaped, at least to some extent, by popularity linked to trust: Reputable vendors attract more clients and more transactions than other vendors. The power few vendors thrive on trust dynamics within the ecosystem: Placing trust in these prominent entities frequently appears to be the more secure option for users, despite the accompanying array of possible hazards.

Localisation and Trust

Directly linked to the issue of trust, Norbutas (2018) noticed that Abraxas' transactional network exhibited a significant degree of localisation, with segmentation occurring primarily along geographical lines: Vendors mainly ship to buyers within the same country. This finding challenges the prevailing notion that cryptomarkets are transnational platforms facilitating transactions among individuals from diverse geographical locations. Instead, cryptomarkets may potentially consolidate domestic trading by confining the circulation of illicit products to within a nation's boundaries.

Thus, buyers frequently prefer local dealers since they perceive them to offer a sense of familiarity, which they associate with decreased risk. This feature of cryptomarkets is linked to the concept of homophily, which suggests that people with comparable characteristics tend to connect and form affiliations more frequently than those with distinctive characteristics (Oksanen et al., 2020; see more broadly in McPherson et al., 2001). The preference for local merchants in cryptomarkets may be attributed to cultural homophily. The thinking is that if vendors and buyers who share a culture, place of living or background have previously engaged in successful transactions with a local vendor, then it is more probable that the buyer will also have a favourable experience. The apparent collective achievement among persons with cultural similarities enhances trust, increasing local businesses' attractiveness within cryptomarkets.

In addition to cultural homophily, practical considerations also influence the dynamics of trust within cryptomarkets. For example, international shipping is perceived as riskier than domestic shipment, due to intricate logistical processes and heightened visibility. The potential for customs checks, seizures or the participation of third-party businesses (Demant et al., 2018) increases the perceived risk for buyers. Transnational consignments depend on global shipping enterprises and are potentially subject to greater legal risks. These issues may prompt participants in cryptomarkets to prioritise local suppliers, perceiving them as more secure and reliable.

The Abraxas Network as a Case Study

In the following sections, the available literature and gathered evidence is used to respond to four overarching inquiries. While each of these questions is relevant to the broader academic debates over cryptomarkets, they will also be of interest to practitioners aiming to dismantle or mitigate the impact of cryptomarkets.

This study relies on data from the Abraxas network, a prominent clandestine online marketplace that could previously be accessed using the TOR network. Like its contemporaries, the platform functioned as a central point of exchange for a wide range of commodities and services, many of which were classified as unlawful or illicit. The offerings included (but were not limited to) drugs, counterfeit cash, fake documents and hacking tools. The life cycle of the Abraxas market exhibited the typical characteristics observed in other darknet platforms throughout the mid-2010s. The operational window of Abraxas was brief. Darknet markets are often ephemeral, either because of law enforcement interventions or internal disintegration.[1] Sufficient data from transactions and ratings of vendors are needed to understand the role of trust in cryptomarket transactions.

Research Questions

The first research inquiry aims to describe the overall framework of Abraxas' transactional network on a global scale. The phenomenon in question has been studied by Duxbury and Haynie (2017) in a different cryptomarket. However, there are gaps in our understanding of the orientation of vendors and buyers within the

---

[1] Speculation over the occurrence of an Abraxas "exit scam" was as a prominent topic of controversy. Within the clandestine recesses of the darknet, exit scams refer to instances wherein platform administrators abruptly terminate operations and embezzle customers' funds, leaving vendors and buyers in a state of uncertainty and disadvantage. Such scams have been a regular occurrence in darknet markets and have significantly influenced the dynamics of trust within these digital subcultures.

transactional network they are a part of. While it is evident that vendor reputations play a pivotal role in distinguishing vendors of superior quality from those of inferior quality, additional factors seem not to have been thoroughly examined. Additionally, there is a lack of clarity regarding the impact of trust on the overall network architecture of a cryptomarket and the potential implications for interventions. According to Barratt and Aldridge (2016), investigating the network structure of cryptomarkets can offer valuable insights into the concealed transactional dynamics that contribute to the stability of these illicit online marketplaces. If one can better understand these dynamics, it is possible to identify potential opportunities to cause destabilisation.

The second research question aims to gain insight into the attributes and makeup of discernible communities within the context of Abraxas. Duxbury and Haynie (2017) conducted analyses that reveal how users of cryptomarkets tend to form subgroups, wherein individual vendors engage in transactions with multiple buyers. The transactional network within the cryptomarket can be likened to small islands specific to certain products and countries. This characteristic is essential in designing law enforcement interventions with a potential focus on communities rather than individual users. Significantly, there has been no prior research that has applied community detection techniques to analyse a transactional network within a cryptomarket. Therefore, further investigation is necessary in this domain to comprehend its efficacy for professionals. Community detection analysis will facilitate a deeper comprehension of the network topology exhibited by cryptomarkets.

The third research inquiry aims to ascertain the attributes that most effectively forecast the choice of vendor. Although the existing study conducted by Décary-Hétu and Quessy-Doré (2017) provides insights into the popularity of various vendors, it does not explain the underlying reasons for buyers' choices. Gaining insight into buyers' decision-making process when selecting vendors is of utmost importance in comprehending the formation of the network structure within a cryptomarket. The central focus of this inquiry is the concept of trust. More specifically, the objective is to quantify the market-level metrics that serve as predictors for vendor selection across three proxy variables associated with trust. Gaining a comprehensive understanding of the nature and significance of these metrics and their operational implications can potentially enhance the effectiveness of law enforcement interventions. Furthermore, law enforcement must comprehend the significance of trust in cryptomarkets, as well as the factors that may undermine it.

According to Gambetta (2000), trust is operationalised in this chapter as "a specific degree of the subjective likelihood that an individual evaluates regarding the performance of a specific action by another individual or a collective of individuals" (p. 29). Therefore, the suggested metrics at the market level can be utilised as indicators or game-theoretic tools for buyers to evaluate the likelihood of a vendor fulfilling their obligations in a predetermined transactional agreement. A total of 14 predictors that span three distinct conceptualisations of vendor trustworthiness are employed. This endeavour can be considered the most comprehensive undertaking thus far.

The objective of the fourth research inquiry is to examine the developmental trajectory of vendors in cryptomarkets, focusing on whether vendors who are deemed most trustworthy continue to thrive as the market experiences growth. The level of continuity and potential growth or decline of vendors operating on these platforms is not thoroughly comprehended by practitioners in this field. This inquiry provides valuable insights into the reciprocal relationship between market and vendor growth. Suppose a scenario exists where a limited number of reputable vendors are responsible for most transactions in a cryptomarket. In this case, it can be inferred that the market's sustained functioning and expansion depend on the efficacy of a central group of vendors. For professionals in the field, understanding the developmental paths of individual vendors is essential in mitigating the impact of these actors and the overall expansion of the market. Law enforcement agencies can employ trajectory models to identify and mitigate potential threats within cryptomarkets.

Methods

Data

In this study, a dataset obtained from the Abraxas cryptomarket is utilised, as documented by Branwen et al. (2015). Other than the anonymous cryptomarket examined by Duxbury and Haynie (2017, 2019), this marketplace is the sole platform where distinctive identifiers are accessible to purchasers. Significantly, Norbutas (2018) employed Abraxas in a study investigating the spatial dispersion of transactions. To fulfil the objectives of this study, a bipartite buyer–seller trade network was built. This network encompasses a total of 5434 transactions involving illicit goods and services. The transactions occurred between 269 distinct sellers and 2794 unique buyers over 7 months, specifically from 2014 to 2015.

According to Norbutas (2018, p. 93), the dataset compiled by the independent researchers Branwen et al. (2015) encompasses data from various cryptomarkets and is acknowledged to have limitations in terms of its comprehensiveness. To clarify, it is possible that the Abraxas marketplace was not comprehensively captured during the routine data extraction processes conducted by Branwen et al. in 2015. Norbutas (2018) compared the number of crawled item pages in the data and the observed number of items presented on Abraxas' home page at various dates. The analysis revealed evident inconsistencies. More broadly, Norbutas (2018) noted that the mean proportion of retrieved items in Branwen's crawls was 92.4%, though it ranged from 26% to 100% depending on the specific crawl (p. 93). Moreover, a significant number of scraped webpages were found to be nonfunctional, resulting in incomplete documentation of market transactions. This limitation is evident as the analysis was restricted to a subset of the Abraxas cryptomarket. To a certain degree, it can be argued that this transactional network lacks completeness, as not all transactions were documented or recorded. Using Norbutas' (2018) methodology, data from multiple daily crawls of item pages were compiled. Consequently, duplicate transactions were identified and removed. The resulting dataset comprises 269 distinct sellers, 2794 distinct buyers and 5434 transactions.

To establish a two-mode transactional network comprising exchanges between individual buyers and sellers, it was necessary to assign each feedback message to a specific buyer. In a broad sense, feedback functions as tangible evidence that a transaction has occurred. According to Martin (2014), customer feedback encompasses a diverse range of expressions, including elaborate remarks regarding the duration of shipping, discreet packaging methods, the perceived effectiveness of illegal substances and a straightforward rating system using five stars (p. 41). It is worth noting that although all cryptomarkets rely on a feedback system, there may be variations in their policies regarding the obligatory nature of buyer feedback. Certain cryptomarkets require buyers to provide feedback following each transaction, whereas others do not impose such a requirement. Abraxas belongs to the former category: All transactions carried out during the market's operational period were meticulously recorded through buyer feedback.

The presence of feedback data in network-based cryptomarket datasets is typically challenging because of partially or fully anonymised buyer usernames. However, Abraxas included distinct buyer profile identifiers for each feedback message. These identifiers were found within the HTML code of item pages. The buyer identifiers were used to consolidate the feedback messages provided by individual buyer accounts. After eliminating duplicate entries, a two-mode transactional network was built for vendors and buyers on Abraxas from 15 January 2015 to 4 July 2015.

Although these analyses successfully identified the purchases made by individual buyer accounts, the dataset lacked information regarding the buyers' country of residence. While direct observation of buyers' geographic location was not possible, making inferences about the clustering of buyers in the marketplace by analysing their choice of vendors located in specific countries was possible. The transactions were systematically classified into different categories to facilitate analysis. The categorisation system consisted of a broad category encompassing all types of items, a subcategory that divided the items into more specific categories and a secondary subcategory that offered more detailed information about each item. Every individual item was manually coded. Regarding pricing, all transactions were converted from Bitcoin to USD using a dynamic exchange rate from the United States. Although this approach may potentially yield less precise pricing information due to the inherent volatility of cryptocurrencies, it also leads to alterations in the listed prices. Implementing a stable exchange rate rather than a fluctuating one would inadequately reflect fluctuations in listed prices.

Statistical Analyses

Descriptive statistics were employed to provide a concise and accessible summary of the 5434 transactions. The aim of this summary was to provide a comprehensive understanding of the characteristics and constituents of illegal transactions occurring on the Abraxas platform. Descriptive statistics, as a whole, offer a simple, transparent and comprehensive means of viewing the data. Social network analysis was performed to investigate Abraxas' network structure. Four distinct analytical approaches are utilised: descriptive network analysis, community detection analysis, statistical modelling and trajectory modelling. The network statistics, modelling and visualisations were performed using R and Microsoft Excel software programmes.

Descriptive Network Analysis

The network structure of Abraxas is summarised at a preliminary level using standard network measures based on social network analysis. It is of utmost significance to ascertain the existence of a connection between two actors by examining whether feedback has been provided following a transaction. The existence of feedback serves as tangible proof that a transaction has taken place. Bichler et al. (2017) have argued that researchers must elucidate the methodology employed in constructing the networks utilised for social network analysis. A network comprising vendors and buyers was created based on the 5434 illicit transactions. The network was built using only transactions involving a known vendor and a buyer. Vendors were identified by their distinct vendor names, whereas the identification of buyers was accomplished using their HTML code. The transactional network comprised 5434 transactions involving 269 distinct vendors and 2794 distinct buyers. A correlation can be established between acting professionals if they have participated in a joint transaction (McGloin & Kirk, 2011).

Network Analysis

In this study, four network measures were employed: network density, in-degree centralisation, out-degree centralisation and eccentricity. The concept of density was used to quantify the level of interconnectedness within a network. To clarify, this metric calculates the ratio of the actual number of connections between actors to the maximum potential number of connections that could exist. The measurement is represented by a coefficient between 0 and 1. In the context of this dataset, a score close to 1 signifies a high level of buyer engagement with multiple vendors, reflecting the extensive interconnections within the network. On the contrary, density scores closer to 0 suggest that buyers engage in transactions with a limited number of vendors, resulting in a dispersed network.

According to Duxbury and Haynie (2017), centralisation refers to the extent to which a few actors possess significant control over the overall network structure (p. 23). In this study, the concept of centralisation is used to represent the extent to which vendors (out-degree centralisation) or buyers (in-degree centralisation) exert influence over the network structure of the Abraxas transactional network. Centralisation was calculated using the degree of centrality of each node. According to Duxbury and Haynie (2018), the calculation determines the total disparities between the actor with the highest centrality score and all other actors within the network. This total is then divided by the maximum possible number of disparities obtained from a hypothetical matrix of equivalent dimensions (p. 929). The outcome of this calculation yields a numerical value that falls within the range of 0 to 1. A higher value on this scale signifies a stronger indication of central tendency within a network, as described by Wasserman and Faust in 1994. In network analysis, eccentricity is a metric that quantifies the maximum distance between a given node and any other node within the network. The eccentricity of a node in a connected network is defined as the maximum distance between that particular node and all other nodes in the network.

Each of these measurements was chosen to assess the interconnectedness of Abraxas' global network structure and the significance of individual nodes within the network. Alternative measurements, such as closeness and betweenness centrality, could have been used in this analysis. However, these measurements would not have yielded meaningful insights due to the rigid categorisation of nodes as either buyers or vendors.

Community Detection

Although standard network measures offer valuable information about the overall characteristics of a network, they have limited ability to reveal the underlying structural features of the network. However, this objective can be accomplished by employing community detection analysis. According to Yang et al. (2013), community detection identifies groups of interconnected vertices, also known as nodes, within a network based on their structural characteristics (p. 15). In brief, community detection algorithms aim to partition nodes into separate communities by considering the extent of their connections with other nodes within the network. While there may be occasional deviations, networks typically comprise individuals who interact more frequently with certain individuals than with others.

In this study, the Walktrap community detection algorithm is used (Pons & Latapy, 2005; Newman, 2003, 2006) to ascertain the subgroup configuration of the Abraxas transactional network. According to Pons and Latapy (2005), the Walktrap algorithm detects various potential community structures by employing a random sequence of walks. According to the source, the graph is divided into distinct communities at each stage, with the merging of communities occurring when the distance between them is deemed sufficiently small (p. 6). The Walktrap method is well suited for analysing extensive, directed networks like the Abraxas network.

The metric Q, the modularity score, was employed to assess the degree of congru-ence between the communities generated by the Walktrap community detection algorithm. A community is commonly defined as a group of nodes within a network that exhibit stronger connections among themselves than with other nodes. Modularity is a statistical measure that accounts for chance, with values ranging from −0.5 to 1. According to Blondel et al. (2008, p. 43), the term "modularity" refers to the difference between the actual proportion of connections within specific groups and the expected proportion of randomly distributed connections.

The calculation of modularity is defined as:

$$Q = \Sigma \left(e_{bd} - a_b^2 \right)$$

According to Duxbury and Haynie (2018, p. 930), the variable "e" represents the proportion of ties that connect community b and community d, while the variable "a" represents the proportion of ties that are connected to community b. A network's level of segmentation increases as its modularity score increases. Values exceeding 0.3 are indicative of a substantial community structure.

Model Estimation

To address the third research question, three regression models were formulated. In all models, identical explanatory and control variables were employed, except for one variable. In the evaluated model that assessed cumulative revenue generated, the inclusion of cumulative purchase price as an explanatory variable was not con-sidered due to its role as the dependent variable.

Estimating Trustworthiness

To assess the trustworthiness of vendors, three proxy variables were generated: suc-cess, popularity and affluence. The various manifestations of trust are reflected in these dependent variables, each representing a crucial aspect of trust. Success was defined in this context as the total number of transactions conducted by a vendor, explicitly referring to the number of sales made. The quantity of sales generated by a vendor serves as an indicator of the enduring quality of their service provision. Trust is established and sustained through the consistent display of professionalism by both the truster and the trustee, as noted by Gambetta (2009) and Przepiorka et al. (2017). Consequently, it can be inferred that vendors who generate higher sales volumes, including both new and repeat customers, are perceived as more trustworthy by buyers who have made an initial purchase and are likely to engage in future transactions. The operationalisation of popularity in this study was defined as the cumulative count of distinct purchasers with whom a vendor has engaged in business transactions. The number of distinct clients in a vendor's client list is a more comprehensive and widespread manifestation of trust. Affluence in this context referred to the vendor's total profit during their period of activity on the Abraxas platform. The sum of the purchase price, denominated in USD, for every transaction a vendor effectively executed was calculated. In this context, trust is represented by the financial benefits esteemed vendors stand to gain from the confidence buyers place in their services. Collectively, these dependent variables provide three distinct yet interconnected indicators for trust. Furthermore, the use of three regression models allowed us to carry out a comparative analysis of the effectiveness of each explanatory variable in accounting for the variability observed in vendor trustworthiness.

Fourteen explanatory variables were formulated and are presented in Table 4.1. Each of the concepts discussed in the scholarly literature on cryptomarket vendors is characterised by a quantifiable attribute (Christin, 2013; Décary-Hétu, 2016; Przepiorka et al., 2017; Norbutas et al., 2020). The explanatory variables can be categorised into six distinct concepts: reputation, affordability, product diversity, openness, risk-taking and accessibility. Each of these concepts contributes, to varying degrees, to the understanding of vendor favourability.

The initial explanatory variable is a cumulative reputation score. Based on the research by Décary-Hétu and Quessy-Doré (2017), the cumulative reputation score is determined by aggregating the ratings assigned to all documented transactions a vendor has successfully carried out. Affordability pertains to the degree of expense associated with a particular vendor. Similar to sellers in legitimate markets, vendors in cryptomarkets must establish prices that are deemed reasonable to incentivise

Table 4.1 Descriptive statistics of variables used in analysis

Variable name	Mean or total	SD	Median	Range
Dependent variables				
Number of transactions	20.2	38.95	7	1–330
Number of unique buyers	14.64	23.24	6	1–179
Cumulative revenue generated	2210.10	5931.95	473.25	0.23–68812.96
Reputation, price and risk				
Cumulative reputation	98.76	191.46	35	0–1628
Average purchase price	105.33	165.72	66.98	0.23–2025.04
Cumulative risk score	42.9	92.41	11	1–929
Items and information				
Unique item listings	5.49	7.42	3	1–58
Unique item categories	1.1	0.46	1	1–5
Unique item subcategories	1.12	0.38	1	1–4
Number of words in item description	2773	7468.18	592	0–73,267
Location shipped from				
Domestic only	1700 (31.3%)	–	–	–
Regional/continental	893 (16.4%)	–	–	–
Worldwide	2374 (43.7%)	–	–	–
Unknown	467 (8.6%)	–	–	–

potential buyers to engage in transactions with them. The concept of affordability was measured by employing two variables: cumulative purchase price and average purchase price. The cumulative purchase price was determined by aggregating the purchase prices of all transactions conducted by a vendor. The average purchase price refers to the mean price at which a vendor sells a product.

Product diversity is a measure of the range of distinct items a vendor provides to customers. The explanatory variable in question implicitly compares the profitability of focusing on a specific product with the profitability of diversifying across multiple products. The understanding of the impact of specialisation and diversification on vendor trustworthiness remains incomplete. Three variables were used to operationalise the concept of product diversity: the number of distinct product listings, the number of product categories and the number of product subcategories. The calculation of each variable involved the aggregate of distinct items or item categories within the respective categories. As proposed by Akerlof (1970), the notion of information asymmetry is mirrored in the concept of openness, which refers to the degree to which vendors divulge product information in a listing. Within each listing, there was a dedicated section for further information about the product being offered for sale. The operationalisation of openness was therefore achieved using a cumulative word count. This metric represents the quantity of words supplied by the seller in the description segment of the listing. The total number of words was determined by aggregating the word count for each transaction completed by a vendor.

The act of shipping goods across international borders is commonly perceived as a hazardous endeavour due to the heightened likelihood of detection, particularly in the case of drug trafficking. Branwen et al.'s (2015) study showed that most cryptomarket vendors arrested (precisely 62%) were apprehended due to their involvement in international shipments. This finding was based on data collected as of May 2015. Therefore, a vendor's readiness to ship internationally can be seen as an indicator of risk-taking. The operationalisation of risk-taking was achieved by utilising a cumulative risk score. A risk score was assigned to each transaction based on the shipping locations specified by the vendor. To minimise the number of control variables, the shipping locations were initially consolidated and represented by four dummy variables, which were used to indicate the distinct shipping categories. Subsequently, risk scores were assigned to each category as follows: unknown or N/A denoted missing data, domestic only was assigned a score of 1 to indicate low risk, continental/regional was assigned a score of 2 to indicate medium risk and worldwide was assigned a score of 3 to indicate high risk. The cumulative risk score was determined by aggregating the risk scores associated with each transaction conducted by a vendor.

The final explanatory factor, accessibility, is closely associated with risk propensity regarding the geographical areas where vendors are willing to deliver their products. The broader the range of shipping destinations a vendor is ready to accommodate, the greater the dilution of exclusivity and the enhanced accessibility of their services to a broader clientele. In contrast to the concept of risk-taking, the variable representing the locations to which items are shipped is categorical. However, similar to risk-taking, the shipping locations were grouped into four dummy variables to accommodate the various shipping categories. The categories encompassed in this classification were domestic only, continental/regional, worldwide with exceptions and worldwide. Significantly, the reference category was established as domestic only.

Trajectory Modelling

In this study, k-means longitudinal modelling was used to ascertain the developmental trajectory of active vendors on the Abraxas platform. Group-based trajectory modelling (GBTM) is a statistical technique introduced by Nagin and Land (1993) to identify distinct subgroups within longitudinal data by examining homogeneous trajectories. Similarly, k-means longitudinal analysis also seeks to identify homogeneous trajectories by grouping data into subgroups. The k-means algorithm, a hill-climbing algorithm, is classified within the expectation–maximisation class. According to Genolini and Falissard (2010), the algorithm initially assigns data points to a particular cluster and then iteratively recalculates each cluster to ensure that each data point is moved closer to the cluster that it most accurately belongs to. The concept of "expectation" entails the identification of the centroid of each cluster, while "maximisation" involves allocating each observation to the closest proximity cluster. The two phases mentioned above are iterated until the clusters reach a state where no additional modifications occur.

The trajectory models were developed using the KmL package in the R programming language, as described by Genolini et al. (2016). Significantly, to address the challenge of determining the precise number of clusters (or trajectories) in advance, and so facilitate the grouping of the data, the Calinski–Harabasz Index was used to ascertain the most suitable number of trajectory groups for each proxy variable, based solely on the clustering results. Andresen et al. (2017) assert that the Calinski–Harabasz Index criterion is a relative metric for comparing various group solutions (p. 434). A trajectory model was developed for each proxy variable mentioned above, representing vendor trustworthiness. These variables included success (measured by completed transactions), popularity (measured by unique buyers) and affluence (measured by revenue).

Results

Descriptive Statistics

Table 4.2 provides a comprehensive set of descriptive statistics about the Abraxas marketplace. When considering the prevalence of drugs, Abraxas exhibits similarities to other cryptomarkets, such as Silk Road 1 (Aldridge & Décary-Hétu, 2016;

Table 4.2 Descriptive statistics on the Abraxas cryptomarket

Descriptive statistics	Mean (SD) or total	Range
Vendor reputation		
Cumulative reputation	98.76 (191.46)	0–1628
Average reputation	4.85 (0.54)	0–5
Cumulative positive reputation	97.43 (189.7)	0–1625
Cumulative negative reputation	1.327 (4.67)	0–59
Ratings		
0	1.4% (74)	–
1	0.4% (23)	–
2	0.2% (10)	–
3	0.5% (26)	–
4	1.1% (59)	–
5	96.5% (5242)	–
Listing categories		
Drugs	92.9% (5050)	–
Digital goods	5.9% (321)	–
Services	0.4% (21)	–
Drug paraphernalia	0.3% (17)	–
Others	0.3% (14)	–
Custom listing	0.2% (11)	–
Listing subcategories		
Cannabis	34.21% (1859)	–
Stimulants	19.38% (1053)	–
Ecstasy	13.8% (750)	–
Opioids	10.8% (587)	–
Psychedelics	6.75% (367)	–
Benzos	3.7% (201)	–
N/A	2.72% (148)	–
Prescription	2.19% (119)	–
Dissociatives	1.25% (68)	–
Information	1.03% (56)	–
E-books	0.98% (53)	–
Erotica	0.9% (49)	–
Fraud	0.59% (32)	–
Steroids	0.35% (19)	–
RCs	0.22% (12)	–
Data	0.2% (11)	–
Drugs (cyber)	0.17% (9)	–
Hacking	0.15% (8)	–
Money	0.11% (6)	–
Weapons	0.11% (6)	–
Electronics	0.09% (5)	–
IDs and passports	0.07% (4)	–

(continued)

Table 4.2 (continued)

Descriptive statistics	Mean (SD) or total	Range
Others	0.06% (3)	–
Software	0.06% (3)	–
Miscellaneous	0.04% (2)	–
Security	0.04% (2)	–
Drug paraphernalia	0.02% (1)	–
Services	0.02% (1)	–
Purchase price (in USD)		
All purchases	109.41 (173.51)	0.23–2800.03
<$1	2.2% (121)	–
$1–$4.99	3.3% (178)	–
$5–$9.99	3.1% (168)	–
$10–$19.99	8.7% (472)	–
$20–$49.99	24.7% (1344)	–
$50–$99.99	28.2% (1532)	–
$100–$199.99	16.3% (884)	–
$200–$499.99	10.8% (589)	–
$500–$999.99	1.9% (201)	–
>$1000	0.8% (44)	–
Locations shipped from		
Australia	8.74% (475)	–
Belgium	0.83% (45)	–
Belize	0.02% (1)	–
Bulgaria	0.64% (35)	–
Canada	0.61% (33)	–
China	0.02% (1)	–
Colombia	0.02% (1)	–
Czech Republic	0.09% (5)	–
Denmark	0.81% (44)	–
Europe/EU	7.19% (391)	–
France	0.74% (40)	–
Germany	25.10% (1364)	–
Hungary	0.06% (3)	–
India	0.18% (10)	–
Italy	0.99% (54)	–
Mexico	0.02% (1)	–
Netherlands	9.22% (501)	–
Norway	0.29% (16)	–
Poland	0.11% (6)	–
South Africa	0.2% (11)	–
Spain	2.37% (129)	–
Switzerland	0.39% (21)	–
UK	13.78% (749)	–

(continued)

Table 4.2 (continued)

Descriptive statistics	Mean (SD) or total	Range
United States	19.34% (1051)	–
Unknown or N/A	8.23% (447)	–
Locations shipped to		
Australia	8.19% (445)	–
Europe	15.73% (855)	–
Europe and United States	0.07% (4)	–
Europe except Italy	0.18% (10)	–
Europe except United Kingdom	0.48% (26)	–
Germany	1.23% (67)	–
Switzerland	0.13% (7)	–
United Kingdom	4.42% (240)	–
United States	17.32% (941)	–
United States and Canada	0.04% (2)	–
Worldwide	36.53% (1985)	–
Worldwide with exceptions	7.16% (389)	–
Unknown or N/A	8.60% (463)	–

Christin, 2013) and Agora (Van Buskirk et al., 2016). Among the various categories of listings, 92.9% (5050) involve drug-related products. In comparison, digital goods account for only 5.9% (321) of the total products sold. A more detailed analysis of the various categories reveals that cannabis comprises the most significant proportion (34.21%), followed by stimulants (19.38%), ecstasy (13.8%), opioids (10.8%) and psychedelics (6.75%). These five categories collectively represent the most prominent products in terms of sales. The pattern above is evident, too, in the monetary value of transactions involving the various substances: Cannabis accounts for $198,745.16, stimulants for $149,078.46, ecstasy for $95,949.28, opioids for $94,480.70 and psychedelics for $19,952.46. In total, the monetary value of transactions in the cryptomarket under investigation amounted to $594,517.50 during the designated research period. Compared to well-established platforms, such as Silk Road 1, Evolution, AlphaBay, Hansa and Wall Street, the total value of transactions in this particular cryptomarket can be considered relatively modest.

In terms of pricing, it is observed that 28.2%, 24.7% and 16.3% of the products were sold at price points falling within the intervals of $50–99.99, $20–49.99 and $100–199.99, respectively. This finding implies that purchasers of Abraxas products generally did not allocate a disproportionately high sum of money towards their purchases. On the contrary, most of the items acquired were moderately priced. However, there were a total of 44 transactions that surpassed the threshold of $1000. Following the trend mentioned earlier, these particular acquisitions involved cannabis (18), opioids (11), ecstasy (8) and stimulants (7). In the context of transaction ratings, the mean rating observed was 4.85, with a substantial majority of transactions (96.5%) receiving a rating of 5. This observation suggests that a significant proportion of purchasers express a high level of satisfaction with the services provided by vendors. However, it is crucial to consider the possibility that the Abraxas rating system may be influenced by the Pollyanna principle, which suggests a tendency towards a positive bias. The top five shipping nations, in terms of origin of the goods shipped, are Germany, the United States, the United Kingdom, the Netherlands and Australia. These countries account for 25.1%, 19.34%, 13.78%, 9.22% and 8.74% of the total number of shipments made, respectively. In addition, it is worth noting that the global distribution of shipped locations was as follows: the world accounted for 36.52%, the United States for 17.32% and Europe for 17.73%. Significantly, this showcases the vendors' inclination to ship without discrimination to all destinations.

Network Structure of Abraxas, Interconnectedness and Organisational Framework

The Abraxas transactional network consists of a total of 2794 distinct actors who are involved in 5434 transactions. Among these actors, there are 269 unique vendors and 2525 unique buyers. In addition, a total of 3935 distinct dyadic pairings exist. Moreover, it is worth noting that the network does not contain any isolates as every buyer is connected to at least one vendor. Importantly, the inability to match unique URL tags for buyers with unique vendor IDs prevented the identification of buyers who also operated as vendors. Due to this constraint, the computation of reciprocity or transitivity metrics was impossible. The network composition and characteristics are presented in Fig. 4.1 and Table 4.3, respectively.

The Abraxas transactional network exhibits low network density, precisely measured at 0.0007. Therefore, a mere 0.07% of the total potential transactions took place. In a comparative analysis, the study conducted by Duxbury and Haynie (2018) revealed that the cryptomarket transactional network for opioid distribution exhibited a density of 0.002. The complete network comprises 29 components. It is worth noting that one specific component contains the majority of nodes within the network, accounting for 97.6% (2726) of the total nodes. This information can be found in Table 4.4. The remaining connected components comprised 19 dyads, seven triads and individual assortments of components of varying sizes. This study's findings indicate that buyers consistently purchase from a limited number of vendors. This behaviour gives rise to a substantial cluster of users with sparse connections, with only a few isolated cliques of buyers and sellers. In the Abraxas transactional network context, nodes exhibit an average maximum distance of 11.23 units from each other, as determined by the eccentricity measurement. Similar mean values can also be observed for vendors (10.32) and buyers (11.33).

Due to the limited network density observed in Abraxas, buyers exhibited a tendency to restrict their interactions to a select few vendors, relying primarily on those they deemed trustworthy or with whom they had established a sense of comfort. According to the data presented in Table 4.5, it is evident that a significant

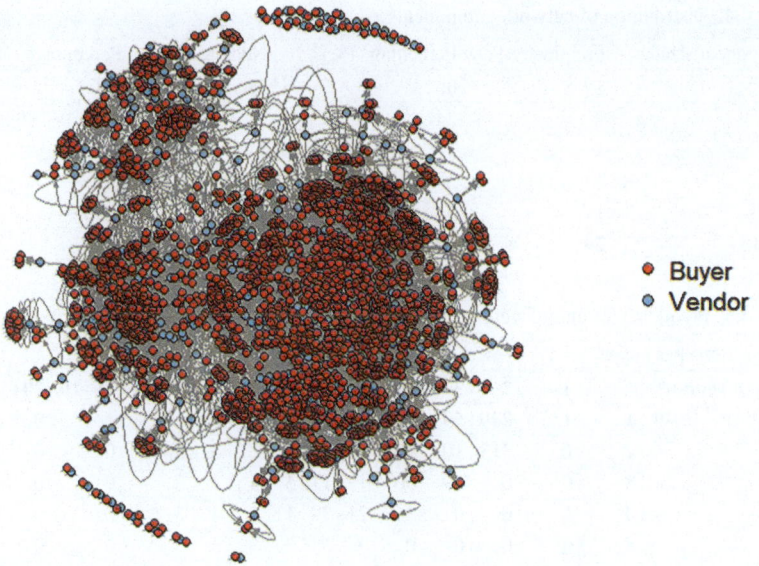

Fig. 4.1 Abraxas transactional network

Table 4.3 Network characteristic

Network characteristics	Mean (SD) or total	Range
Unique actors/nodes	2794	–
Unique vendors	269	–
Unique buyers	2525	–
Isolates	0	–
Total unique edges	3935	–
Density	0.0007	–
In-degree	2.15 (2.2)	1–34
Out-degree	20.2 (39)	1–330
In-degree centralisation	0.01	–
Out-degree centralisation	0.12	–
Eccentricity (All)	11.23 (1.9)	1–16
Eccentricity (vendors)	10.32 (3.38)	1–15
Eccentricity (buyers)	11.33 (1.64)	1–16

proportion of buyers, specifically 34.1% or 860 individuals, made purchases exclusively from two vendors. Indeed, most buyers (67.5% or 1702 individuals) purchased solely from a single vendor. It is clear that purchasers exhibit a preference for engaging in transactions with a limited number of suppliers rather than a diverse range of options. This preference results in a market imbalance characterised by a concentration of transactions among a limited number of vendors. This information can also be inferred from the out- and in-degree centrality measures. On average, buyers engaged in transactions with 2.15 vendors, whereas vendors had an average

Table 4.4 Distribution of network components

Component size	Frequency	Percentage (%)	Node total	Percentage (%)
2	19	66	38	1.4
3	7	24	21	0.8
4	1	3	4	0.1
5	1	3	5	0.2
1000+	1	3	2726	97.6
Total	**29**	**100**	**2794**	**100**

Table 4.5 Frequency of unique vendors purchased from by number of transactions

Transactions per buyer													
Unique vendors purchased from		**1**	**2**	**3**	**4**	**5**	**6**	**7**	**8**	**9**	**10–14**	**15–19**	**20+**	**Total**
	1	1350	249	59	18	15	3	1	3	0	3	1	0	1702
	2	0	313	107	45	15	11	7	2	3	5	0	0	508
	3	0	0	79	50	17	11	5	4	2	3	0	0	171
	4	0	0	0	36	21	7	11	0	4	3	0	0	82
	5	0	0	0	0	9	5	5	3	3	5	0	0	30
	6	0	0	0	0	0	3	7	4	3	0	1	3	21
	7	0	0	0	0	0	0	0	1	0	0	1	1	3
	8	0	0	0	0	0	0	0	0	1	0	1	0	2
	9	0	0	0	0	0	0	0	0	0	3	0	0	3
	10	0	0	0	0	0	0	0	0	0	1	0	1	2
	11+	0	0	0	0	0	0	0	0	0	0	0	1	1
	Total	**1350**	**562**	**245**	**149**	**77**	**40**	**36**	**17**	**16**	**23**	**4**	**6**	**2525**

of 20.2 buyers (refer to Table 4.6). As mentioned earlier, the findings are consistent with the research conducted by Duxbury and Haynie (2017) and Norbutas (2018).

A more precise representation of the distribution of in- and out-degree centrality can be observed in Table 4.6. A significant proportion of purchasers (53.47%) engaged in transactions exclusively with a single vendor. In the context of Abraxas, it is essential to note that transactions typically involve multiple participants, with 19 dyads being observed. However, it is commonly observed that buyers tend to exhibit a preference for engaging with a single vendor. Furthermore, a notable percentage of buyers, precisely 22.6%, have been involved in transactions with two distinct vendors. The lack of selectivity observed among vendors, with 84.4% having multiple buyers, is comprehensible. Undoubtedly, vendors engage in transactions with a diverse range of buyers.

The out-degree centralisation of Abraxas is 0.12. Once more, this observation serves as evidence that a significant proportion of purchasers tended to engage in transactions with a limited selection of highly influential suppliers. However, specific buyers exhibited higher enthusiasm in their purchasing behaviours than others. In contrast to the average buyer who purchased from only two vendors, the most enthusiastic buyers engaged in transactions with a significantly higher number of vendors, ranging from 1 to 34. Many buyers exhibited infrequent purchasing

Table 4.6 Distribution of in- and out-degree

Degree centrality	Out-degree total (vendor) (%)	In-degree total (buyer) (%)
1	42 (15.6)	1350 (53.47)
2	30 (11.2)	562 (22.26)
3	21 (7.8)	245 (9.7)
4	19 (7.1)	149 (5.9)
5	8 (3)	77 (3.05)
6	11 (4.1)	40 (1.58)
7	7 (2.6)	36 (1.43)
8	10 (3.7)	17 (0.67)
9	7 (2.6)	16 (0.63)
10–14	27 (10)	23 (0.91)
15–19	18 (6.7)	4 (0.16)
20–29	15 (5.6)	5 (0.2)
30–49	25 (9.3)	1 (0.04)
50–99	22 (8.2)	–
100+	7 (2.6)	–
Total	**269 (100)**	**2525 (100)**

behaviour as the in-degree centralisation of Abraxas was 0.001. Determining the underlying factors driving a buyer's purchasing pattern is a complex task due to the many potential reasons that may influence the decision-making process. These buyers may have transitioned to an alternative cryptomarket or ceased their activities on the dark web entirely due to the inherent risks involved.

Notably, although a minority of vendors were responsible for the majority of sales, the vendors beyond this dominant group encountered challenges in sustaining their livelihoods on Abraxas. As mentioned earlier, the phenomenon can potentially be ascribed to the influence of trust and reputation. Vendors possessing superior reputations consistently generate sales, thereby intensifying the obstacles new vendors face when entering the market. A vendor's average cumulative reputation score is 98.76, with a standard deviation of 191.46. The observed scores exhibited a wide range from 0 to 1628. Vendors with a strong reputation tend to attract more buyers as they leverage their established track record of reliable service as a significant factor in their sales strategy. This information can be inferred from the results of the community detection analysis below.

Community Detection Analysis

Community detection analysis allows us to identify significant attributes that help improve our understanding of the fundamental organisation of the Abraxas transactional network. Abraxas exhibited a total of 158 distinct communities established based on the preferences of the most prominent vendors (see Fig. 4.2). Furthermore,

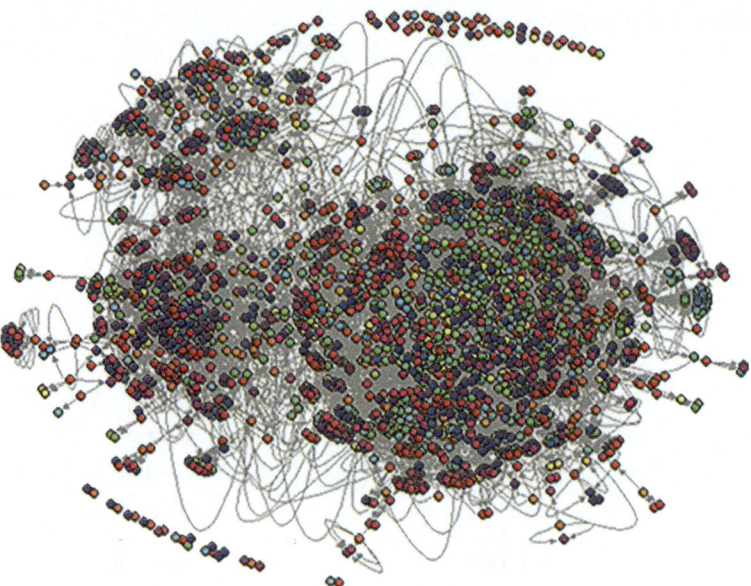

Fig. 4.2 Abraxas transactional network by community

Table 4.7 Community network characteristics

Network characteristics	Mean (SD)	Range
Community size	17.7 (44.7)	2–390
Community density	0.26 (0.19)	0.01–1
Edges	26.96 (85.81)	1–810
Within community transactions	34.39 (103.03)	1–921
Average cumulative vendor reputation	66.09 (87.97)	1–550
Avg. outdeg (vendor)	10.33 (12.72)	1–85
Avg. indeg (buyer)	1.29 (0.31)	1–2.17
Number of vendors	1.7 (2.87)	1–29
Number of buyers	15.98 (42.03)	1–373

the community detection analysis yielded a modularity score of 0.72, indicating a relatively high Q value. This observation suggests that the network exhibited significant segmentation, with numerous distinct communities. The largest community comprised 390 members, while the smallest 111 communities had less than ten members each (refer to Table 4.7). In this regard, it is noteworthy that 35 communities were classified as dyads, consisting of two members, while 20 communities were categorised as triads, comprising three members. The top 20 communities were responsible for a significant portion of activity in the market, accounting for 63% (1763) of the total number of actors and 71.9% (3909) of the transactions. Furthermore, it is worth noting that the typical community exhibited an average of 1.7 vendors and 15.98 buyers. To clarify, it can be stated that each vendor, along with their corresponding buyers, formed distinct communities.

In terms of community composition, communities with larger membership exhibited higher average vendor reputation scores, as depicted in Table 4.8. These communities also revealed the highest concentration of vendors. Most transactions conducted on Abraxas can be attributed to these communities, as many buyers were drawn to a limited number of reliable vendors. Nevertheless, it is plausible that the size of these communities influences this phenomenon, as larger communities tend to have a more significant number of engaged participants. In this sense, Abraxas can be described as a collection of transactional entities that revolve around multiple widely recognised vendors, attracting numerous purchasers. The average ratio of vendors to buyers in these communities is 1:19, with a range from 1:6.5 to 1:57. Indeed, there are three communities that a single vendor completely controls. As expected, the network density of a community tends to increase as its size grows.

In addition, these communities are limited to specific countries and products, as indicated in Table 4.9. Communities, on average, exhibit significant concentration (96.7%) in terms of the origin country from which the traded items were shipped. Furthermore, within a community, the items shipped tended to be classified within the same category, exhibiting an average rating of 97.6%. Hence, the transactional communities within Abraxas are characterised by their specific geographical locations and limited to a particular category of items. As an illustration, a community may engage primarily in the exchange of drug paraphernalia that is exclusively

Table 4.8 Community network measures (top 20 based on community size)

Community size	Community density	Edges	Within community transactions	Cumulative reputation (M)	Vendors	Buyers
390	0.01	810	921	266.06	17	373
337	0.01	574	748	126.69	29	308
139	0.02	331	373	153.58	12	127
129	0.01	202	247	135.78	9	120
96	0.02	151	210	166.33	6	90
91	0.02	149	176	109.5	8	83
82	0.02	117	196	294.67	3	79
58	0.03	97	105	510	1	57
53	0.03	71	111	550	1	52
52	0.02	66	89	109.75	4	48
52	0.02	65	99	246	2	50
44	0.04	85	97	121.25	4	40
38	0.04	55	71	106.67	3	35
38	0.06	80	95	237	2	36
38	0.03	45	55	251	1	37
32	0.04	36	52	82	3	29
32	0.05	53	62	102.67	3	29
32	0.04	40	64	156.5	2	30
30	0.05	40	58	72.25	4	26
30	0.05	41	74	119	3	27

Table 4.9 Communities by item categories and country shipped from (top 20 based on community size)

Community size	Custom listing (%)	Digital goods (%)	Drug paraphernalia (%)	Drugs (%)	Others (%)	Services (%)	Shipping country 1 (%)	Shipping country 2 (%)	Shipping country 3 (%)	Shipping country 4 (%)	Shipping country 5 (%)	Shipping country 6 (%)	Shipping country 7 (%)
390	0	0	0	100	0	0	93.16	2.71	1.95	1.74	0.33	0.11	–
337	0	85.45	0	14.55	0	0	36.10	28.74	6.42	5.88	5.35	4.95	3.07
139	0	0	0	100	0	0	92.76	6.97	0.27	–	–	–	–
129	0.40	0.27	0	99.33	0	0	96.36	3.24	0.40	–	–	–	–
96	0	0	0	100	0	0	68.10	23.33	5.71	1.90	0.95	–	–
91	1.72	0	0	98.28	0	0	99.43	0.57	–	–	–	–	–
82	0	0	0	100	0	0	100	–	–	–	–	–	–
58	0	0	0	100	0	1.88	100	–	–	–	–	–	–
53	0.80	6.97	0.27	90.08	0	0	100	–	–	–	–	–	–
52	0.11	1.95	0	97.94	0	0	96.63	3.37	–	–	–	–	–
52	0	0	0	95.77	0	4.23	83.84	13.13	1.01	1.01	1.01	–	–
44	1.02	0	0	98.98	0	0	100	–	–	–	–	–	–
38	0	0	0	100	0	0	92.96	4.23	2.82	–	–	–	–
38	0	0	0	100	0	0	100	–	–	–	–	–	–
38	0	0	0	100	0	0	100	–	–	–	–	–	–
32	0	0	0	100	0	0	100	–	–	–	–	–	–
32	0	0	0	100	0	0	100	–	–	–	–	–	–
32	0	0	0	96.91	3.09	0	79.69	18.75	1.56	–	–	–	–
30	0	0	0	100	0	0	65.52	22.41	12.07	–	–	–	–
30	0	0	0	100	0	0	97.30	2.70	–	–	–	–	–

imported from Canada. This implies that trust in Abraxas is potentially influenced by factors beyond a vendor's reputation, such as the country of origin for shipping and the specific product(s) being sold. This observation indicates a bias towards a particular vendor and contradicts the argument set out in Barratt and Aldridge (2016) that cryptomarkets operate as a globally interconnected network for transactions. According to Norbutas (2018), the transactional network of Abraxas exhibits a significant degree of localisation in its structure. These findings provide more comprehensive documentation of this particular trend.

Regression Results and Power Few Distributions

The results of the multiple linear regression models for vendor success, popularity and affluence are displayed in Table 4.10. The cumulative reputation score exhibits a positive and statistically significant trend across all three models. It is evident that a vendor's reputation plays an essential role in determining trust levels across the three proxy variables. This is consistent with the findings of previous studies

Table 4.10 Results of regression models

Variable name	Number of transactions (success)		Number of unique buyers (popularity)		Cumulative revenue generated (affluence)	
	Coefficient	SE	Coefficient	SE	Coefficient	SE
Intercept	−0.79**	0.27	−0.33	1.03	2389.86***	657.76
Cumulative reputation	0.1949***	0.0016	0.077***	0.006	37.86***	3.04
Average purchase price	−0.0003	0.0005	−0.0001	0.001	5.58***	1.17
Cumulative purchase price	0.0001**	0.00002	−0.0001	0.0001	–	–
Cumulative risk score	0.02***	0.003	0.059***	0.011	−35.52***	7.099
Items and information						
Unique items listings	−0.079**	0.026	0.33***	0.098	−41.97	64.01
Item categories	0.67*	0.29	1.298	1.098	−3777.36***	675.32
Item subcategories	0.38***	0.11	0.831*	0.404	314.88	263.70
Number of words in item description	0.00004*	0.00002	0.0001	0.0001	0.18***	0.044
Shipped to locations						
Continent/region	0.118	0.2625	0.79	0.991	539.78	646.98
Worldwide	−0.228	0.1986	0.0022	0.75	592.76	488.63
AIC	832.8	–	1496.88	–	4737.46	–
BIC	878.5	–	1542.66	–	4779.71	–

AIC Akaike information criteria, *BIC* Bayesian information criteria
*p < 0.05; **p < 0.01; ***p < 0.001

(Décary-Hétu, 2016; Décary-Hétu & Quessy-Doré, 2017; Duxbury & Haynie, 2017), despite their broader scope. Furthermore, cumulative risk demonstrates statistical significance as a predictor in all three models. While the coefficient estimate displays a positive value for the number of transactions and the number of distinct buyers, it exhibits a negative value for the cumulative revenue generated. This intriguing development requires further analysis based on extensive qualitative data to provide a thorough explanation. The outcome aligns with logical reasoning concerning the number of transactions and the number of distinct buyers. The adage "no risk, no reward" remains applicable in Abraxas. The vendor's willingness to assume the risks associated with international shipping, especially on a global scale, enhances their capacity to engage in more transactions and expand their customer base. Therefore, the success and popularity of a vendor are enhanced when they possess the willingness and capability to access a broader market. A logical correlation could be postulated between the revenue generated and the measured variables in the model. However, the model suggests otherwise.

It is essential to note that each model exhibits variations in the specific estimates that account for the variability in vendor success, popularity and affluence. Regarding the achievement of a vendor, the combined purchase price, categories of items and subcategories of items also serve as positive indicators. The impact of the cumulative purchase price on a vendor's success is found to be insignificant. However, the vendor's probability of achieving success is positively influenced by the ability to provide customers with a greater variety of items (in terms of item category and subcategory). Unique item listings and subcategories also serve as positive indicators of the popularity of vendors. This concept is logically sound, as a vendor with a more comprehensive range of products is more likely to appeal to a broader group of buyers with varying purchasing preferences. Ultimately, the product description's mean acquisition cost and word count emerge as the sole indicators of vendor prosperity. This concept is logical to a certain extent, as there is a positive correlation between the average price of a product and the potential revenue a vendor can generate. Furthermore, when an excessively high price is associated with a product, the vendor must provide the buyer with a guarantee of the utmost quality of the purchased item. Therefore, it can be inferred that including additional words in product descriptions decreases information asymmetry, as suggested by Akerlof (1970).

Figure 4.3 illustrates the power law distributions of vendor success, popularity and affluence. The phenomenon observed in Abraxas can be characterised by a power law distribution, wherein a minority of vendors are responsible for most transactions, unique buyers and generated revenue. In this study, it was found that 9.3% of vendors were responsible for 50% of the total completed transactions. Additionally, 10% of vendors accounted for 47% of unique buyers, while a smaller group of 5.2% contributed to 50.1% of the total revenue generated. As with numerous natural (Zipf, 1949; Simon, 1955) and criminological phenomena, Abraxas is indeed influenced by a select group of individuals with significant authority. The significant degree of preferential attachment observed underscores trust's critical role in shaping Abraxas' transactional network.

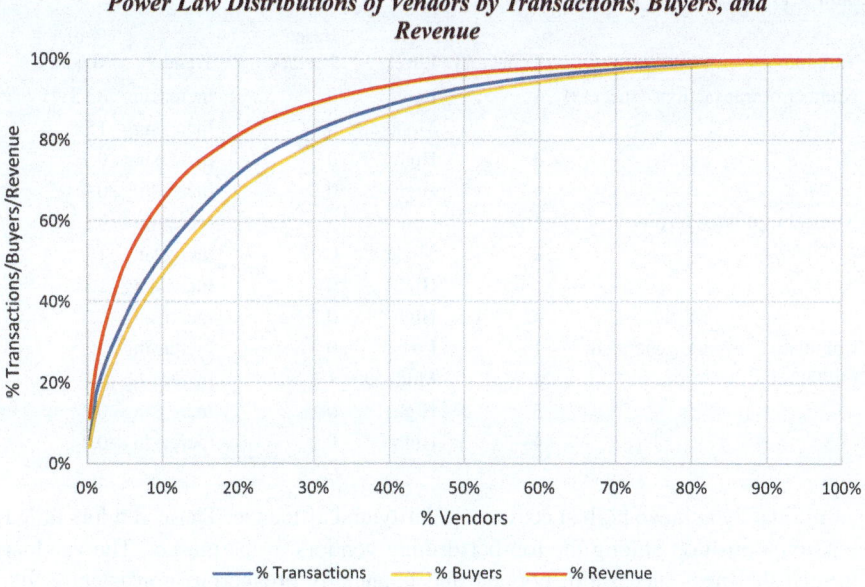

Fig. 4.3 Power law distributions of vendors by transactions, buyers and revenue

Trajectory Analyses

The results of the k-means trajectory models are presented in Table 4.11. The table provides information on three proxy variables, including the count of trajectories in each model, the relative level of each trajectory concerning the specific variable, the base crime count in January (the first month of Abraxas' operation), the trend and the percentage of vendors within each trajectory group. These trends are identified by applying regression analyses to the vendors' data over time, within each trajectory group. According to Andresen et al. (2017), a trajectory can be considered stable if the slope parameter falls within the range of −0.2 to 0.2. If the slope parameter is below −0.2, the trajectory is deemed to be decreasing, while if it is above 0.2, it is classified as increasing.

Utilising the Calinski criterion score, it was determined that a k-means partition of four groups is optimal for models assessing success, popularity and affluence. Importantly, the first trajectory in each model comprises over 80% of the total number of vendors on Abraxas. This finding suggests that a significant proportion of vendors did not engage in a high number of transactions, interact with many vendors or generate considerable revenue during their time in the market. In essence, most vendors had a negligible impact on market dynamics within the Abraxas platform, as they could not stimulate growth. Likewise, the second trajectories observed in both models indicate that moderately successful, popular and affluent vendors exhibited consistent growth within these respective categories. However, they did

Table 4.11 Summary of k-means trajectories

Variable	Trajectory	Level	Base, January	Trend	% of vendors
Number of transactions (success)	1	Low	0	Increasing	83.3
	2	Moderate	0.07	Increasing	15.6
	3	High	0	Increasing	0.7
	4	High	0	Increasing	0.4
Number of unique buyers (popularity)	1	Low	0	Increasing	82.2
	2	Moderate	0.07	Increasing	16
	3	High	0	Increasing	1.1
	4	High	0	Increasing	0.7
Cumulative revenue generated (affluence)	1	Low	0.3	Increasing	90.3
	2	Moderate	1.4	Increasing	8.6
	3	High	0	Increasing	0.7
	4	High	0	Increasing	0.4

not ultimately achieve high success, popularity and affluence. These vendors failed to reach a position among the top-performing vendors in the market. The vendors deemed the most successful, popular and financially prosperous consistently followed a similar trajectory in both the third and fourth models, maintaining this trend until the eventual closure of Abraxas. These vendors achieved significant prominence within the market and maintained their dominant position throughout their tenure in the market.

The trajectories of each model over Abraxas' operational timeline are depicted in Fig. 4.4. Each line in the regression output represents the average values of the results. In both models, the third and fourth trajectories demonstrate substantial growth as a limited number of vendors achieve significant success, popularity and affluence within a relatively brief timeframe. Interestingly, the vendors above displayed relatively low activity levels during the initial 2 months but experienced a notable surge in prominence during April, exhibiting exponential growth. Both the revenue and affluence models exhibit a comparable pattern. To provide further details, the fourth trajectory within the success model indicates a mean of zero transactions during January and February, followed by an increase to three transactions in March. Subsequently, the trajectory experienced a significant surge, reaching 41, 108 and 129 transactions in April, May and June, respectively. In a similar vein, the fourth trajectory within the revenue model exhibits an initial average cumulative revenue of $0 during January and February, followed by a substantial surge to $17,865.2, $30,276.7 and $18,024.6 in April, May and June, respectively. In the popularity model, the fourth trajectory exhibits an initial absence of unique buyers in January and February, followed by a subsequent increase to 68, 80.5 and 60.5 in April, May and June, respectively. Interestingly, a significant majority of trajectories in every model exhibit a downward trend after May. The reasons behind this phenomenon remain unclear, despite potential factors such as market competition and the unpredictable nature of the dark web.

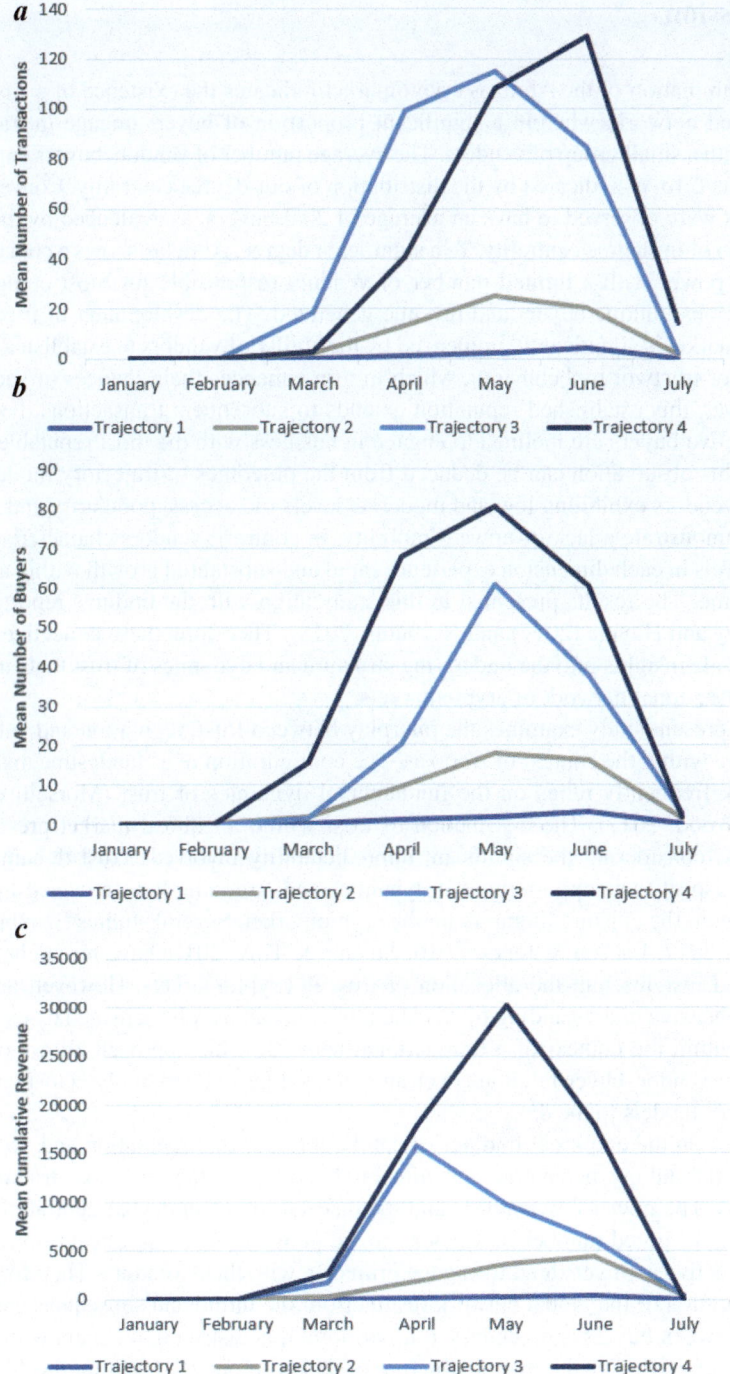

Fig. 4.4 K-means trajectories

Discussion

The examination of the Abraxas cryptomarket indicates the existence of a vast and dispersed network, wherein a significant proportion of buyers engage in transactions with a small group of vendors. The average number of vendors buyers engaged with was 2.15, as indicated by the distribution of out-degree centrality. Conversely, vendors were observed to have an average of 20.2 buyers, as evidenced by the distribution of in-degree centrality. To a significant degree, Abraxas shows a concentration of power with a limited number of vendors responsible for most completed transactions, unique buyers and revenue generated. The development of trust in a cryptomarket is significantly influenced by the ability of vendors to establish a reputation for trustworthy behaviour, which in turn enhances their chances of success. Moreover, this established reputation extends to subsequent transactions, because prospective buyers are inclined to engage in business with the most reputable vendors. This observation can be deduced from the outcomes of trajectory models, in which vendors exhibiting low and moderate levels of success, popularity and affluence demonstrate a lack of upward mobility. In contrast, vendors characterised by high levels in each dimension experience rapid and substantial growth within a brief timeframe. The results presented in this study align with the findings reported by Duxbury and Haynie (2017) and Norbutas (2018). Therefore, these collective studies provide insights into the underlying structure and dynamics of trust that support the transactional network of cryptomarkets.

The present study examines the interplay between trust, reputation and network structure within the context of Abraxas. The configuration of a clandestine market's network frequently relies on the fundamental dynamics of trust (Morselli et al., 2007; Wood, 2017). The distribution of trust within an illegal market presents a paradox, considering the significant unpredictability involved. Trust dynamics, a crucial aspect that supports market dynamics and structure, have received limited attention in the existing literature on the cryptomarket. Several studies (Duxbury & Haynie, 2017; Lacson & Jones, 2016; Janetos & Tilly, 2017) have researched and provided insights into the allocation of trust in cryptomarkets. However, a more comprehensive understanding of this phenomenon can only be achieved by examining it within the context of a transactional network. This approach allows one to quantify vendor–buyer relations over an extended period and apply statistical and trajectory models to the data.

Based on the empirical findings, it can be inferred that reputation and, to some extent, risk-taking behaviour are influential factors in the network structure of Abraxas. The power few analysis and the distribution of in-degree centrality indicate that a limited number of vendors are responsible for a significant portion of market activity. Buyers tend to engage primarily with these vendors. Therefore, the configuration of the global network results from the initial and subsequent interactions between buyers and vendors. Furthermore, this distribution occurs within the framework of the local network structure of this cryptomarket. Within the Abraxas ecosystem, each vendor and their corresponding buyers form distinct communities.

As mentioned earlier, the communities also tend to be geographically situated and focused on specific products, indicating the significance of geographic proximity and specialised markets in shaping the network structure. It was observed that, on average, approximately 96.7% of the commodities exchanged within a given community originate from a single nation. Moreover, these items were classified under the same product category in 97.6% of cases.

Therefore, the transactional communities within Abraxas are geographically bound and limited to a specific category of products. This contradicts the argument made by Barratt and Aldridge (2016), who suggest that cryptomarkets operate as globally interconnected trading networks, facilitating transactions between buyers and vendors across various nations and involving a diverse range of products and services. In essence, trust in Abraxas is intricately linked to multiple factors, such as the vendor's reputation, the country of origin for shipping and the nature of the product(s) being sold. However, this observation may indicate buyer preferences rather than an accurate measure of vendor trustworthiness. Purchasers may prefer to engage in transactions with vendors who specialise in a particular product and operate from a specific geographical location, driven by subjective inclinations or the desire for ease and convenience. This is of central importance since the fact that illicit transactions are guided by the specific preferences of buyers, in addition to the trust they place in vendors, is frequently overlooked. While the primary focus of this chapter has been on the dynamics of trust, buyer preferences cannot be disregarded.

Summary and Conclusion

This chapter has examined the allocation of trust on the platform known as Abraxas. Significantly, a notable prevalence or consolidation of trust among buyers towards a limited group of vendors exists. Although the available data does not provide conclusive evidence on the finite nature of trust within Abraxas, there are indications that it follows a Pareto distribution. However, buyers depend on data concerning vendors' previous actions when deciding which vendor to choose. The data presented herein is derived from feedback voluntarily submitted by previous clients. Vendors who are new to the market and lack a proven track record of ethical behaviour can enhance their reputation by offering price discounts to buyers. By accruing a growing number of favourable ratings, individuals or businesses can offset their initial investment by commanding a higher price based on their reputation.

Trust in Abraxas is a coordination mechanism facilitated by the established feedback and reputation system. The feedback provided by a buyer serves as an indicator of their level of trust, or lack thereof, in a vendor. Prospective buyers can subsequently access this data to assess the reliability of the vendor in question. Akerlof (1970) was one of the early scholars to highlight the potential for market failure when buyers cannot examine products before purchase and are left with uncertainty regarding the quality of the products. The negative experiences of buyers who transact with sellers of low-quality products lead to a decline in quality standards and a diminishing willingness to pay the appropriate price for high-quality products. According to Shapiro (1983), one potential solution to address the information asymmetry between buyers and sellers that hinders trade is for sellers of high-quality products to establish a reputation upon entering the market.

The regression models indicate that vendor reputations serve as a form of brand name, conveying to buyers the reliability and excellence of a vendor. According to Akerlof's seminal work in 1970, the adverse consequences of a market characterised by information asymmetry can be alleviated if a buyer can determine the quality of the goods being sold. In the context of Abraxas, reputation plays a crucial role in distinguishing the quality of goods and mitigating uncertainty in a volatile setting. In this scenario, prospective and existing consumers will decline to engage in future transactions with a vendor of substandard quality.

In summary, reputation scores serve as a predictive indicator of consumer behaviour. Acknowledging that reputation scores indicate a seller's overall performance and dependability is essential. However, it is plausible that sellers with solid credibility and high-quality products may occasionally deceive buyers by overemphasising the product's quality or misrepresenting its attributes. With this in mind, it is plausible that a purchaser may experience heightened apprehension when evaluating a vendor with a less established reputation, as the overall perception of said vendor relies heavily on a limited number of concluded transactions. In contrast, buyers are reassured by vendors who have completed numerous transactions, as observed. Therefore, satisfactorily completed transactions may help reduce information asymmetry and address a buyer's apprehensions. Buyers may seek certain information regarding a vendor's transactional history to facilitate their decision-making process when purchasing. This observation provides insights into the mechanisms employed to address information asymmetry within cryptomarkets, such as Abraxas. Regardless of whether the feedback is positive or negative, vendors gain more recognition as their feedback increases. Consequently, the network architecture of Abraxas may potentially result from this particular dynamic.

Ultimately, drawing from the outcomes of the trajectory models, a limited subset of vendors emerges as remarkably prosperous, renowned and financially well-off within a relatively brief timeframe. This phenomenon may be attributed to how trust is established and disseminated within a cryptomarket. As stated earlier, the extent to which trust can be considered a finite resource in cryptomarkets remains uncertain. However, trust is not evenly distributed among a limited number of vendors who disproportionately benefit from it. Furthermore, this level of trust, or the absence thereof, persists over time. In this particular scenario, it appears probable that trust in Abraxas is based on a "winner-takes-all" framework, wherein certain vendors who successfully establish trust with buyers gradually assume market dominance throughout its operation. In terms of functionality, vendors who are unable to establish rapport with buyers will experience limited transactional activity and subsequently generate minimal revenue. Consequently, once trust has been established with certain vendors, it becomes challenging for new vendors to displace them. From a certain perspective, trust can be perceived as a metaphorical moat, serving as a strategic advantage that distinguishes a select group of vendors from the remaining competitors in the market.

Moreover, the trajectory models illustrate that the initial stages of the market did not witness the presence or activity of the leading vendors on Abraxas. However, these vendors eventually emerged as dominant market players upon their engagement with buyers. This phenomenon may be indicative of a transactional cascade. Undoubtedly, upon the entrance of particular vendors into a market and their initiation of transactions with novel buyers, their engagement rapidly intensifies, resulting in a substantial share of market activity within a relatively brief timeframe. However, there remains ambiguity regarding whether these particular vendors were previously successful sellers on other platforms before transitioning to Abraxas, or if their success was primarily derived from this specific market. Therefore, it is indeterminate whether their achievement on Abraxas was a result of organic development or if it was transferred from another market. On the other hand, the vendors in the initial trajectories exhibited limited growth concerning each proxy variable over time. Furthermore, it should be noted that these vendors were involved from the beginning of Abraxas, engaging in a limited number of transactions during January. This suggests that the absence of a first mover principle on Abraxas results in early entrants' eventual dominance of market activity.

In conclusion, the points mentioned above suggest that trust is an inherent component of any network that engages in the transportation, exchange and commerce of goods and services, irrespective of their legal status. The network structure of cryptomarkets such as Abraxas and the one investigated by Duxbury and Haynie (2017) is based on the trust buyers place in the vendors they engage in transactions with. Trust plays a crucial role in facilitating the smooth functioning of transactional networks; however, it can also introduce disruptions to their operational efficiency. In the present scenario, trust emerges as a fragile component of the Abraxas transactional network. Suppose law enforcement agencies were to formulate a strategy to impede trade on Abraxas. It is plausible that they would prioritise targeting vendors with high credibility and trustworthiness among buyers. After all, this select group of individuals is responsible for propelling market activity on the Abraxas platform. It is highly probable that the elimination of these actors would result in a cessation of market activity or, at the very least, a reduction in its pace to some extent.

The practical implications of this study are apparent in this context. In order to effectively mitigate the activities of these illicit entities, law enforcement agencies should prioritise gaining a comprehensive understanding of their underlying dynamics of trust. This would entail identifying the vendors that are most responsible for market activity. Law enforcement officers might then compile a roster of appropriate subjects for apprehension. The primary objective of this strategy is to disrupt a criminal network by focusing specifically on those individuals with the highest level of trust within the network. The hypothetical elimination of these actors would potentially deprive a transactional network of its most crucial economic resources, compelling buyers to transition to an unfamiliar supplier or withdraw from the market entirely.

Although the rationale behind this specific strategy aligns with the present study's findings, the adverse consequences of such targeted interventions are inadequately understood. What might be the impact on the overall level of trust in the market if a reliable vendor were to be eliminated? What methods might be employed to quantify this phenomenon? Would purchasers opt for an alternative vendor within the same market, or would they transition to an entirely different market to conduct their business? The upcoming chapters will address these questions, simulating and evaluating the effectiveness of eliminating trusted cryptomarket users as a comprehensive law enforcement strategy.

References

Akerlof, G. A. (1970). The market for lemons: Qualitative uncertainty and the market mechanism. *Quarterly Journal of Economics, 84*, 488–500.

Aldridge, J. & Décary-Hétu, D. (2016). Cryptomarkets and the future of illicit drug markets. In European Monitoring Centre for Drugs and Drug Addiction, J. Mounteney, A. Bo, & A. Oteo (Eds.), *The internet and drug markets (EMCDDA Insights 21)* (pp. 23–30). Publications Office of the European Union. https://data.europa.eu/doi/10.2810/324608

Andresen, M. A., Curman, A. S., & Linning, S. J. (2017). The trajectories of crime at places: Understanding the patterns of disaggregated crime types. *Journal of Quantitative Criminology, 33*, 427–449.

Ashton, S. A., & Bussu, A. (2022). The social dynamics of adolescent co-offending. *Youth Justice, 23*(3), 350–371. https://doi.org/10.1177/14732254221136044

Baker, T., & Piquero, A. R. (2010). Assessing the perceived benefits—Criminal offending relationship. *Journal of Criminal Justice, 38*(5), 981–987.

Barratt, M., & Aldridge, J. (2016). Everything you always wanted to know about drug cryptomarkets* (*but were afraid to ask). *International Journal of Drug Policy, 35*, 1–6.

Batikas, M., & Kretschmer, T. (2018). Entrepreneurs on the darknet: Reaction to negative feedback (Unpublished paper). https://doi.org/10.2139/ssrn.3238141.

Bichler, G., Malm, A., & Cooper, T. (2017). Drug supply networks: A systematic review of the organizational structure of illicit drug trade. *Crime Science, 6*(2), 63–73.

Blondel, V., Guillaume, J., Lambiotte, R., & Lefebvre, E. (2008). Fast unfolding of communities in large networks. *Journal of Statistical Mechanics: Theory and Experiment, 2008*, P10008. https://doi.org/10.1088/1742-5468/2008/10/P10008

Branwen, G., Christin, N., Décary-Hétu, D., Andersen, R. M., StExo, E. P., Anonymous, L., Sohhlz, D., Kratunov, D., Cakic, V., Buskirk, V., Whom, M., Goode, S. (2015, July 12). *Dark net market archives, 2011–2015*. https://www.gwern.net/DNM-archives

Bright, D. A., Koskinen, J., & Malm, A. (2017). Illicit network dynamics: The formation and evolution of a drug trafficking network. *Journal of Quantitative Criminology, 35*(2), 237–258.

Catino, M. (2014). How do mafias organize? Conflict and violence in three mafia organizations. *European Journal of Sociology, 55*(2), 177–220.

Christin, N. (2013). Traveling the Silk Road: A measurement analysis of a large anonymous online marketplace. In *Proceedings of the 22nd international conference on World Wide Web* (pp. 213–224). Association for Computing Machinery. https://doi.org/10.1145/2488388.2488408.

Décary-Hétu, D. (2016). Policing cybercrime and cyberterror. *Global Crime, 17*(1), 123–125.

Décary-Hétu, D., & Dupont, B. (2013). The social network of hackers. *Global Crime, 13*(3), 1–16.

Décary-Hétu, D., & Quessy-Doré, O. (2017). Are repeat buyers in cryptomarkets loyal customers? Repeat business between dyads of cryptomarket vendors and users. *The American Behavioral Scientist, 61*(11), 1341–1357.

Demant, J., Munksgaard, R., Décary-Hétu, D., & Aldridge, J. (2018). Going local on a global platform: A critical analysis of the transformative potential of cryptomarkets for organised illicit drug crime. *International Criminal Justice Review, 28*(3), 255–274.

Dumouchel, P. (2005). Trust as an action. *European Journal of Sociology, 46*(3), 417–428.

Duxbury, S., & Haynie, D. (2017). The network structure of opioid distribution on a darknet cryptomarket. *Journal of Quantitative Criminology, 34*(4), 921–941.

Duxbury, S., & Haynie, D. (2018). Building them up, breaking them down: Topology, vendor selection patterns, and a digital drug market's robustness to disruption. *Social Networks, 52*, 238–250.

Duxbury, S., & Haynie, D. (2019). Criminal network security: An agent-based approach to evaluating network resilience. *Criminology, 57*(2), 314–342.

Englefield, A., & Ariel, B. (2017). Searching for influencing actors in co-offending networks: The recruiter. *International Journal of Social Science Studies, 5*(5), 24–45.

Fader, J. J. (2016). Criminal family networks: Criminal capital and cost avoidance among urban drug sellers. *Deviant Behavior, 37*(11), 1325–1340.

Free, C., & Murphy, P. R. (2015). The ties that bind: The decision to co-offend in fraud. *Contemporary Accounting Research, 32*(1), 18–54.

Gambetta, D. (Ed.). (1988). Trust: Making and breaking cooperative relations. .

Gambetta, D. (2000). Can we trust trust? In D. Gambetta (Ed.), *Trust: Making and breaking cooperative relations* (pp. 213–237). University of Oxford.

Gambetta, D. (2009). *Codes of the underworld: How criminals communicate.* Princeton University Press.

Gambetta, D., & Bacharach, M. (2001). Trust in signs. In K. Cook (Ed.), *Trust and society* (pp. 148–184). Russell Sage Foundation.

Genolini, C., & Falissard, B. (2010). KmL: k-means for longitudinal data. *Computational Statistics, 25*(2), 317–328.

Genolini, C., Ecochard, R., Benghezal, M., Driss, T., Andrieu, S., & Subtil, F. (2016). kmlShape: An efficient method to cluster longitudinal data (time-series) according to their shapes. *PLoS One, 11*(6), e0150738. https://doi.org/10.1371/journal.pone.0150738

Hardy, R., & Norgaard, J. (2016). Reputation in the Internet black market: An empirical and theoretical analysis of the Deep Web. *Journal of Institutional Economics, 12*(3), 515–539.

Herley, C., & Florencio, D. (2010). Nobody sells gold for the price of silver: Dishonesty, uncertainty and the underground economy. In T. Moore, D. Pym, & C. Ioannidis (Eds.), *Economics of information security and privacy* (pp. 35–53). Springer.

Holt, T., & Lampke, E. (2010). Exploring stolen data markets online: Products and market forces. *Criminal Justice Studies, 23*(1), 33–50.

Holt, T., Strumsky, D., Smirnova, O., & Kilger, M. (2012). Examining the social networks of malware writers and hackers. *International Journal of Cyber Criminology, 6*(1), 891–903.

Janetos, N., & Tilly, J. (2017). Reputation dynamics in a market for illicit drugs (Unpublished paper).

Jaspers, J. D. (2017). Managing cartels: How cartel participants create stability in the absence of law. *European Journal on Criminal Policy and Research, 23*, 319–335.

Kenney, M. (2007). The architecture of drug trafficking: Network forms of organisation in the Colombian cocaine trade. *Global Crime, 8*(3), 233–259.

Lacson, W., & Jones, B. (2016). The 21st century darknet market: Lessons from the fall of Silk Road. *International Journal of Cyber Criminology, 10*(1), 40–61.

Lantz, B., & Ruback, R. B. (2017). The relationship between co-offending, age, and experience using a sample of adult burglary offenders. *Journal of Developmental and Life-Course Criminology, 3*, 76–97. https://doi.org/10.1007/s40865-016-0047-0

Malm, A., & Bichler, G. (2011). Networks of collaborating criminals: Assessing the structural vulnerability of drug markets. *Journal of Research in Crime and Delinquency, 48*(2), 271–297.

Martin, J. (2014). *Drugs on the dark net*. Palgrave Macmillan.

McGloin, J. M., & Kirk, D. (2011). An overview of social network analysis. *Journal of Criminal Justice Education, 2*(2), 169–181.

McPherson, M., Smith-Lovin, L., & Cook, J. M. (2001). Birds of a feather: Homophily in social networks. *Annual Review of Sociology, 27*(1), 415–444.

Morselli, C. (2009). *Inside criminal networks*. Springer.

Morselli, C., Giguere, C., & Petit, K. (2007). The efficiency/security trade-off in criminal networks. *Social Networks, 29*(1), 143–153.

Morselli, C., Turcotte, M., & Tenti, V. (2011). The mobility of criminal groups. *Global Crime, 12*(3), 165–188.

Nagin, D., & Land, K. (1993). Age, criminal careers and population heterogeneity: Specification and estimation of a nonparametric, mixed Poisson model. *Criminology, 31*(3), 327–362.

Natarajan, M. (2006). Understanding the structure of a large heroin distribution network: A quantitative analysis of qualitative data. *Journal of Quantitative Criminology, 22*(2), 171–192.

Newman, M. E. J. (2003). The structure and function of complex networks. *SIAM Review, 45*(2), 167–256. https://doi.org/10.1137/S003614450342480

Newman, M. E. J. (2006). Modularity and community structure in networks. *Proceedings of the National Academy of Sciences, 103*(23), 8577–8582.

Norbutas, L. (2018). Offline constraints in online drug marketplaces: An exploratory analysis of a cryptomarket trade network. *International Journal of Drug Policy, 56*, 92–100. https://doi.org/10.1016/j.drugpo.2018.03.016

Norbutas, L., Ruiter, S., & Corten, R. (2020). Believe it when you see it: Dyadic embeddedness and reputation effects on trust in cryptomarkets for illegal drugs. *Social Networks, 63*, 150–161.

Oksanen, A., Miller, B. L., Savolainen, I., Sirola, A., Demant, J., Kaakinen, M., & Zych, I. (2020, July). Illicit drug purchases via social media among American young people. In G. Meiselwitz (Ed.), *Social computing and social media. Design, ethics, user behavior, and social network analysis. HCII 2020. Lecture Notes in Computer Science: Vol. 12194* (pp. 278–288). Springer.

Papachristos, A. V. (2009). Murder by structure: Dominance relations and the social structure of gang homicide. *American Journal of Sociology, 115*, 74–128.

Papachristos, A. V. (2014). The network structure of crime. *Sociology Compass, 8*, 347–357.

Pettit, P. (2004). Trust, reliance and the internet. *Analyse & Kritik, 26*(1), 108–121.

Pons, P., & Latapy, M. (2005). Computing communities in large networks using random walks. In P. Yolum, T. Güngör, F.Gürgen, & C. Özturan (Eds.), *Computer and Information Sciences—ISCIS 2005. Lecture Notes in Computer Science: Vol. 3733* (pp. 284–293). Springer.

Przepiorka, W., Norbutas, L., & Corten, R. (2017). Order without law: Reputation promotes cooperation in a cryptomarket for illegal drugs. *European Sociological Review, 33*(6), 752–764.

Sarnecki, J. (2001). *Delinquent networks: Youth co-offending in Stockholm*. Cambridge University Press.

Serva, M. A., Fuller, M. A., & Mayer, R. C. (2005). The reciprocal nature of trust: A longitudinal study of interacting teams. *Journal of Organizational Behavior, 26*(6), 625–648.

Shapiro, C. (1983). Premiums for high quality products as return to reputation. *Quarterly Journal of Economics, 98*, 659–680.

Simon, H. (1955). On a class of skew distribution functions. *Biometrika, 42*, 425–440.

Smith, C. M., & Papachristos, A. V. (2016). Trust thy crooked neighbour: Multiplexity in Chicago organized crime networks. *American Sociological Review, 81*(4), 644–667.

Tzanetakis, M., Kamphausen, G., Werse, B., & von Laufenberg, R. (2016). The transparency paradox. Building trust, resolving disputes and optimising logistics on conventional and online drugs markets. *International Journal of Drug Policy, 35*, 58–68. https://doi.org/10.1016/j.drugpo.2015.12.010

Van Buskirk, J., Naicker, S., Roxburgh, A., Bruno, R., & Burns, R. (2016). Who sells what? Country specific differences in substance availability on the Agora cryptomarket. *International Journal of Drug Policy, 35*, 16–23. https://doi.org/10.1016/j.drugpo.2016.07.004

van Hout, M., & Bingham, T. (2013a). 'Surfing the Silk Road': A study of users' experiences. *International Journal of Drug Policy, 24*(6), 524–529. https://doi.org/10.1016/j.drugpo.2013.08.011

von Lampe, K. (2016). The ties that bind: A taxonomy of associational criminal structures. In G. A. Antonopoulos (Ed.), *Illegal entrepreneurship, organized crime and social control: Essays in Honor of Professor Dick Hobbs* (pp. 19–35). Springer.

von Lampe, K., & Johansen, P. (2004). Organized crime and trust: On the conceptualization and empirical relevance of trust in the context of criminal networks. *Global Crime, 6*(2), 159–184.

Wasserman, S., & Faust, K. (1994). *Social network analysis: Methods and applications.* Cambridge University Press.

Weerman, F. M. (2003). Co-offending as social exchange: Explaining characteristics of co-offending. *British Journal of Criminology, 43*(2), 398–416.

Williamson, O. (1993). Calculativeness, trust, and economic organization. *Journal of Law and Economics, 36*(1), 453–486.

Wood, G. (2017). The structure and vulnerability of a drug trafficking collaboration network. *Social Network, 48*, 1–9.

Yang, S., Keller, F., & Zheng, L. (2013). *Social network analysis: Methods and examples.* Sage Publications.

Zipf, G. (1949). *Human behavior and the principle of least effort: An introduction to human ecology.* Addison-Wesley Press.

Chapter 5
Agent-Based Modelling for Criminal Network Interventions

Introduction

Emerging threats from cyberspace have engendered proactive efforts from law enforcement to curtail and counteract these malicious actors and organisations. These strategies and tactics will differ in their operational parameters and functional objectives. Some interventions may seek to stem the flow of new actors, while others aim to thoroughly dismantle the structure of criminal organisations in their entirety (Morselli, 2009). Regardless of the nuances of the intervention, one fundamental question remains: How effective was it? This question of what works and what does not work has not been extensively applied to the study of cryptomarkets.

A relatively new criminal phenomenon, cryptomarkets are illicit online marketplaces facilitating the trucking, bartering and trading of various illegal goods and services between buyers and vendors. At the same time, governments and law enforcement agencies worldwide have made numerous attempts to disrupt the ease of operation of these illicit entities as they have metastasised, adopting new methods for both securitising their continued operation and expanding their scope and influence (Shortis et al., 2020). As such, it is unclear whether these interventions have had pronounced impacts on the cryptomarket ecosystem. Nevertheless, a growing number of studies (Malm & Bichler, 2011; Natarajan, 2006; Wood, 2017) have provided empirical evidence of the utility of social network analysis in understanding the structural composition of criminal organisations. Moreover, cryptomarket scholars (Duxbury & Haynie, 2018, 2020) have begun testing the efficacy of strategic interventions.

While traditional methods of targeting criminal networks have prioritised the identification and removal of "kingpins", Morselli (2009) contends that the fluidity and flexibility of the structure of certain illicit networks makes them resilient to traditional law enforcement strategies. Crucially, Duxbury and Haynie (2020) note that prior research (Holt et al., 2012; Kenney, 2007; Morselli, 2009; Malm & Bichler, 2011; Natarajan, 2006; Wood, 2017) that used social network analysis to measure the structure and actors within a criminal network has failed to apply supplementary simulation methods that isolate probable vulnerabilities in the criminal network. In short, these studies have not accounted for possible network adaptation following intervention. This can be applied to generate informed strategies that can better disrupt the operation of criminal networks (Duxbury & Haynie, 2019). Thus, studies that leverage computer simulations to understand the impact of strategic interventions must consider probable adaptation on the part of actors within the network.

This chapter details the theoretical and practical elements of agent-based modelling (ABM) as a methodological and strategic tool for interventions against criminal organisations and networks. To this extent, this chapter explains the intricacies and aims of agent-based modelling and then examines practical ABM use cases in various domains, focusing on law enforcement and criminal justice.

This study utilised sequential node deletion to measure the efficacy of six different targeting strategies in disrupting the ease of operation of the transactional network of Abraxas, the cryptomarket examined in Chap. 4. These include (1) lead k, (2) eccentricity, (3) total revenue generated, (4) cumulative reputation score, (5) listing amount and (6) random targeting. To this extent, five outcome variables are used to measure the performance of each targeting strategy: (1) number of isolates, (2) number of components, (3) average number of nodes in components, (4) average geodesic distance and (5) number of nodes in the largest component. This model will set parameters to govern the purported behaviour of actors when nodes are removed. As such, the transactional network's overall behaviour can be accurately modelled (Bright et al., 2017) through evidence-based calculus. The basis for these decisions is explored in the forthcoming sections.

Literature Review

What Is Agent-Based Modelling?

Agent-based modelling is a tool for studying complex social systems through programmable adaptations. At their very core, agent-based models are computer simulations whose artificial agents behave and interact based on a set of rules and environmental conditions programmed by the designer (Miller & Page, 2007). These interactions between agents within their environment are aggregated to understand more significant phenomena. It is these emergent patterns that are of interest to scientists attempting to understand patterns within the natural world. As Bruch and Atwell (2015) note, "because agent-based models explicitly link individuals' characteristics and behaviour with their collective consequences, they provide a powerful tool for exploring the social consequences of individual behaviour".

Indeed, even a simple agent-based model can exhibit complex behavioural patterns and provide valuable information about the dynamics of the real-world system that it emulates. "By using ABM as computational laboratories, one may test systematically different hypotheses related to attributes of the agents, their behavioural rules, and the types of interactions, and their effect on macro-level stylised facts of the system" (Janssen, 2005, p. 1).

Methodologically speaking, agent-based models combine the precision of restrictive, formal models with the malleability and richness of qualitative descriptions (Holland & Miller, 1991). Moreover, agent-based models lend themselves to incorporating multilayered empirical data on human behaviour and social environments from various sources. To this extent, these models can successfully integrate the granularity of information that traditional statistical and mathematical models do not easily handle. This combination makes it ideal for understanding and exploring patterns in human systems, both large and small.

To be clear, agent-based models are systems comprised of three constituent elements: (1) agents, (2) an environment and (3) rules. O'Sullivan and Haklay (2000) define an agent as "an autonomous, goal-directed software entity" (p. 13). As such, agents are autonomous decision-making entities whose actions are contingent on preprogrammed rules. These rules are conceived a priori and implemented by the model developer. Importantly, agents will assess their environment and proximity to other agents to make decisions. In addition, agents may be capable of evolving, allowing unanticipated behaviours to emerge. Moreover, repetitive interactions between these agents over some iterations of the model constitute the backbone of this technique. These dynamics are quantified through pure mathematics via a computer system. It is important to note that agents can be construed as individuals, neighbourhoods, organisations, governments and others with unique characteristics and rule-based behaviours. "The characteristics of agents can be randomly assigned so that specific societal averages are produced, and the possibility of systematic bias is all but eliminated" (Groff, 2007, p. 76). At the simplest level then, agent-based models describe a collective of agents and the relationships between them. As such, the agent-based mindset is predicated on describing a potentially complex system from the perspective of its constituent parts (Bonabeau, 2002).

Crucially, agents and their respective behaviour within an environment is an area of research. A subfield of artificial intelligence, multi-agent systems research examines the adaptive behaviour of autonomous actors in the physical and digital world (Janssen, 2005). In agent-based modelling, the challenge of programming relevantly complex agents lies in balancing reactive and goal-oriented behaviour. As humans are neither task-driven nor hyperresponsive, the key is finding a golden mean between the two when programming agents. Moreover, models of bounded rationality should also include concepts from psychology, such as emotions, motivations and perceptions.

Environments, the second element of ABMs, describe the "sandbox" in which agents interact and make decisions. The environmental fundamental determines the logical extent to which agents' actions can be made and their impact at the micro- and macro-levels. Environments affect agents and are similarly affected by agents.

Of course, environments are not static systems that are not subject to change. As in real-life ecological systems, the behaviour of actors within a system can change the underlying and overarching principles that determine the system's structure over a long enough period. As such, while environments influence agents' behaviour, agents also affect the structure of the environment.

The third element, rules, is the fundamental conditions that govern agents' actions and the environment's structure. Rules are conceptual routines and subroutines that determine how an agent-based model operates. The rules, and in some cases constraints, are based on patternable behaviours that the designer expects from real-life agents and their environments. Rules can be simple or complex, goal-driven or reactive. Regardless, they must reflect a guided belief system about how agents and environments behave and operate. The closer the rules of an agent-based model are to reality, the better the model should perform in measuring and explaining the dynamics of complex systems.

Using dynamic interactions between agents at the micro-level to understand macro-level patterns, agent-based modelling explores and elaborates theory without the expenditure associated with sizeable, randomised controlled trials (Dowling, 1999; O'Sullivan, 2004). Indeed, agent-based models address the "micro-macro problem" in which there is a lack of clarity and understanding of how individual actions give rise to social organisations and dynamics (Coleman, 1994; Granovetter, 1978). All human behaviour is interdependent, with present and future actions contingent on the past decisions of agents and those around them. More generally, individuals' actions are enabled or constrained by their social context (e.g. network structure, social institutions and demographic composition) that shape available opportunities for action. Moreover, this social context is a product of the accumulation of previous actions individuals have made within their environment. This interdependence between agents' behaviour has implications for both micro- and macro-level trends as agents respond to their environment while the accumulation of their actions changes the environment.

Unlike statistical models like multiple linear regression, which uses inputs and outputs to describe a relationship between the data, agent-based models incorporate and actively test the elements of a more significant phenomenon under investigation. In general, agent-based simulations are premised on a bottom-up schema in which agents are imbued with rule-based idiosyncrasies and behaviours that emerge at the macro-levels once agents interact with one another and their environment (Epstein & Axtell, 1996). In short, an excellent agent-based model allows researchers to understand how, and perhaps why, some interactions between agents might generate specific collective results. Moreover, an agent-based approach might help inform statistical models and broader data collection processes when operated iteratively in a research setting.

Nevertheless, agent-based modelling is not necessarily a novel concept as it merely quantifies reality (Gilbert & Terna, 1999; Schelling, 1971; Simon, 1952). Of course, how faithfully a model represents reality depends on how structurally valid a model's parameters are. This is the underlying challenge of agent-based models, as the reality they describe is based on a set of rules judged to be in unity with the natural world by the model designer. Of course, it is generally the case that modelling efforts must hold to the principle that simplicity is better. In this case, a model builder must ensure that the fundamental building blocks of the social system they are looking to model are well understood before greater complexity can be added (Macy & Willer, 2002). Indeed, one must first learn to walk before one runs.

Relative to standard methodological techniques, the advantages of agent-based models are manifold. Nevertheless, Bonabeau (2002) captured these advantages across three broad statements: (1) ABM captures emergent phenomena, (2) ABM provides a natural description of a system and (3) ABM is flexible. Beginning with the first statement, emergent phenomena are events whose existence is born out of interactions between their constituent parts. For example, a car accident is a product of drivers on the road and the various decisions they make behind the wheel in response to specific environmental stimuli. By its very nature, ABM is the canonical approach to modelling emergent phenomena as it simulates the behaviour and interactions of a system's agents through a bottom-up logic structure. Assuming agents follow the rules, and the environment does not change substantially, the collective behaviour of agents can be predicted. As Axtell (2000, p. 3) notes, agent-based models allow for the "entire dynamical history of the process under study" to be examined by constantly integrating new information.

Regarding the second statement, whether scientists are attempting to model a traffic jam, the stock market or the operation of an environment, agent-based modelling seeks to replicate the system to an accurate degree. Moreover, "simulation allows heterogeneity among individuals that more closely approximates the variety found in everyday life and can accommodate the non-linear relationships present in dynamic and complex interactions" (Groff, 2007, p. 77). Finally, the flexibility of agent-based models can be observed through their provision of a natural framework for tuning the complexity of agents and altering the level of description and aggregation of a system and its agents.

While the statements above represent the methodological advantages of this technique, there are logistical advantages as well. First, agent-based models are quite cheap to design and run relative to randomised controlled trials or long-term subject-based studies. Second, similar to Bayesian methods, they allow for integrating and testing a researcher's subjective perceptions about a phenomenon. Third, agent-based models are relatively simple to run relative to dense mathematical models or logistically complex experiments.

While the advantages of agent-based models are apparent, there are nevertheless clear limitations that must be acknowledged. First, agent-based models are limited by the assumptions and rules on which they are based. According to Groff (2007),

> Agent-based models reflect the quality of the theoretical and empirical research available, data sources, and the choices about how they are implemented in the model. Specifically, the relationships depicted, data sources, parameter values, and decision rules within the model all influence the relationships observed within the model and the outcomes. (p. 77)

In contrast, the subjectivity of agent-based models can be advantageous in testing hypotheses; it can harm the model results if the core assumptions and rules do not reflect the system or process under examination.

Another limitation of agent-based modelling is the utility of the findings derived from an artificial society. In short, these findings have not been derived from an empirical test but rather from a computer simulation that sought to test the plausibility of a theory. Should an agent-based model produce findings relevant to a policy, how would policymakers grapple with the results, much less implement them? The answers to these questions are not clear. While some domains (epidemiology, medicine, etc.) might readily consider the results of an agent-based model, other domains (criminal justice, labour, etc.) might be less inclined to do so. A third limitation relates to the programming of agents, particularly those that represent humans. In this regard, human agents are often complex to model, given their potentially irrational behaviour, subjective choices and complex psychology. In short, soft, distinctive factors and randomness might represent difficult-to-program elements, and human agents are not rigid or perfectly rational actors in all situations and at all times.

While the advantages and disadvantages of agent-based models have been laid out, it is essential to outline when this technique should be used. According to Bonabeau (2002, p. 7282), agent-based models should be used:

1. When the interactions between the agents are complex, nonlinear, discontinuous or discrete, for example, when the behaviour of an agent can be altered dramatically, even discontinuously, by other agents.
2. When space is crucial, the agents' positions are not fixed.
3. When the population is heterogeneous, each individual is (potentially) different.
4. When the topology of the interactions is heterogeneous and complex. In this regard, when interactions are homogeneous and globally mixing, there is no need for agent-based simulation, but social networks are rarely homogeneous. They are characterised by clusters, leading to deviations from the average behaviour.
5. When the agents exhibit complex behaviour, including learning and adaptation.

In sum, agent-based approaches are ideal when agent behaviour is a complex function of agent attributes and characteristics, environments and inter-agent interaction over time. These models allow macro-level behavioural patterns to emerge from explicitly described micro-level behaviours, interactions and movements of agents in their environments.

Real-World Applications of Agent-Based Modelling

Agent-based models are used ubiquitously throughout all human systems and domains of research. Applications include the flow of raw materials in a factory, inventory control in a warehouse, state legitimacy and imperialist policy, urban traffic, migration, disease transmission, demographic changes in a world system and ecological limits to growth (Forrester, 1971; Meadows et al., 1974; Hanneman et al., 1995). As Caldwell (1997) indicates, agent-based modelling is a "bottom-up" strategy for modelling the interacting behaviour of decision-makers (such as individuals, families and firms) within a larger system. This modelling strategy utilises data on representative samples of decision-makers, along with equations and algorithms representing behavioural processes, to simulate the evolution through time of each decision-maker, and hence of the entire population of decision-makers.

Therefore, when agent-based models engage in micro-simulation (e.g. using observable population distributions to estimate more significant parameters), they allow researchers to potentially understand complex systems when systemic patterns emerge from the aggregated decision-making of agents.

Bonabeau (2002) notes that there are four broad areas in which agent-based models are applied in business: flows (evacuation, traffic and customer flow management), markets, organisations (operational risk and organisational design) and diffusion (diffusion of innovation and adoption dynamics). Epidemiology and urban planning are two areas in which agent-based models have been rigorously applied with success (Bruch & Atwell, 2015). Within epidemiology, Shamil et al. (2021) utilised agent-based modelling to simulate the spread of COVID-19 among the inhabitants of a city. The model considered each person as an agent who was susceptible to COVID-19 and who could transmit the disease. The model is validated by comparing the simulation to actual data. Different interventions, including contact tracing, are applied on a scaled-down version, and the parameters that lead to a controlled epidemic are determined. Overall, the model suggests that the transmission rate could be effectively curtailed through contact tracing via smartphones, with more than 60% of the population owning a smartphone combined with a city-wide lockdown.

The Models of Infectious Disease Agent Study (MIDAS) is an epidemiological project that draws together multiple interdisciplinary teams of researchers at different sites to investigate how to use agent-based models of disease transmission to understand infectious diseases. MIDAS has developed several high-yield models incorporating detailed geographic, demographic, social, biological and epidemiological information to model the H5N1 and H1N1 outbreaks. A similar undertaking was conducted by Frias-Martinez Williamson and Frias-Martinez et al. (2011), who leveraged agent-based models to measure the spread of H1N1 in Mexico and the effectiveness of government policies to curtail the disease. The model used social interactions and individual mobility patterns extracted from call detail records to accurately model virus spreading. The authors demonstrated that mobility restrictions by the Mexican government reduced infection rates by 10% at the outbreak's peak while postposing the pandemic's peak by 2 days.

UrbanSim was an experimental urban planning laboratory that utilised agent-based modelling to examine urban policy, transportation and development (Borning et al., 2008). The model merges individual, organisational and infrastructural data with a realistic geographic landscape, and it has been pivotal in guiding decision-making in urban transportation investments in light rail, freeway extensions and land-use zoning. Interestingly, another model, the Artificial Anasazi project, leveraged archaeological, anthropological and ecological data to explore the rise and fall of the Anasazi culture in the Long House Valley in north-eastern Arizona between 1800 BCE and 1300 CE (Dean & Gumerman, 2000).

Agent-based modelling has been applied sparingly in criminal justice and criminology relative to other analytic and methodological techniques. Nevertheless, agent-based models have grown in frequency in criminological studies over the past decade. Applying routine activities theory, Birks and Davies (2017) sought to examine the occurrence of residential burglaries when motivated offender agents found attractive targets in the absence of capable guardians. In short, the authors endeavoured to measure how systemic manipulation of street networks shapes crime patterns and the knock-on effects on the volume and distribution of property crime. Running different permutations of the simulation, Birks and Davies (2017) found support for routine activities theory in explaining burglaries but did not find a clear correlation between street permeability and crime. Agent-based modelling has been used in separate studies on hotspot policing conducted by Eck and Liu (2008), Groff and Birks (2008) and Weisburd et al. (2017). Each study simulated the impact of hotspot policing on burglaries based on different assumptions and found varying levels of crime reduction.

Malleson et al. (2014) used agent-based modelling to better understand burglaries in an urban setting. More specifically, the authors constructed an artificial city based in Leeds, United Kingdom, and a synthetic population to explore the main processes and drivers behind burglaries. In short, the model's results validated many of the hypotheses the authors proposed, providing a clear understanding of the processes behind burglaries and the most effective crime prevention strategies. A similar study by Zhu and Wang (2021) used census data and time geography to create an artificial population and city to simulate robberies in Baton Rouge, Louisiana. The authors replicated prominent robbery hotspots in the study area with various degrees of success, with target definitions and offender strategies having an outsize effect on model performance.

In a state-of-the-art literature review of all publications using ABM to simulate urban crime patterns, Groff et al. (2019) found 45 publications. The authors concluded that many publications lacked sufficient detail to enable replication as they did not disclose a rationale for modelling choices, parameter selection or calibration. Moreover, these parameters were rarely calibrated using empirical data. Nevertheless, Groff et al. (2019) did conclude that, despite the absence of plausible research, agent-based modelling offered great potential for criminological enquiry.

Criminal Networks and Agent-Based Modelling

When dealing with criminals, law enforcement officials are constantly playing a game of cat and mouse in which adaptations made by criminals force law enforcement to make counter-adaptations. This iterative game is particularly prominent within cyberspace, where innovation and progress are the norm (Wall, 2001). Nevertheless, this should not and does not stop law enforcement from testing new strategies for disrupting criminal activity and destabilising criminal networks. Law enforcement, while often slow in responding to emerging cyber threats, has increased its efforts to curtail these burgeoning threats. This is no different for cryptomarkets. According to Martin (2014), law enforcement organisations worldwide have undertaken several interventions to destabilise these illicit online marketplaces, including market infiltration, digital forensics, vendor arrests, mail scanning and market takedowns.

Of course, the principal dilemma facing law enforcement agencies tasked with combating cryptomarkets is where to target scarce resources. This is further complicated by the difficulties of the highly volatile cryptomarket environment. Indeed, the short lifecycle of these illicit marketplaces (Christin, 2013; Soska & Christin, 2015) makes investigating these entities particularly difficult, as a market may cease to exist before the investigation is completed. Furthermore, constantly improving security and encryption protocols compounds the difficulty of adequately policing these entities. According to Van Buskirk et al. (2014), "Administrators are heeding the lessons of prior market closures and are taking extra steps to fortify their sites against external penetration" (p. 54). In short, disrupting the ease of operation of cryptomarkets grows increasingly difficult, while the resources required for such undertakings remain scarce.

However, criminologists (McGloin & Rowan, 2015; Shaw & McKay, 1942; Warr, 2002) have increasingly observed that a large portion of criminal activity is group-based. Indeed, criminals often do not act alone but are embedded in a network of similarly motivated actors. To this extent, researchers have increasingly relied on social network theory and methods to understand the structure, operation and vulnerabilities of varying-sized criminal entities (Kennedy, 2008; McGloin, 2005; Papachristos, 2009, 2011, 2014). Indeed, a myopic focus on single individuals on the part of law enforcement is unlikely to bear fruit when combatting an association of actors. To this extent, a growing area of research examines how criminal networks respond to disruption (Duijn et al., 2014; Malm & Bichler, 2011; Morselli, 2009).

Consider the research by Krebs (2001), which documented the structural properties of the 9/11 terrorist attack. According to the author, the criminal network's extreme diffusion made it remarkably resilient to disruption. Indeed, any single actor could only incriminate a maximum of four other network members if identified and arrested. In contrast, Wood (2017), examining the structure of an international heroin trafficking network, found that the removal of 20% of all actors had a considerable disruptive effect on the network.

For the resilience and behaviour of a criminal network to be understood, researchers have turned to examining the topology of networks (Duxbury & Haynie, 2018). Indeed, the network structure will often determine how it responds to law enforcement intervention. Notably, the topology of a criminal network is often unique and is organised based on differences in security concerns and constraints on the efficient mobilisation of resources (Raab & Milward, 2003). No two criminal networks are the same. According to research from Morselli et al. (2007), drug distribution networks typically rely on a hierarchical network structure in which high-profile distributors insulate themselves from the brunt of the network activity by connecting to only a few actors. This ensures a certain level of protection, as constant exposure to other actors and elements within the network increases the likelihood of arrest.

This is not the same for all networks. Alternatively, research on social commerce networks by Diekmann et al. (2014) and Stephen and Toubia (2009) revealed that these networks are premised on preferential attachment. As such, these networks possess scale-free properties in which a few desirable, trusted actors retain many customers within the market. Such power law dynamics are not exceptionally reliable in the criminal context as scale-free criminal networks are more vulnerable to crippling targeted interventions given the presence of highly connected vertices. Research (Raab & Milward, 2003) suggests that criminal networks will often veer away from highly centralised topologies to ensure greater structural robustness when confronted with interventions against them.

However, this aversion to scale-free properties is not universal across all criminal networks, as some network topologies will naturally abide by power law dynamics. Indeed, preferential attachment is unavoidable in environments in which trust is scarce and difficult to establish. Past research demonstrates that skewed degree distributions are also a characteristic feature of criminal networks. Among cannabis cultivators, Duijn et al. (2014) present a pronounced power law distribution in which a small number of actors produced and traded a disproportionate amount of cannabis. In a similar study of a drug trafficking network, Natarajan (2006) discovered a small number of disproportionately high-degree traffickers among a large contingent of actors of low degree. This is similar to Varese's (2010) examination of a Russian Mafia group in Italy, which revealed a heavy-tailed degree distribution. As such, Varese concluded that the group was hierarchically structured and polycentric. While Krebs (2001) demonstrated that the 9/11 terror cell was a diffuse network, this is not the case for all terrorist networks. The degree distribution can vary considerably in a terrorist network. For example, Morselli et al. (2007) and Qin et al. (2005) found truncated power law distributions in the terrorism networks they examined.

Significantly, criminal organisations vary in their prioritisation of security or efficiency. Regarded as the security–efficiency trade-off (Morselli, 2009), the objectives of a criminal organisation might engender a focus on efficiency in the form of accomplishing a specific goal or security in the form of protecting the entity from detection and infiltration by law enforcement or other harmful actors. Moreover, one of these features comes at the cost of the other, as prioritising efficiency comes at the expense of security and vice versa. Crucially, for criminal organisations to be successful against law enforcement intervention, they must be flexible in their response to harmful stimuli by adjusting how they balance these two principles. Resilient criminal organisations can respond quickly and effectively to disruptions, enabling them to maintain illegal activities over time.

According to Newman (2002), removing a highly connected vertex often fractures the network into numerous distinct components. This reflects degree-mixing patterns that characterise scale-free networks (Newman, 2003). To elaborate, Alm and Mack (2017) contend that networks in which high-k actors are connected to low-k actors (degree mixing or disassortative mixing) are more susceptible to the disruptive impact of essential vertex removal relative to networks in which degree mixing does not occur (assortative mixing). Wood (2017) documented disassortative mixing in several drug distribution networks, corroborating Kennedy's (2008) contention that many real-world drug markets are highly susceptible to law enforcement intervention. As it relates to cryptomarkets, Barrattet al. (2016a, b) initially speculated that these online markets were subject to low disassortative mixing as many buyers reported experimenting with new products and vendors. Moreover, there is relatively less risk in purchasing goods and services through online markets.

Given the inherent difficulties associated with the procurement and cleanliness of criminal network datasets, studies on simulated law enforcement interventions are scarce relative to studies documenting the structure of criminal networks. Moreover, studies examining simulated interventions may not necessarily account for network adaption due to the security–efficiency trade-off. Duijn et al. (2014) observed that the pace of network recovery is a critical component of network resilience. Indeed, criminal networks are comprised of agentic actors with a rational incentive to maintain their network activity. To this extent, Morselli (2009) contended that the likelihood that criminal networks exhibit adaptive responses to disruption is high as actors wish to continue operations.

Criminal network structures are, indeed, known to be very complex systems. As Morselli (2009, p. 8) describes, "Criminal networks are not simply social networks operating in criminal contexts. The covert settings surrounding them call for specific interactions and relational features within and beyond the network". Nevertheless, unlike dark networks like terrorist rings, traditional criminal networks are generally action-oriented, preferring flexibility and agility in carrying out their operations over outright secrecy (Duijin et al., 2014); this complexity makes criminal networks a problematic area of study for researchers, particularly for those leveraging simulation-based methods.

When combining social network analysis and agent-based modelling to examine the expected effect of law enforcement interventions, it is essential to ensure that several key elements of research are present and accounted for. First, crime researchers leveraging this combination of methods must have an adequate data source that reflects reality. In this case, what is required is real-life criminal justice data as simulated or hypothetical data, while a potentially viable alternative has lower construct validity. Second, the researcher must select law enforcement interventions from which to test. This can range from simplistic strategies like sequential node deletion according to the centrality of actors to more complex techniques such as targeting agents that fulfil a critical operational role in the criminal organisation.

Third, simulation studies must specify outcome measures for network disruption and dismantlement. While this can vary depending on the network typology, outcome or performance measures examine the relative effectiveness of law enforcement interventions. Moreover, pre- and post-measures of dismantlement variables offer one approach to quantifying the efficacy of particular law enforcement strategies. Measures of dismantlement include number of isolates, number of components, average number of nodes in components, average geodesic distance and number of nodes in the most significant element. According to Duijin, Kashirin and Sloot (2014), there are three broad indicators of network destabilisation: "a reduction in the rate of information flow in the network, a reduction in the ability to conduct its tasks or a failure, or significant slowing down of the decision-making process" (p. 2).

Finally, researchers must consider network adaption processes following law enforcement intervention (Morselli et al., 2007; Bright & Delaney, 2013). It is essential to remember that criminal organisations are not static entities but dynamic collectives that change and adjust their typology and operation to account for interventions that seek to damage and dismantle them. Eilstrup-Sangiovanni and Jones (2008) note that "a fluid structure is said to provide networks with a host of advantages including adaptability, resilience, and capacity for rapid innovation and learning, and wide-scale recruitment" (p. 8). To this extent, criminal networks will replenish these losses, filling their depleted ranks by recruiting new members to replace arrested actors or to gain access to particular skills or knowledge.

Regardless, much can be gleaned from the studies that have evaluated simulated interventions against criminal networks. One such study by Keegan et al. (2010) contrasted the structural robustness of a drug trafficking network with a proxy gaming network. Applying k-based sequential node removal to each network, the authors observed that removing the top 5% of nodes based on degree centrality dismantled both networks. In contrast, the random removal of 5% of nodes failed to yield a comparable result. In short, Keegan et al. (2010) demonstrated the disruptive impact of k-degree removals in both licit and illicit networks. In contrast, Xu and Chen (2003) used a simulation methodology to examine terrorist, methamphetamine trafficking and gang networks. The authors concluded that targeting hubs and brokers was ineffective in disrupting the network's ease of operation. In contrast, strategies prioritising brokers' targeting proved more effective as these specific actors were responsible for keeping the network together. Together, these studies demonstrate that differences in the topology of a criminal network will yield different vulnerabilities that require various strategic interventions. Indeed, one targeting strategy will not be equally effective on all networks if their structural compositions differ.

Applying computer simulations to evaluate the impact of law enforcement interventions on two drug trafficking networks, Bright et al. (2014) focused on the removal of hubs. As with previous studies, the researchers found that removing key actors by law enforcement can create a relatively speedy structural collapse. Furthermore, Brightet al. (2017), investigating the effectiveness of six law enforcement intervention strategies against a drug market against three outcome measures, found that removing actors with betweenness centrality was the most effective strategy. This was followed by eliminating actors who made the most money.

Examining four criminal networks with varying network structures, Duxbury and Haynie (2019) applied agent-based modelling to evaluate how criminal networks respond to disruptions. The authors arrived at two important conclusions. First, "isolated law enforcement disruptions may be unsuccessful at reducing future crime levels in efficiency-oriented networks" (Duxbury & Haynie, 2019, p. 335). Second, disruption tends to yield time-persistent damage to a network prioritising security. This suggests that future law enforcement interventions should attack security-oriented criminal networks. Another study by Calderoni et al. (2022) used agent-based modelling to measure the effects of four policy scenarios on recruitment into organised crime groups: (1) targeting organised crime leaders, (2) targeting facilitators for imprisonment, (3) providing educational and welfare support to children and their mothers while separating them from organised crime fathers and (4) increasing educational and social support to at-risk schoolchildren. All the model's main parameters were based on data from Palermo or Sicily, with theories of peer effects (differential association, social learning), social embeddedness of organised crime and the general theory of crime being tested. The authors found that the model generated realistic outcomes, with all interventions reducing the total number of members, whereas all but primary socialisation reduced newly recruited members. Nevertheless, the intensity of the effects differed across dependent variables and models.

While it is imminently clear from Chap. 3 that extensive market closures are not the way forward, there is an open question as to what is. Scholars have increasingly focused on the network dynamics within cryptomarket transactional networks to understand their structural vulnerabilities. As with studies in this particular subfield, these studies seek to identify the structural vulnerabilities in a cryptomarket and the strategies that might best take advantage of these vulnerabilities. This is a potentially fruitful avenue of research as the results might inform strategic decision-making regarding cryptomarket interventions. Duxbury and Haynie (2018, 2019) have made the most progress in applying adaptive computer simulations to test the theoretical effect of law enforcement interventions on a cryptomarket transactional network.

Building off their prior work on the network structure of a cryptomarket, Duxbury and Haynie (2018) conducted disruption simulations on the same opioid market. In particular, the authors identified vendor selection patterns using exponential random graph models and evaluated the network's robustness using vertex removal simulations. Given that this opioid network was characterised by degree scaling properties under a preferential selection of vendors on the part of buyers, the size and scope of the market were reduced with the sequential removal of the top vendors therein. To this extent, the size of the most significant components shrank. In contrast, as more vendors were removed, the proportion of potential components and the number of isolates in the network decreased and increased. This study demonstrates two interrelated principles concerning the network structure of cryptomarkets. First, Duxbury and Haynie (2018) observe that the evidence of preferential attachment mechanisms "lends greater support to the influence of trust than the effect of product differentiation or affordability" (p. 246). Second, this trust can be exploited by interventions seeking to disrupt a cryptomarket's ease of operation. According to the authors (Duxbury & Haynie, 2018), "these results suggest that targeting any available combination of high-profile distributors may be an alternative strategy to leading distributor removal when leading distributors are difficult to isolate or identify" (p. 245). Consistent with research in drug distribution networks (Carley, 1995; Duijn et al., 2014; Wood, 2017), the authors found that removing the most prolific vendors sequentially fragmented the network in relatively little time.

In their second study, Duxbury and Haynie (2019) designed an agent-based simulation to assess the network responsiveness of a larger darknet drug market. The authors considered three attack strategies: (1) weak link attacks that delete large numbers of weakly connected vertices, (2) signal attacks that saturate the network with noisy signals and (3) targeted attacks that delete structurally integral vertices. The authors demonstrated that targeted attacks generally succeeded in disrupting the market when adopted at a large scale. The authors (Duxbury & Haynie, 2019) conclude that "these two processes undermine long-term network robustness and increase network vulnerability to future attacks". They also found that intentional attacks were generally more effective as actors grew more cautious about forging ties when the network was attacked. Under these conditions, network robustness was undermined in the long term.

Given the nature of adaptive computer simulations, it is essential to emphasise that these results should not be accepted dogmatically. Scholars leveraging adaptive computer simulations are merely making educated guesses on the assumed rational behaviour of actors in a criminal network. Therefore, modelling parameters are based on these assumptions. Whether cryptomarket actors behave in this manner is another matter altogether. In short, while adaptive computer simulations go some way towards identifying structural vulnerabilities in cryptomarkets, they should not be accepted as the complete truth. The behaviour of licit actors, much less criminal, cannot be perfectly simulated given the probabilistic nature of human behaviour. While general patterns in human behaviour are observable, strict obedience to these patterns will differ from actor to actor.

Regardless, the results of these studies are promising for designing effective law enforcement strategies to combat cryptomarkets. Adaptive rule-based sequential node removal somehow mimics the operation of a cryptomarket when pressurised by a targeted intervention. Law enforcement might find use in applying this methodological technique when deciding which actors to take and how removing these actors might affect the overall structure and operation of the market. However, there is a pressing need for more studies that simulate law enforcement interventions in real-world cryptomarket transactional networks to evaluate the impact of specific targeting strategies. In particular, such studies should test the efficacy of individual targeting strategies, determining their ability to disrupt the operation of a cryptomarket and how this performance stacks up against other targeting methods. Furthermore, these studies must incorporate some form of network adaption to mimic the purported behaviour of actors when the market is disrupted. Given that criminal networks are comprised of human actors whose behaviour is liable to change in the face of an attack, studies that leverage computer simulations to understand the impact of strategic interventions must consider probable adaptation on the part of actors within the network.

Designing an Agent-Based Model to Test the Disruption of a Dark Web Marketplace

By their orientation in a network, the behaviour of each node is dependent on the behaviour of every other node within the network (Bright et al., 2017). Just because two nodes are unconnected does not necessarily mean they do not affect one another in some capacity. Indeed, downstream effects are plausible (Newman, 2003) as the removal or inclusion of new nodes changes the dynamic of a network and, by extension, the behaviour of the actors within it (Namatame & Chen, 2016). Criminal networks comprise individual actors whose mutual relationships strengthen or dissipate when internal and external stimuli are added to the network. Thus, criminal networks are not static entities. The structure of a network may change based on the behaviour of the actors within it. This fact cannot be ignored when examining the efficacy of interventions on criminal networks. These considerations are, moreover, important when designing an agent-based model.

For law enforcement organisations, agent-based models represent a novel means of testing their hypotheses about the behaviour of criminal networks and the actors within them. Furthermore, agent-based models represent a cheap, low-risk method of identifying vulnerabilities and potentially disrupting criminal networks in an age of increasing austerity and public scrutiny. Nevertheless, the effective use of agent-based models hinges on two elements: (1) the use of real-world data from which the efficacy of models can be measured and (2) accurate a priori observations about the rules that govern the behaviour of actors and the structure of the environment they interact within. Beyond this, law enforcement officials' adoption of agent-based models will fundamentally rest on the openness of police leaders to incorporate computer simulations into their investigative repertoire. This is perhaps the most pernicious element preventing the widespread use of agent-based models within policing.

This chapter delves into the intricacies of designing an agent-based model. More specifically, it will develop a model that tests the effectiveness of several law enforcement strategies against a criminal network. To do this, this chapter first examines the fundamental principles of designing an agent-based model to disrupt illegal networks. Particular attention is paid to the processes and rationale of prior criminological studies that have designed agent-based models for the disruption of criminal networks. Following this, the principal research questions guiding the design of the agent agent-based model are discussed. These research questions will also have some associated hypotheses from which the model will be accessed. This chapter will then examine the overarching analytic design of the model.

Designing an Agent-Based Model

Agent-based models are a helpful method for testing theoretical suppositions and measuring the effectiveness of policies. In this regard, Groff et al. (2019) note that approximately 40% of criminological studies utilising agent-based models examined policy, while the other 60% explored theory. The authors noted that "Policy-focused publications tended to examine policing-related topics. Over half modelled different patrol strategies such as random, directed hotspots and problem-oriented policing. ABM's standard practice is to use theory as a foundation for selecting the agent sample and the behavioural rules used" (Groff et al., 2019, p. 167). Routine activities theory (Cohen & Felson, 1979) was mentioned in 58% of studies concerning the theories used as the basis for agent behaviour in models. In contrast, crime pattern theory (Brantingham & Brantingham, 1984) and rational choice theory (Clarke & Cornish, 1985) were mentioned in 29% and 27% of the studies reviewed, respectively (Groff et al., 2019). Social disorganisation or collective efficacy was used in models in 20% of the publications, while near-repeat victimisation informed 9% of publications.

As is apparent from these results, criminological studies differ in how agent-based models are designed and applied. Nevertheless, most studies use opportunity theories to structure and define agents' behaviour. While the theoretical bases of these models might differ, so too do their parameter calibration strategies and their use of empirical data. Here, it is considered how an agent-based model might be designed for measuring crime reduction, with a thematic focus on the simulated disruption of criminal organisations. It is important to note that agent-based models cannot incorporate all the factors that might influence agents' decisions and activities in the real world. There is, therefore, a preference for parsimony in model building.

> Additionally, models incorporate stochastic effects either to model random factors that might influence crime pattern formation, such as the presence of a bystander at a given time or to model uncertainty in agent decision-making. Since this stochasticity will mean that model results vary from one run to the next, an important question concerns if and how modellers assess the consistency of model outcomes across simulation runs and how they determine the number of runs necessary to produce stable estimates and draw conclusions. (Groff et al., 2019, 172)

A fundamental element of designing a robust agent-based model is determining the number of times a model will be run. Simply running a model once does not guarantee that the results will accurately describe the phenomenon under observation. To this extent, model builders should strive to run their model multiple times and then determine the average results from the aggregated runs. The number of runs has implications for processing time as more runs of a model increase the time of model completion. According to Groff et al. (2019), 44% of the criminological publications they examined reported using between 11 and 100 runs, with only 9% reporting more than 100 runs. Notably, 27% of publications did not disclose the number of runs, and 76% of publications did not explain the number of runs. As the number of runs is vitally essential for contending with the stochasticity of agent-based models, it is crucial to explain why a specific number of runs were selected.

Deciding what sort of model to design in the first place is as important as determining how many times a model should be run. Gilbert (2008) summarises two model types by their specific aims. First, "middle-range agent-based models simulate particular social behaviour such as committing a specific type of crime, or offender targeting strategies" (Gilbert, 2008, p. 176). In these models, specific locations are not used, but landscapes are applied to implement the model, with empirical data informing the characteristics of agents and the stylistic patterns of crime. Second, facsimile models "exactly match a particular location in the real world and rely upon specific empirical data for calibration and validation" (Gilbert, 2008, p. 176). One of the outstanding challenges of building an agent-based model for crime is the model validation process when a crime is under-reported or unreported. As such, there does not exist an accurate baseline with which to compare the results of agent-based models of crime (Eck & Liu, 2008). In this case, crime modellers (Birks et al., 2012, 2014; Eck & Liu, 2008; Groff, 2007; Wang et al., 2014) lacking empirical data will validate their model by comparing patterns in model outcomes to stylistic patterns that are widely recognised in the empirical data. While this is not necessarily ideal, it is a viable option.

That said, modellers often use agent-based models to test assumptions and measure outcomes when they know little about overarching patterns and there is no empirical data.

> This is because ABM offers the researcher a way of systematically testing theories in silico for which (nonlinear) complex interactions and feedback loops would be difficult or impossible to anticipate in thought experiments, or where primary data collection is impractical. (Groff et al., 2019)

To this extent, Groff et al. (2019) found that 38% of criminological publications used empirical data to validate their models, while 33% and 24% of publications used stylised distributions and theoretical distributions, respectively.

In one study that sought to test the structural robustness of a cryptomarket transactional network, Duxbury and Haynie (2018) applied a sequential node deletion or k-based removal process in which vendors were arranged in descending order based on the number of buyers they possessed. The researchers noted that "decreasing k is ideal for examining drug market disruption because most enforcement agencies seek to prosecute high-profile offenders" (Duxbury & Haynie, 2018, p. 240). Notably, the researchers tested the disruptive impact of five interventions: (1) betweenness centrality, (2) degree centrality, (3) cut-set, (4) actors who possess money and (5) actors who possess precursor chemicals. These five interventions are compared with each other and with random (opportunistic) removal of actors in two settings: (1) with network adaptation incorporated into the simulations and (2) without network adaptation.

Moreover, Duxbury and Haynie (2018) assessed the impact of each vendor removal as the number of components remaining in the graph, the size of the largest component and the number of remaining isolates. This captures the number of elements split from the largest component, how each removal impacts the size of the most significant element and the count of isolated buyers with each split. Duxbury and Haynie (2018) expand this method further by identifying all vendors with a degree centrality of 50 or higher in their weighted network. These vendors were removed in all possible triadic combinations to evaluate the average impact on the overall network. This method offers insight into the potential impact of coordinated law enforcement efforts against high-profile distributors. To determine how vendors situated over structural holes impact the network, the researchers compared the results of these calculations to the triadic removal of vendors that broker structural holes.

In another study utilising agent-based modelling to simulate the disruption of a dark network, Bright (2015) examined the efficacy of four law enforcement strategies: (1) sequential removal of the nodes that ranked highest in degree centrality, (2) sequential removal of nodes that played critical functional roles in the network, (3) sequential removal of nodes based partly on centrality scores and partly on the roles played by actors and (4) the random removal of nodes. Bright (2015) measured the impact of these strategies in two ways: (1) counting the number of nodes in the largest component and (2) counting the number of nodes in the largest remaining connected component in combination with a measure of these nodes' role-based importance in the network. This methodology assessed each actor's relative importance in the criminal network, gauging their roles and responsibilities. The researchers used weight as a proxy for the importance of the role and for the difficulty an illicit network might encounter if they needed to replace a lost node.

Based on previous research (Bright et al., 2017), strategies for criminal network disruption can be divided into two categories: the network approach and the human capital approach. The network approach focuses on individual actors that occupy strategic positions within criminal networks (Sparrow, 1991; Schwartz & Rouselle, 2008). These predominantly revolve around common centrality measurements such as degree centrality, betweenness centrality and eccentricity. Because high scores across these metrics are associated with better access to resources, these actors are related to influential and powerful positions within social networks.

> Since they are important for the flow of information and resources throughout the network, these actors are called hubs. Hubs have a major influence on overall network structure; networks that gravitate around a few hubs, for instance, are defined as 'scale-free' (centralised) networks. (Duijn et al., 2014, p. 2 s).

In economics, human capital encompasses "the competencies, knowledge, social and personality attributes, including creativity, embodied in the ability to perform labour to produce economic value" (Duijin et al., 2014, p. 4236). In the context of illegal markets, human capital is assembled and integrated in the form of trust. However, this might also come in the form of an actor's specific business process or role, which translates to some value brought to the overall network. This value is represented by specialised skills and knowledge that make an actor invaluable to the operation to the point where their loss would hamper the fluid operation of the criminal enterprise or organisation.

The forthcoming sections will detail some primary methodological elements of designing an agent-based model. More specifically, the Abraxas transactional network from Chap. 4 will be utilised as the operative example of simulated interventions against a cryptomarket.

Research Questions

Before an agent-based model is designed, it is crucial to consider the research questions that will guide its overall purpose and design. Indeed, regardless of the methodology or analytical design, research questions are a vital element that gives structure to a research project. Moreover, research questions might also merge with the extant scholarly literature, offering new insights into aspects of a topic that has not been extensively explored, or remains entirely unexplored. To this extent, this chapter proposes three research questions that will guide the development of the agent-based model:

1. Which of the six proposed disruption strategies offers the most significant initial damage to the Abraxas transactional network?
2. For which of the first 100 nodes that are removed from each disruption strategy does the impact carry over across all outcome measures?
3. What do these strategies tell us about the efficacy of dark web disruption strategies?

Given the absence of research on this topic, scholars and law enforcement are generally uncertain about the measurable impact of cryptomarket disruption strategies. The effectiveness of cryptomarket intervention strategies is an area in which knowledge is lacking (Shortis et al., 2020). While Duxbury and Haynie (2020) have applied sequential node removal to one cryptomarket, it is unclear how generalisable these findings are. As criminal networks are adaptive and dynamic, different disruption strategies will likely yield different results. When it comes to cryptomarkets, it is unclear which strategies work and which ones do not. The first and second research questions will address this critical gap in the scholarly literature, comparing and contrasting the effectiveness of six different disruption strategies across five impact measurements. As such, the explicit focus of this research is not on the structural robustness of cryptomarket transactional networks but on the efficacy of strategic interventions that might be used against these networks.

This expands on Duxbury and Haynie's (2020) study, which leveraged three intervention strategies (high k vendors, low k buyers and vendor rating) across three impact measurements (number of ties, number of transactions and network density). To this extent, the objective was to utilise agent-based modelling to determine which strategies are most effective across a single outcome and all measures. In addition, this represents a novel opportunity to identify inherent differences in each strategic intervention. Indeed, it may be the case that, while each strategy possesses a different targeting objective, they may target the same actors within the network. As a result, these interventions, while purported to be strategically distinct, are functionally similar, if not identical.

The third research question seeks to leverage the findings of the first and second research questions to speculate on the overall efficacy of law enforcement interventions. The structure of a criminal network naturally lends itself to generating disruption strategies. In short, this question evaluates how different unlawful network disruption strategies might affect the immediate and long-term impact of dark web criminal networks. Network activity in the aftermath of disruption provides insight into how criminal organisations behave in unstable environments. Social network theory and analysis are ideally suited to understanding how disruption efforts affect crime groups' behaviour, coordination and recovery time. Moreover, combined social network analysis and computer simulations overcome the well-known methodological and data collection problems of examining dark networks (Bright & Delaney, 2013; Bright et al., 2018; Morselli, 2009; Wood, 2017). Thus, in addition to making theoretical advancements in understanding organised crime and informing criminal intelligence, this question will also provide methodological contributions, demonstrating the utility of computational methods and social network analysis in understanding criminological phenomena.

Based on these three research questions, this chapter proposes a series of ancillary hypotheses that are linked to the use of agent-based modelling:

H1: Reputation and total purchase price targeting will be the most effective targeting strategies across all outcome metrics.

H2: Random targeting will be the least effective targeting strategy.

H3: Several targeting strategies will perform similarly, indicating the interchangeability of targeting strategies.

H4: The impact of removing the first 100 nodes carries over to all outcome measures for all targeting strategies.

Data and Methods

Again, a buyer–seller dataset from the Abraxas cryptomarket is used (Branwen et al., 2015). Apart from the anonymous cryptomarket analysed by Duxbury and Haynie (2019), this is the only marketplace in which unique identifiers are available for buyers. From the 5434 illicit transactions, a single two-mode network featuring vendors and buyers was created. Vendors were identified based on their unique vendor name, while buyers were identified based on their HTML code. The transactional network comprised 5434 pairs, with 269 vendors and 2794 individual buyers. This analysis used directed ties.

Table 5.1 presents the descriptive network statistics of Abraxas' transactional network. First, the network is diffuse with a network density of 0.0007. As such, only 0.07% of all possible transactions occurred. Furthermore, the complete network consists of 29 components, with one component containing 97.6% (2726) of

Table 5.1 Network
characteristics

Network characteristics	Mean (SD) or total	Range
Unique actors/nodes	2794	–
Unique vendors	269	–
Unique buyers	2525	–
Isolates	0	–
Total unique edges	3935	–
Density	0.0007	–
In-degree	2.15 (2.2)	1–34
Out-degree	20.2 (39)	1–330
In-degree centralisation	0.01	–
Out-degree centralisation	0.12	–
Eccentricity (all)	11.23 (1.9)	1–16
Eccentricity (vendors)	10.32 (3.38)	1–15
Eccentricity (buyers)	11.33 (1.64)	1–16

all nodes within the network. The remaining connected components consisted of 19 dyads, seven triads and single assortments of components of various sizes. As expected, there are no isolates, as a transaction must involve both a buyer and a vendor. Based on the eccentricity measurement, nodes within the Abraxas transactional network have an average distance of 11.23 from one another. Comparable mean values can also be observed for vendors (10.32) and buyers (11.33).

Research into the disruption of criminal networks has posited several methods of reducing the ease of operation of these networks. In curbing the network activity of a drug market, Kennedy (2008) advocates for a "focus deterrence" strategy that simultaneously removes multiple influential criminals in a single stroke. This is done to reduce the likelihood of a resultant power vacuum by removing the actors most responsible for activity within a network. This method of targeting the most influential actors is challenged by methods that maintain that network disruption is best achieved by targeting brokers within the network (Burt, 2000). These brokers bridge structural gaps in a network, connecting segments via the maintenance of pathways. This is particularly important for strategies targeting gangs because a more significant disruptive impact may be achieved if actors spanning local network clusters are targeted for removal. Indeed, this strategy posits the targeting of connectors as opposed to distributors.

Based on numerous studies examining real and hypothetical law enforcement interventions (Morselli, 2009; Wood, 2017; Alm & Mack, 2017; Duxbury & Haynie, 2020), the most common method of testing the structural robustness of a network is to "remove vertices in descending order of magnitude and to measure the proportion of network features as a function of the actor's removal" (Duxbury & Haynie, 2018, p. 245). Importantly, this chapter does not endeavour to measure the structural robustness of Abraxas but rather the efficacy of proposed strategic interventions that target the actors therein. Nevertheless, this method can also be applied to measure the efficacy of strategic interventions. Furthermore, this research deviates from other studies (Duxbury & Haynie, 2018, 2020) measuring cryptomarket intervention. It places each targeting strategy into two categories for disrupting criminal networks: network and human capital.

This study employs sequential node deletion according to six law enforcement strategies: lead k (degree centrality), eccentricity, unique items bought/sold, cumulative reputation score, total purchase price and random targeting. Mirroring Bright et al. (2017), each strategy is premised on law enforcement's hypothesised aims and falls under either a social or human capital approach. Each targeting strategy begins with all 2794 actors within the network and then deletes one node at a time based on the strategic objective of the intervention. Isolates are then given the choice of rejoining the network before calculating the output measures. This simulation strategy was selected due to its successful use by Bright et al. (2017) and Gilbert and Troitzsch (2005). The six targeting strategies are as follows:

1. Random targeting: Targets are selected at random regardless of their role in the market. This targeting strategy possesses no overt strategic objective. It is premised on opportunistic intervention

   Interventions that target only network capital:

2. Degree centrality targeting: Lead k actors are removed in descending order. These are the actors within Abraxas with the highest number of trade partners. This is a fairly standard measurement by which network-based node removal is conducted.
3. Eccentricity targeting: Nodes in the network will be removed based on their distance from a specific node to any other node. Eccentricity measures the maximum distance of one node to any other node in the network. As such, the eccentricity of a node in a connected network is the maximum distance between that node and another over all nodes in the network.

   Interventions that target only human capital:

4. Unique items bought/sold targeting: Nodes are removed based on the number of unique items bought or sold by an actor

   Total purchase price targeting: Nodes are removed based on an actor's total revenue generated or spent.

   Reputation targeting: Deletions are based on the cumulative reputation score of actors.

   Finally, the five outcome variables used to assess the efficacy of each strategy are:

1. Mean geodesic distance in the network.
2. Number of nodes in the most significant components of the networks.
3. Average number of nodes in components.
4. Number of components.
5. Number of isolates.

The first outcome variable examines the mean of the shortest path lengths between any two actors in the network. Smaller mean geodesic distances indicate that information and resources can travel more quickly throughout the network, promoting criminal activity. Thus, increases in mean geodesic distances indicate more significant network damage. The second, third and fourth variables measure network hierarchy and actors' integration into a centralised organisation. Thus, they provide a measure of hierarchical network cohesion, in which decreases in the size of the most significant component, the average number of nodes in components and the number of components reflect more substantial network damage. The fifth variable measures the market fragmentation based on the number of nodes without a tie. As the number of isolates increases, the network grows more fragmented and is generally less capable of achieving its organisational goals as a cohesive unit.

It is, nevertheless, essential to clarify differences between this simulation strategy and those pursued in other studies measuring the impact of interventions on cryptomarkets. Duxbury and Haynie (2019) leveraged three intervention strategies in their first study of a dark web opioid network: (1) high k vendors, (2) low k buyers and (3) vendor rating. The impact of these interventions was measured across three impact measurements: the number of ties, the number of transactions and network density. In their second study, Duxbury and Haynie (2020) used three attack strategies: (1) weak link attacks that delete large numbers of weakly connected vertices, (2) signal attacks that saturate the network with noisy signals and (3) targeted attacks that delete structurally integral vertices. These interventions were measured across the number of ties, network density and number of isolates within the network.

While this study shares some targeting strategies (lead k and vendor reputation) and outcome measurements (number of isolates) with the studies mentioned earlier, it provides a broader array of targeting strategies and outcome measurements that have not been attempted. Therefore, this study offers a more in-depth look at the efficacy of cryptomarket targeting strategies, building upon prior research by more closely examining each targeting strategy's relative and comparative impact. This adaptive simulation strategy qualifies as the most extensive within the scholarly literature on cryptomarkets. Moreover, network and human capital frameworks add a more rounded analytical focus, segmenting the targeting strategies based on a higher-order functional objective premised on network position or human competency. This has not been attempted in previous cryptomarket simulation studies.

Like Bright et al. (2017) and Gilbert and Troitzsch (2005), 100 simulation iterations for each target strategy were performed. Each outcome measure is then averaged over the 100 runs to produce plots of the average value over time (Birks & Davies, 2017; Birks et al., 2012; Groff et al., 2019; Weisburd et al., 2017). One hundred runs were chosen as they represent standard practice in the design of agent-based models and are not computationally tasking.

Network Adaptation Procedures

Real-world data on criminal networks are typically drawn from captured networks, rendering observations of the network before and after disruption almost impossible (Bright et al., 2018; Morselli, 2009). Sequential node deletion simulations must incorporate network adaption and preferential selection processes that are premised on some basic truth. Following Bright et al.'s (2017) adaptation procedure, network adaptation was modelled by allowing the network to replace an actor that was removed due to sequential node deletion. In this study, it is assumed that replacement actors should possess three necessary characteristics: (1) the same product bought/sold as the deleted actor, (2) the same shipped to/from location as the deleted actor and (3) the highest possible reputation score of all eligible replacements. While the first two characteristics were chosen purely out of common-sense logistical reasoning, as buyers will purchase a specific product from a vendor relative to them, the third characteristic requires further explanation.

Like Clearnet markets, cryptomarkets employ an evaluation system by which purchases are ranked with visible comments from each buyer (Resnick & Zeckhauser, 2002; Van Der Heide et al., 2013). That is, vendor reputations are established by consumers who are encouraged by administrators to provide publicly available feedback on their experience with a vendor. Hardy and Norgaard (2016) use data from Silk Road to study the relationship between reputation and prices and to show that investment in reputation provides a premium to entrepreneurs. Online black markets manage to alleviate moral hazards predominantly because negative feedback leads to sales reductions. In short, providing buyers with the opportunity to air their grievances and praise vendors of whom they approve helps the overall health of a dark market. Finally, Armona (2017) measured the impact of informal communication (through forum discussions) in anonymous marketplaces and found evidence that product demand grows as the number of messages grows.

Janetos and Tilly (2017) show that a mature, highly rated cryptomarket vendor charges 20% higher than an adult, low-rated vendor. Vendors with more reviews charge a higher price than sellers with fewer reviews, regardless of rating. As such, it is speculated that vendors with a more extended and more successful transactional history are more likely to cash in on this history. In other words, reputable vendors can exercise their brand to profit more significantly on future transactions than vendors without a history of successful exchanges. However, bad (i.e. low-ranked) sellers prefer to exit the market than decrease their prices in response to negative feedback.

This is similar to the findings of Batikas and Kretschmer (2018), who, studying the Agora marketplace, found that cryptomarket vendors are likelier to exit following negative feedback. Therefore, receiving negative feedback early on in a vendor's career can reduce their chances of continued operation in a market. Negative feedback stands out more when it is not situated amidst positive feedback. Once a vendor is marked as untrustworthy, it is difficult to change because buyers will not take the risk of doing business with a vendor without a proven track record for reputable economic transactions. Furthermore, a vendor's accumulated transaction experience on the platform negatively moderates market exit as a longer transactional history is correlated with continued market participation.

Finally, Przepiorka et al. (2017) use longitudinal data from Silk Road to determine the extent to which buyers consider sellers' reputations when making purchasing decisions. The authors conclude that "vendors react to changes in their reputation by adjusting the prices of their goods, with well-reputed vendors reaping market benefits by increasing prices" (Przepiorka et al., 2017, p. 39). The authors also found that vendors with higher ratings were more successful in selling goods. Again, successful cryptomarket vendors can leverage their reputation to create more transactions at higher prices in the future. From this research, it is imminently clear that vendor reputation constitutes a critical factor in buyer decision-making.

Each of these replacement criteria was weighed the same. In other words, replacement actors must match the base-level profile of the deleted actor while also possessing a relatively high level of trustworthiness so that surrounding nodes would comfortably do business with them. Once a node had been removed in each sequential deletion, the first step was identifying how many nodes were isolated due to the deletion. Second, a single replacement node in the network with the above three replacement characteristics was identified. Isolates were then allowed to reconnect to the network via the specified replacement node. Notably, the reconnection probability was set to 0.5, indicating that the isolate had a 50% reconnection probability. All told, the network would replace an actor who was removed with the most suitable candidate. The isolate did not rejoin the network if there was no suitable candidate.

This adaptation process is based on network redundancy. Redundancy, in this case, refers to the number of relationships between network actors. Notably, the more redundancy in a network, the more viable options for replacing lost human capital. In short, replacements in Abraxas with a reliable reputation and suitable shipping country and product listing will serve as replacements if similar actors are deleted from the market. Key to this is information asymmetry, which is modelled in some respect.

Criminal and lawful markets are often plagued by information asymmetry whereby buyers' and sellers' knowledge about goods and services is not uniform. This can lead to a market for substandard goods in which consumers possess less valid or reliable information about the quality of the goods relative to vendors. According to Herley and Florêncio (2009), the uncertainty created by low-quality vendors imposes a tax on every transaction conducted in the market. That is, high-quality vendors stand to make less, as the presence of low-quality vendors discourages buyers from engaging in transactions and drives down the price of goods and services. This general uncertainty created by the presence of bad-faith vendors imposes a tax on every transaction conducted in the market.

According to Thomaz et al. (2020), "Cryptomarkets consist of two tiers of players: experts with more information, and newcomers who not only have less information but also do not know how to weigh sources of information and reputational cues properly". This creates a fascinating situation in which these naïve players abide by the rules established by knowledgeable players, while those knowledgeable players put little to no trust in others. Moreover, the knowledgeable actors benefit from new market entrants who are naïve and do not understand the market conditions. A market will disintegrate without trust, but trust must first be predicated on spreading information about who is trustworthy. In essence, trust is predicated on information, whether naïve or competent. Indeed, buyers on Abraxas must accumulate enough evidence to convince themselves of the likelihood of a positive outcome: that they are likely to get what they paid for and not get their money stolen or be arrested for their activities. Therefore, entire narratives are created around the trustworthiness of specific vendors.

To this extent, finalising early and the Pollyanna principle are possible features of healthy information flows on Abraxas, resulting in a lack of information asymmetry. To this extent, the predominance of five-rated transactions is possibly due to the singling out of trustworthy and reputable vendors through a natural process of selection and elimination. Therefore, information on a vendor is created by past buyers who either applaud or chastise their respective transactions with the said vendor. Indeed, a prospective buyer's knowledge and desire to transact with a vendor is based on what previous buyers have suggested. This is an information cascade whereby buyers' preference for a particular vendor is compounded across multiple transactions.

Functionally, these information cascades minimise information asymmetry on Abraxas as buyers know which vendors are reputable. In contravention of information asymmetry, this level of certainty created by the presence of reputable vendors would not impose a tax on every transaction conducted on the market. Buyers and vendors can transact in a reasonably transparent and collegial manner. Buyers are perhaps less likely to be afflicted by the fear of fraud or duplicity by vendors. As such, in cryptomarkets like Abraxas, buyers are more likely to have a pleasant experience than in terrestrial markets with fewer checks and balances that mitigate fraudulent vendor activity. This might explain the Pollyanna principle on Abraxas, in which most transactions receive a five-star rating. Indeed, given the abundance of five-star ratings on the market, buyers are simply reporting on their pleasant experiences on cryptomarkets relative to less enjoyable experiences on terrestrial markets, rather than inflating their scores.

Results

Below, the results of the agent-based model are examined. In particular, each of the research questions proposed earlier is examined, with the results being carefully parsed out. Each targeting strategy's baseline results are examined across all outcome measurements. The results of single node deletion under each targeting strategy and outcome measure carry-over and node characteristics are explored. Finally, the results are discussed, outlining the implications of each targeting strategy and the overarching impact of law enforcement interventions against cryptomarkets.

This chapter demonstrates to practitioners how their results might be structured and what measurements to consider in determining the value of the results of their agent-based model.

Baseline Simulation Results

Table 5.1 displays the results of all six simulated interventions across the five outcome measures. To facilitate comparisons across law enforcement strategies, the five outcome measures are plotted on five separate graphs: number of active components (Fig. 5.1a), number of isolates (Fig. 5.1b), average number of nodes in components (Fig. 5.1c), number of nodes in most significant component (Fig. 5.1d) and average geodesic distance (Fig. 5.1e). All five plots show the results of simulations in which network adaptation is included. For each plot, the x-axis indicates the number of steps performed, operationalised as the number of nodes deleted sequentially. At each step, one actor is removed. The y-axis reflects the specific outcome measure featured in the simulation.

Table 5.2 demonstrates the impact of deleting a single node per intervention across all outcome measurements. Based on the number of isolates and components, it is readily apparent that eccentricity and random targeting are the least effective targeting strategies, producing the lowest average results per deleted node. Interestingly, degree centrality, reputation, total purchasing price and unique items bought/sold each performed similarly across these two measurements. While the average is exceptionally stable for each targeting strategy across the average number of nodes in components, the number of nodes in the largest component and the average geodesic distance, clear differences are apparent based on the standard deviation and range. Again, eccentricity and random targeting are the least effective at disrupting the transactional network. Furthermore, degree centrality, reputation, total purchasing price and unique items bought each perform similarly across these three measures, offering tremendous disruption per node deleted. Nevertheless, a closer look at the speed of disruption for each targeting strategy across the five measures is warranted.

Regarding the number of components, the maximal effect is measured as the highest number of components created on intervention. In short, if the intervention is successful, node deletion should yield a sizable increase in the number of components within the network (see Fig. 5.1a). An increase in the number of components reflects network fragmentation and disruption of information flow. Upon closer examination, it is evident that degree centrality targeting yielded the fastest speed (by the narrowest margins) of relative disruption. Deleting 251 nodes (9% of all nodes) produced 2310 total components, a 7866% increase from the original 29 components. In comparison, reputation targeting yielded 2312 components after 244 nodes were deleted, while total purchasing price targeting and unique items bought/sold resulted in 1948 and 2061 components after 288 and 422 nodes were deleted, respectively. Perhaps unsurprisingly, random targeting yielded a high of

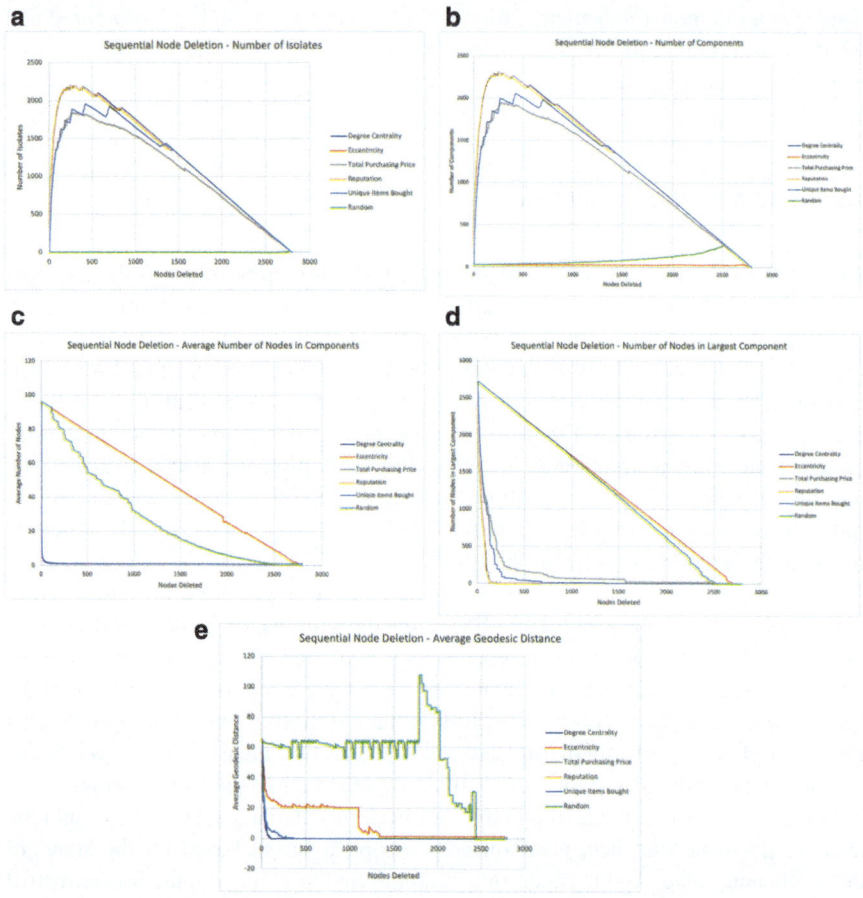

Fig. 5.1 Sequential node deletion (**a**) Number of components (**b**) Number of isolates (**c**) Average number of nodes in components (**d**) Number of nodes in largest component (**e**) Average geodesic distance

269 components once 2525 nodes were deleted. Curiously, eccentricity offered the least disruption with a high of 38 components once 2702 (96.7%) nodes were deleted.

Concerning the number of isolates, the maximal effect is measured as the highest number created upon intervention (see Fig. 5.1b). Reputation targeting appears to be the most effective strategy, as deleting the top 299 nodes (10.7%) yielded 2202 isolates within the network. Degree centrality targeting offered the second fastest disruption, producing 2201 isolates when the top 300 nodes were deleted. In this case, both strategies provided nearly identical results. Total purchasing price targeting and unique items bought/sold targeting created the third and fourth fastest

Table 5.2 Impact of single node deletions by strategy and outcome

Measures	Initial value	Mean	SD	Range
Isolates[a]				
Degree centrality[b]	0	1.77	4.46	0–91
Eccentricity[b]	0	0.03	0.18	0–3
Random[b]	0	0.03	0.18	0–3
Reputation[b]	0	1.77	4.46	0–91
Total purchasing price[b]	0	1.7	4.52	0–91
Unique items bought[b]	0	1.67	4.52	0–90
Components [a]				
Degree centrality[b]	29	1.76	4.58	0–91
Eccentricity[b]	29	0.02	0.16	0–3
Random[b]	29	0.18	0.45	0–5
Reputation[b]	29	1.75	4.58	0–91
Total purchasing price[b]	29	1.69	4.64	0–91
Unique items bought[b]	29	1.66	4.63	0–90
Average number of nodes in components [a]				
Degree centrality[b]	96.35	0.04	1.35	0–70.48
Eccentricity[b]	96.35	0.04	0.06	0–2.72
Random[b]	96.35	0.04	0.16	0–3.12
Reputation[b]	96.35	0.04	1.35	0–70.48
Total purchasing price[b]	96.35	0.04	1.35	0–70.48
Unique items bought[b]	96.35	0.04	1.36	0–71.41
Average geodesic distance [a]				
Degree centrality[b]	64.62	0.04	0.63	0–30.45
Eccentricity[b]	64.62	0.05	0.38	0–12.44
Random[b]	64.62	0.2	1.56	0–43.24
Reputation[b]	64.62	0.04	0.63	0–30.45
Total purchasing price[b]	64.62	0.04	0.51	0–23.24
Unique items bought[b]	64.62	0.04	0.51	0–23.24
Number of nodes in largest component [a]				
Degree centrality[b]	2726	0.98	6.47	0–169
Eccentricity[b]	2726	0.98	0.59	0–27
Random[b]	2726	0.98	1.31	0–39
Reputation[b]	2726	0.98	6.34	0–159
Total purchasing price[b]	2726	0.98	5.65	0–102
Unique items bought[b]	2726	0.98	6.11	0–117

[a]Indicates outcome measure; [b]Indicates targeting strategy

disruptions, respectively. Total purchasing price yielded a high of 1841 isolates after 288 nodes were deleted, while unique items bought/sold yielded 1559 isolates after 422 were removed. Eccentricity and random targeting offered the same maximal disruption, with 19 isolates created after 2765 nodes were deleted. These are particularly poor showings.

The average number of nodes in a component reflects the average size of components within the network. As such, maximal disruption is premised around reductions in the average number of component nodes. The smaller the components, the more fragmented the transactional network. Based on rank-order vertex removal simulations, the size of components plummets as the number of nodes is removed. This is particularly the case for degree centrality targeting, total purchasing price targeting, reputation targeting and unique items bought/sold targeting following a similar pattern (see Fig. 5.1c). Degree centrality targeting yielded the fastest disruption, with 44 (1.6%) node deletions reducing the average component size to 1.99 nodes (a 97.9% reduction from the original 96.35 average). Similarly, reputation targeting yielded nearly identical disruption as the rank-ordered deletion of 47 nodes reduced the average number of nodes within components to under two. To reduce the average number of nodes to 1.99, 70 and 71 nodes must be deleted for total purchasing price and unique items bought/sold, respectively. Random and eccentricity targeting yielded the slowest disruption, requiring the random deletion of 2381 (85.2%) and eccentricity-based deletion of 2938 (98%) nodes to reduce the average component size to 1.99 nodes.

Regarding the number of nodes in the largest component, the maximal disruptive effect is measured as the lowest number of nodes in the largest component following the intervention. In other words, the smaller the largest component, the more fragmented the network (see Fig. 5.1d). Degree centrality targeting yielded the fastest speed of relative disruption as the deletion of 562 nodes reduced the largest component to three nodes. In comparison, reputation targeting yielded the same result after 815 nodes were deleted. Total purchasing price targeting and unique items bought/sold produced the same measure result (three nodes) after 2621 and 1351 nodes were deleted, respectively. Random and eccentricity targeting yielded the same outcome after 2507 and 2736 nodes were deleted, respectively.

While decreases in the average geodesic distance typically reflect improved communication between nodes as the distance from one node to all other nodes is short, this is not necessarily the case for the Abraxas transactional network. In this case, consistent decreases in the average geodesic distance according to sequential node deletion are a product of a shrinking share of nodes that can be connected. In short, the average geodesic distance decreases as fewer nodes connect to it. Reputation targeting appears to be the most effective strategy, as deleting the top 99 nodes (10.7%) yielded an average geodesic distance of 0.41. Degree centrality targeting offered the second fastest disruption by deleting 96 nodes, delivering an average geodesic distance of 0.93. Unique items bought/sold targeting and total purchasing price targeting created the third and fourth fastest disruptions, with the deletion of 226 and 230 nodes yielding an average geodesic distance of 0.8. Eccentricity and random targeting were again the least effective strategies, producing averages of 0.5 and 0.3 once 2792 and 2240 nodes were deleted, respectively.

Node Deletion Impact

Not every deleted node will have the same disruptive effect on a criminal network. Removing specific nodes will disproportionately impact a network's ease of operation according to their influence and place within the network structure. Figure 5.2a–e illustrate the percentage of node deletion by the percentage of disruption impact for each strategic intervention across all outcome measures. It is immediately apparent from these figures that the effect of node deletion can be either linear, curvilinear

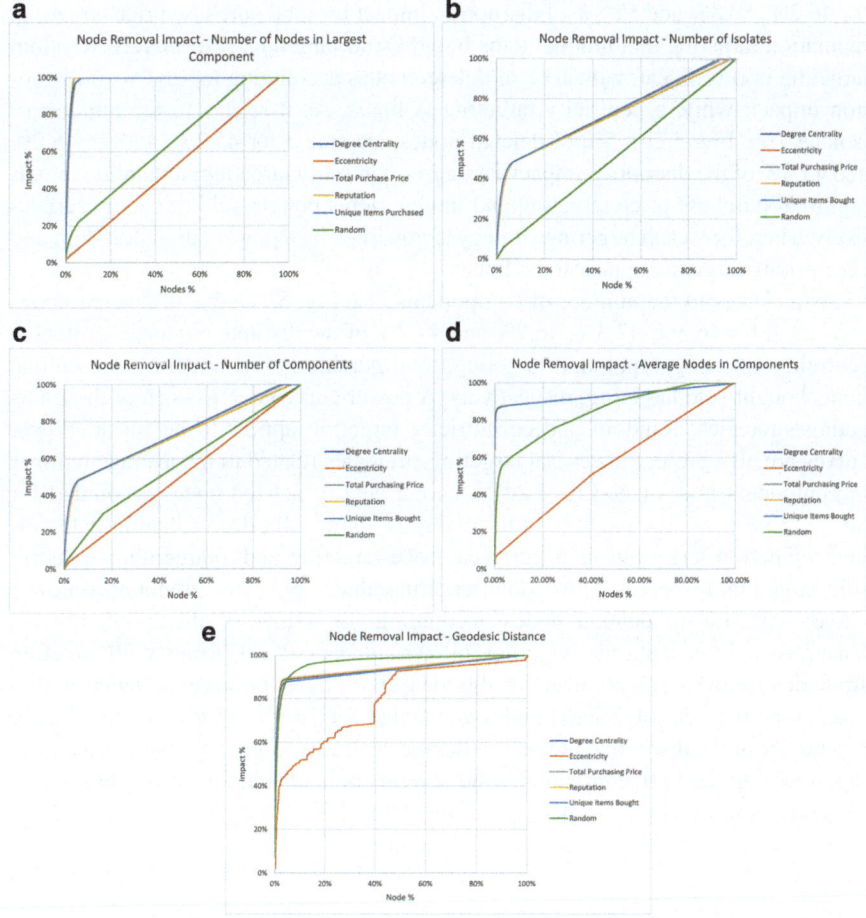

Fig. 5.2 Node removal impact: **a)** Number of nodes in largest component; **b)** number of isolates; **c)** number of components; **d)** average nodes in components; **e)** geodesic distance

or power law. A linear relationship means that node deletion and disruption impact are proportional, implying that removing a large number of nodes will result in an equally significant level of disruption. A curvilinear relationship means a moderate number of deleted nodes account for a large disruption impact. Finally, a power law curve implies that a small number of deleted nodes accounts for an outsized portion of disruption impact.

Based on Fig. 5.2a, degree centrality targeting, reputation targeting, total purchase price targeting and unique items bought/sold targeting are each based on a power law regarding the number of nodes in the largest component. In degree centrality targeting, 1% of deleted nodes accounted for 51.5% of disruption impact. This is also the case for the other three strategies, as 1% of deleted nodes accounted for 46.2%, 50.8% and 52.8% of disruption impact for total purchase price targeting, reputation targeting and unique items bought/sold targeting, respectively. Random targeting is curvilinear, with 10% of deleted nodes accounting for 26.6% of disruption impact, while eccentricity targeting is linear. As it relates to the number of isolates (see Fig. 5.2b), 5% of deleted nodes accounted for 45.2%, 45.8%, 45.2% and 45.8% of the disruptive impact for degree centrality targeting, reputation targeting, total purchase price targeting and unique items bought/sold targeting, respectively. Therefore, each targeting strategy is governed by a power curve. Random and eccentricity targeting appear to be linear.

As it relates to the number of components (see Fig. 5.2c), 5% of deleted nodes accounted for 46.3%, 47.3%, 46.9% and 47.2% of the disruptive impact for degree centrality targeting, reputation targeting, total purchase price targeting and unique items bought/sold targeting, respectively. A power curve governs each of these targeting strategies. Random and eccentricity targeting appear to be linear. Power curves are also present in several targeting strategies related to the average number of component nodes (see Fig. 5.2d). One per cent of deleted nodes accounted for 86.3%, 85.8%, 86.2% and 86% of the disruptive impact for degree centrality targeting, reputation targeting, total purchase price targeting and unique items bought/sold targeting, respectively. Random targeting abides by a less pronounced power curve, with 1% of deleted nodes accounting for 41.3% of disruption impact. Unsurprisingly, eccentricity targeting follows a linear curve. Curiously, all targeting strategies follow a power curve for the measured effects on average geodesic distance. One per cent of deleted nodes accounted for 73.8%, 85.8%, 74.6%, 60.3% and 60.3% of the disruptive impact for degree centrality targeting, reputation targeting, total purchase price targeting, unique items bought/sold targeting and random targeting, respectively. Five per cent of the deleted nodes targeted based on eccentricity accounted for 46.1% of impact disruption.

Outcome Measure Carry-Over and Node Characteristics

Table 5.3 shows the percentage of the top 100 deleted nodes for each target strategy that is common to the targeting strategy for each outcome measure. In short, this table shows how many nodes within the top 100 simulated deletions are held in common by all targeting strategies. Based on these results, it is apparent that most (> 50%) of deleted nodes show common outcome measures for degree centrality targeting, reputation targeting, total purchase price targeting and unique items bought/sold targeting. There appears to be a 90% or greater congruence for isolates and components. This partly explains why the disruption impact was so similar for these targeting strategies; the deleted nodes were the same actors. Moreover, these four targeting strategies did not share the same nodes with eccentricity and random targeting. This again explains the sharp differences in their disruption performances. The same actors were not targeted for deletion as they were for degree centrality targeting, reputation targeting, total purchase price targeting and unique items bought/sold targeting.

Table 5.4 presents a complete array of descriptive statistics for the top 100 deleted nodes that are held in common across all outcome measures. Of the top 100 nodes deleted based on degree centrality targeting, 78 were shared across the five outcome measures. Notably, eccentricity and random targeting yielded no common deleted nodes across the outcome measures. Of the targeting strategies with commonly held deleted nodes, an overwhelming majority sold or bought drugs, with stimulants, cannabis and ecstasy being the products of choice. To this extent, these particular actors predominantly dealt with one product type but could diversify with two to three additional products. The United States, United Kingdom and the Netherlands were the top three countries of origin or destination. These findings indicate that the actors most influential in the network stability of Abraxas bartered primarily in stimulants and were affiliated with the United States in some capacity. Notably, all deleted nodes across the applicable interventions were vendors.

Discussion

Adaptive sequential node deletion was applied to test the efficacy of six law enforcement strategies in disrupting the ease of operation of the Abraxas cryptomarket. In a real-world setting, this mimics law enforcement efforts to target, apprehend and arrest individual actors within a network's value chain. The results showed that random targeting was the least effective strategy across the five outcome measures, producing minimal disruptive effects at a relatively slow pace. These results are consistent with findings from other criminal network research (Keegan et al., 2010; Westlake et al., 2011) that found that random interventions perform poorly compared with strategies that target specific actors.

Curiously, random targeting was not the poorest performing strategy, as eccentricity targeting proved to be the least disruptive. It is unclear why this is the case, as eccentricity measures the distance of one node from every other node in a network so it should prove effective as a calibrated intervention. However, from closer examination, it appears that the eccentricity values of the nodes were so similar that this intervention provided little strategic value because it targeted nodes that yielded negligible disruptive impact. In other words, there was no power law distribution in the eccentricity scores, so no influential nodes could be removed from the network.

Table 5.3 Top 100 actors held in common across targeting strategies

Metrics	Degree centrality	Eccentricity	Total purchasing price	Reputation	Unique items bought
Isolates					
Eccentricity	10%	–	–	–	–
Total purchasing price	95%	9%	–	–	–
Reputation	99%	10%	95%	–	–
Unique items bought	94%	10%	95%	95%	–
Random	7%	5%	7%	7%	8%
Components					
Eccentricity	6%	–	–	–	–
Total purchasing price	92%	5%	–	–	–
Reputation	100%	6%	92%	–	–
Unique items bought	93%	6%	95%	93%	–
Random	0%	3%	0%	0%	0%
Average number of nodes in components					
Eccentricity	4%	–	–	–	–
Total purchasing price	85%	5%	–	–	–
Reputation	92%	5%	85%	–	–
Unique items bought	76%	4%	68%	73%	–
Random	2%	2%	3%	2%	6%
Average geodesic distance					
Eccentricity	0%	–	–	–	–
Total purchasing price	73%	0%	–	–	–
Reputation	86%	0%	74%	–	–
Unique items bought	49%	0%	45%	46%	–
Random	0%	7%	2%	1%	1%
Number of nodes in largest component					
Eccentricity	2%	–	–	–	–
Total purchasing price	85%	2%	–	–	–
Reputation	97%	2%	85%	–	–
Unique items bought	78%	3%	78%	79%	–
Random	0%	2%	2%	1%	3%

Table 5.4 Descriptive statistics for top 100 actors held in common across targeting strategies

Descriptive statistics	Degree centrality (78)	Eccentricity (0)	Total purchasing price (68)	Reputation (76)	Unique items purchased (43)	Random (0)
Actor designation						
Vendor	100% (78)	–	100% (68)	100% (76)	100% (43)	–
Buyer	0% (0)	–	0% (0)	0% (0)	0% (0)	–
Number of unique item categories						
1	85.9% (67)	–	83.8% (57)	85.5% (65)	74.4% (32)	–
2	10.3% (8)	–	11.8% (8)	10.5% (8)	18.6% (8)	–
3	0% (0)	–	0% (0)	0% (0)	0% (0)	–
4	1.3% (1)	–	1.5% (1)	1.3% (1)	2.3% (1)	–
5	2.6% (2)	–	2.9% (2)	2.6% (2)	4.7% (2)	–
Listing categories						
Custom listing	7.7% (6)	–	8.8% (6)	7.9% (6)	14.0% (6)	–
Digital goods	7.7% (6)	–	4.4% (3)	9.2% (7)	16.3% (7)	–
Drug paraphernalia	2.6% (2)	–	4.4% (3)	2.6% (2)	4.7% (2)	–
Drugs	96.2% (75)	–	100% (68)	94.7% (72)	90.7% (39)	–
Others	3.8% (3)	–	4.4% (3)	3.9% (3)	7.0% (3)	–
Services	6.4% (5)	–	5.9% (4)	6.6% (5)	11.6% (5)	–
Number of unique item subcategories						
1	35.9% (28)	–	35.3% (24)	34.2% (26)	18.6% (8)	–
2	23.1% (18)	–	25% (17)	23.7% (18)	18.6% (8)	–
3	23.1% (18)	–	23.5% (16)	23.7% (18)	32.6% (14)	–
4	3.9% (3)	–	2.9% (2)	4% (3)	4.7% (2)	–
5	6.4% (5)	–	5.9% (4)	6.6% (5)	11.6% (5)	–
6	2.6% (2)	–	2.9% (2)	2.6% (2)	4.7% (2)	–
7	1.3% (1)	–	1.5% (1)	1.3% (1)	2.3% (1)	–
8	2.6% (2)	–	1.5% (1)	2.6% (2)	4.7% (2)	–
9	0% (0)	–	0% (0)	0% (0)	0% (0)	–
10+	1.3% (1)	–	1.5% (1)	1.3% (1)	2.3% (1)	–
Listing subcategories						
Benzos	11.5% (9)	–	10.3% (7)	11.8% (9)	14% (6)	–
Cannabis	43.6% (34)	–	47.1% (32)	44.7% (34)	48.8% (21)	–
Data	3.8% (3)	–	2.9% (2)	5.3% (4)	9.3% (4)	–
Dissociatives	10.3% (8)	–	10.3% (7)	10.5% (8)	14% (6)	–
Drugs	2.6% (2)	–	0% (0)	2.6% (2)	4.7% (2)	–
Drug paraphernalia	1.3% (1)	–	1.5% (1)	1.3% (1)	2.3% (1)	–
E-books	5.1% (4)	–	2.9% (2)	6.6% (5)	11.6% (5)	–
Ecstasy	34.6% (27)	–	33.8% (23)	34.2% (26)	46.5% (20)	–
Electronics	2.6% (2)	–	2.9% (2)	2.6% (2)	4.7% (2)	–
Erotica	3.8% (3)	–	1.5% (1)	3.9% (3)	7% (3)	–

(continued)

Table 5.4 (continued)

Descriptive statistics	Degree centrality (78)	Eccentricity (0)	Total purchasing price (68)	Reputation (76)	Unique items purchased (43)	Random (0)
Fraud	2.6% (2)	–	1.5% (1)	2.6% (2)	4.7% (2)	–
Hacking	2.6% (2)	–	1.5% (1)	3.9% (3)	7% (3)	–
IDs and passports	1.3% (1)	–	1.5% (1)	1.3% (1)	2.3% (1)	–
Information	5.1% (4)	–	2.9% (2)	5.3% (4)	9.3% (4)	–
Miscellaneous	1.3% (1)	–	1.5% (1)	1.3% (1)	2.3% (1)	–
Money	2.6% (2)	–	1.5% (1)	2.6% (2)	4.7% (2)	–
N/A	12.8% (10)	–	13.2% (9)	13.2% (10)	20.9% (9)	–
Opioids	24.4% (19)	–	25% (17)	25.0% (19)	25.6% (11)	–
Others	1.3% (1)	–	1.5% (1)	1.3% (1)	2.3% (1)	–
Prescription	11.5% (9)	–	11.8% (8)	11.8% (9)	14% (4)	–
Psychedelics	15.4% (12)	–	14.7% (10)	13.2% (10)	20.9% (9)	–
RCs	1.3% (1)	–	1.5% (1)	1.3% (1)	2.3% (1)	–
Security	1.3% (1)	–	1.5% (1)	1.3% (1)	2.3% (1)	–
Software	2.6% (2)	–	1.5% (1)	2.6% (2)	4.7% (2)	–
Steroids	1.3% (1)	–	1.5% (1)	1.3% (1)	2.3% (1)	–
Stimulants	52.6% (41)	–	58.8% (40)	51.3% (39)	51.2% (22)	–
Weapons	1.3% (1)	–	1.5% (1)	1.3% (1)	2.3% (1)	–
Number of unique locations shipped from						
1	76.9% (60)	–	79.4% (54)	76.3% (58)	67.4% (29)	–
2	18% (14)	–	14.7% (10)	18.4% (14)	23.3% (10)	–
3	3.9% (3)	–	4.4% (3)	4% (3)	7% (3)	–
4	1.3% (1)	–	1.5% (1)	1.3% (1)	2.3% (1)	–
Locations shipped from						
Australia	9% (7)	–	11.8% (8)	9.2%	7.1% (3)	–
Belgium	2.6% (2)	–	1.5% (1)	2.6%	–	–
Belize	1,3% (1)	–	1.5% (1)	1.3% (1)	2.4% (1)	–
Bulgaria	1.3% (1)	–	1.5% (1)	1.3% (1)	2.4% (1)	–
Canada	1.3% (1)	–	1.5% (1)	1.3% (1)	–	–
Denmark	1.3% (1)	–	1.5% (1)	1.3% (1)	–	–
Europe/EU	11.5% (9)	–	11.8% (8)	13.2% (10)	21.4% (9)	–
France	2.6% (2)	–	2.9% (2)	2.6% (2)	2.4% (1)	–
Germany	21.8% (17)	–	22.1% (15)	21.1% (16)	21.4% (9)	–
India	1.3% (1)	–	1.5% (1)	1.3% (1)	2.4% (1)	–
Italy	1.3% (1)	–	1.5% (1)	1.3% (1)	2.4% (1)	–
Netherlands	17.9% (14)	–	17.6% (12)	17.1% (13)	19% (8)	–
Norway	–	–	1.5% (1)	–	–	–
Spain	2.6% (2)	–	1.5% (1)	2.6% (2)	4.8% (2)	–
United Kingdom	19.2% (15)	–	17.6% (12)	18.4% (14)	14.3% (6)	–

(continued)

Table 5.4 (continued)

Descriptive statistics	Degree centrality (78)	Eccentricity (0)	Total purchasing price (68)	Reputation (76)	Unique items purchased (43)	Random (0)
United States	19.2% (15)	–	22.1% (15)	19.7% (15)	26.2% (11)	–
Unknown or N/A	14.1% (11)	–	8.8% (6)	14.1% (11)	21.4% (9)	–

This naturally resulted in the low impact of node removals. Nevertheless, degree centrality and reputation targeting were the most effective strategies across all five outcome measures, consistently producing near-identical results.

These strategies are likely interrelated as the specific targeted actors are the same or similar. Degree centrality can be operationalised as the total number of unique buyers with whom a vendor has done business. The size of a vendor's clientele list indicates a more broad-based form of trust. On the other hand, reputation targeting is the preeminent marker of trust in cryptomarkets. The more trading partners an actor has, the more likely they are to have an equally high cumulative reputation score (Christin, 2013; Décary-Hétu & Quessy-Dore, 2017).

While total purchasing price targeting and unique items bought/sold targeting were not quite as effective as degree centrality and reputation targeting, they did provide comparable levels of disruption to the transactional network. The disruption pattern demonstrated by these four targeting strategies was that the proportion of potential measurable values increases or decreases as more actors are removed. These values plateau as the network becomes completely fragmented and the disruptive effect begins to decline as the network size decreases due to vertex deletion.

Targeting Based on Human and Network Capital

This raises an interesting question about the underlying differences between these four targeting strategies. In short, are these strategies the same, given their comparable patterns of disruption? Similarities between disruptive impacts can be attributed more to the similarity of the targeted actors than to the idiosyncrasies of the targeting strategies. To elaborate, an actor with a high degree of centrality and an equally high cumulative reputation is also likely to have a high market share (revenue generated) and a high number of unique items bought or sold. The majority (> 50%) of deleted nodes were held in common among degree centrality targeting, reputation targeting, total purchase price targeting and unique items bought/sold targeting for nearly all outcome measures (see Table 5.2). High-impact nodes are likely to dominate markets across several human and social capital metrics.

This shows that network and human capital metrics may not differ completely if the removed actors are the same. Contrary to previous studies (Bright et al., 2014; Tsvetovat & Carley, 2003), it is posited that targeting criminal actors based on a human capital approach may not always be accurate. In short, if the network and human capital measures are interrelated or correlated to some extent, preferencing one approach over the other is functionally moot as both approaches achieve similar or perhaps near-identical disruptive impact.

However, one element of the human capital approach stands out: the actor's role. As in the study of Duijn et al. (2014), vendor deletion exclusively positively impacted the transactional network (see Table 5.3). Moreover, removing buyers was ineffectual as they were merely customers who did not supply illegal contraband. As such, their reduced engagement with actors on Abraxas precluded their prioritisation by any targeting strategy aside from eccentricity and random targeting. While buyers might move the market, determining the ebb and flow of economic transactions as they purchase the advertised products, vendors ultimately supply these products. Therefore, cryptomarket interventions should be vendor-centric.

Aside from the actor's role, it is evident that the most effective deleted nodes are product specialists based in Western nations like the United States and the United Kingdom (see Table 5.4). The popularity of particular goods (stimulants and marijuana) and the countries from which they are shipped gives us an idea of which products are in demand and where that demand comes from. As it relates to the general distribution of products and countries on Abraxas, cannabis (34.21%), stimulants (19.38%), ecstasy (13.8%), opioids (10.8%) and psychedelics (6.75%) account for the top five products sold. Germany, the United States, the United Kingdom, the Netherlands and Australia accounted for 25.1%, 19.34%, 13.78%, 9.22% and 8.74% of source nations, respectively. Therefore, law enforcement interventions against dark web markets might equally prioritise vendors that sell a specific product or ship from a particular country. As most cryptomarket transactions are conducted by a small number of product- and country-specific vendors, it may be beneficial to calibrate interventions based on these. While most dark web markets will sell a wide assortment of products shipped from a wide variety of nations, it is evident that most transactions involve a small number of product types from a short list of countries.

Metagames and Power Laws

Consistent with research in criminal networks (Druxbury & Haynie, 2019; Wood, 2017), it was found that removing the most prolific vendors in sequential order fragments the network in relatively little time. Indeed, these results are not altogether different from those of Duxbury and Haynie (2020), who documented the existence of a scale-free online drug market and distribution network. To this extent,

disassortative mixing in Abraxas, according to preferential attachment, while necessary for successful transactions at scale, produced apparent vulnerabilities in the
network structure of this market. However, this was only observed for degree centrality targeting, reputation targeting, total purchase price targeting and unique
items bought/sold targeting. In short, Abraxas comprises a small number of influential actors whose deletion would result in a fragmentation cascade. Removing the
top nodes across these four targeting strategies yielded a cross-cutting impact, producing noticeable disruption across all five outcome measures. This is particularly
noteworthy as it implies that removing prolific actors has a universal disruptive
effect on the transactional network.

Furthermore, the findings indicate that, when interventions are successful, the
disruption follows a power law in which a small number of deleted nodes produce
an outsized disruption impact (see Fig. 5.2a-e). This study establishes differences in
linear, curvilinear and power law disruption. A linear relationship means that the
node deletion and disruption impact are proportional, implying that removing a
large number of nodes will result in an equally large level of disruption. A curvilinear relationship means a moderate number of deleted nodes account for a large
disruption impact. Finally, a power curve implies that a small number of deleted
nodes account for an outsized disruption impact. Across the five outcome measures,
degree centrality targeting, reputation targeting, total purchase price targeting and
unique items bought/sold targeting all demonstrated power law properties, but
eccentricity and random targeting generally demonstrated linear properties and
were sometimes curvilinear.

Significantly, the disruptive impact of sequential node removal can be described
as a chess-like metagame. A metagame presupposes underlying rules within a game
so that understanding and abiding by these rules confer strategic dominance over
those who understand and abide by baseline rules. In chess, the metagame involves
anticipating what moves one's opponent might make and making moves that
manoeuvre one's opponent into a position favourable to oneself. Moreover, one
might make certain moves that set up successive moves that have a greater impact.

Sequential node removal has a similar metagame in which disruptive impact can
be maximised if specific nodes are first removed to make way for the removal of
other nodes. In short, initial nodes must be removed to achieve maximal impact
once the network is reformed following the initial intervention. When examining
the disruption impact, it is evident that the nodes that produced the greatest impact
were often those that were not first removed (i.e. that had the highest value per the
parameters of a specific targeting strategy). Nodes with the greatest disruptive
impact were often those outside of the first ten deleted nodes. As it relates to law
enforcement interventions, initial arrests or apprehensions should be used to set up
future arrests or apprehensions that have a greater capacity for disrupting the criminal network.

Conclusion

This chapter examined the fundamental building blocks of agent-based models and developed a model to measure the efficacy of six law enforcement interventions against the Abraxas cryptomarket. However, it is important to note that this study did not possess real-world data to test the overall performance of these interventions. A glaring limitation of this methodology is that there is no data on subject-based targeting of cryptomarket participants by law enforcement organisations. Moreover, the efficacy of these interventions was tested against a relatively small cryptomarket in Abraxas. Therefore, the results of this model cannot be extrapolated to larger markets as they may possess disparate operational dynamics. This study did not consider the migration of Abraxas buyers and vendors to other cryptomarkets.

The results of the agent-based model are presented, with attempted to determine the efficacy of the six law enforcement interventions under observation. Though computer simulations are not a novel technique, their use by criminologists is less common than other techniques, so agent-based modelling offers a potentially worthwhile tool to supplement more costly and less statistically rigorous methods. However, agent-based modelling may serve as an unparalleled method for testing both the efficacy of interventions and their assumptions about the behaviour of criminals for both researchers and policy practitioners. Researchers of organised crime and dark networks can use agent-based models to understand the structure and typology of these entities. It is important to note that agent-based modelling tests assumptions and understands macro-level trends based on the researcher's established rules, so the model's performance should be back-tested against real-world data to gauge its accuracy.

This study designed an agent-based model that measures the efficacy of several law enforcement interventions against a cryptomarket transactional network and—to understand and dismantle criminal networks—this study examined the processes and logic behind how agent-based models are structured. This study showed that adaptive computer simulations represent a novel means of testing the structural robustness of a criminal network and the effectiveness of strategic interventions. However, the results of these analyses are driven by predetermined parameters that govern the behaviour of the actors within the network. While driven by educated and evidence-based suppositions, these parameters are fundamentally speculative, so these results should not be mistaken for actional intelligence gathered from a real-world experiment. They can only go so far in illustrating the true dynamics that undergird the phenomenon of the study. Randomised controlled trials represent the gold standard of research within the social sciences, so adaptive computer simulations are a secondary option. Future research into cryptomarket disruption strategies should consider experiments on live markets with interventions and measured results. While the logistical difficulties of such an undertaking are understandably considerable, such an experiment represents the pinnacle of evidence-based research into cryptomarkets.

References

Alm, J., & Mack, K. (2017). Degree-correlation, robustness and vulnerability in finite scale-free networks. *Asian Research Journal of Mathematics, 2*(5), 1–6.

Armona, L. (2017). *Measuring the impact of formal and informal communication on electronic commerce demand.* Stanford University mimeo.

Axtell, R. (2000). *Why agents? On the varied motivations for agent computing in the social sciences.* The Brookings Institution.

Barratt, M., Ferris, J., & Winstock, A. (2016a). Safer scoring? Cryptomarkets, social supply and drug market violence. *International Journal of Drug Policy, 35*, 24–31.

Barratt, M., Lenton, S., Maddox, A., & Allen, M. (2016b). What if you live on top of a bakery and you like cakes? Drug use and harm trajectories before, during and after the emergence of Silk Road. *International Journal of Drug Policy, 35*, 50–57.

Batikas, M., & Kretschmer, T. (2018). Entrepreneurs on the darknet: Reaction to negative feedback. *SSRN:* https://ssrn.com/abstract=3238141

Birks, D., & Davies, T. (2017). Street network structure and crime risk: An agent-based investigation of the encounter and enclosure hypotheses. *Criminology, 55*(4), 900–937.

Birks, D., Townsley, M., & Stewart, A. (2012). Generative explanations of crime: Using simulation to test criminological theory. *Criminology, 50*(1), 221–254.

Bonabeau, E. (2002). Agent-based modeling: Methods and techniques for simulating human systems. *Proceedings of the National Academy of Sciences of the United States of America, 99*, 7280–7287.

Borning, A., Waddell, P., & Förster, R. (2008). Urbanism: Using simulation to inform public deliberation and decision-making. In H. Chen et al. (Eds.), *Digital government. Integrated Series in Information Systems* (Vol. 17). Springer.

Brantingham, P., & Brantingham, P. (1984). *Patterns in crime.* Macmillan.

Branwen, G., Christin, N., Décary-Hétu, D., Andersen, R. M., StExo, Presidente, E., Anonymous, Lau, D., Sohhlz, Kratunov, D., Cakic, V., Buskirk, V., & Whom. (2015). *Dark Net Market Archives, 2011–2015* [Data set]. https://academictorrents.com/details/1698989f23b60f9118 7d42b031f0ad857793888a

Bright, A. (2015). *Disrupting and dismantling dark networks: Lessons from social network analysis and law enforcement simulations in illuminating dark networks* (pp. 39–51).

Bright, D. A., & Delaney, J. J. (2013). Evolution of a drug trafficking network: Mapping changes in network structure and function across time. *Global Crime, 14*, 238–260.

Bright, D. A., Greenhill, C., & Levenkova, N. (2014). Dismantling criminal networks: Can node attributes play a role? In C. Morselli (Ed.), *Crime and Networks* (pp. 148–162). Routledge.

Bright, D., Greenhill, C., Britz, T., Ritter, A., & Morselli, C. (2017). Criminal network vulnerabilities and adaptations. *Global Crime, 18*(4), 424–441.

Bright, D. A., Koskinen, J., & Malm, A. (2018). Illicit network dynamics: The formation and evolution of a drug trafficking network. *Journal of Quantitative Criminology, 35*(2), 237–258.

Bruch, E., & Atwell, J. (2015). Agent-based models in empirical social research. *Sociological Methods & Research, 44*(2), 186–221.

Burt, R. S. (2000). The Network Structure of Social Capital. *Research in Organizational Behavior, 22*, 345–423.

Calderoni, F., Comunale, T., Campedelli, G., Marchesi, M., Manzi, D., & Frualdo, G. (2022). Organized crime groups: A systematic review of individual-level risk factors related to recruitment. *Campbell Systematic Reviews, 18*(1), 1–87.

Caldwell, S. (1997). *Dynamic Microsimulation and the Corsim 3.0 Model.* Strategic Forecasting.

Carley, K. M. (1995). Computational and mathematical organization theory: Perspective and directions. *Computational and Mathematical Organization Theory, 1*(1), 39–56.

Christin, N. (2013). Traveling the Silk Road: A measurement analysis of a large anonymous online marketplace. In *Proceedings of the 22nd International Conference on World Wide Web.* International World Wide Web Conferences Steering Committee.

Clarke, R., & Cornish, D. (1985). Modeling offenders' decisions: A framework for research and policy. *Crime and Justice, 6*, 147–185.

Cohen, L., & Felson, M. (1979). Social change and crime rate trends: A routine activity approach. *American Sociological Review, 44*(4), 588–608.

Coleman, J. S. (1994). Social capital, human capital, and investment in youth. In A. C. Petersen & J. T. Mortimer (Eds.), *Youth unemployment and society* (pp. 34–50). Cambridge University Press.

Dean, J., & Gumerman, G. (2000). Understanding Anasazi culture change through agent-based modelling. In T. A. Kohler & G. J. Gumerman (Eds.), *Dynamics in human and primate societies: Agent-based modeling of social and spatial processes*. Oxford Academic.

Décary-Hétu, D., & Quessy-Dore, O. (2017). Are repeat buyers in crypto markets loyal customers? Repeat business between dyads of crypto market vendors and users. *The American Behavioral Scientist, 61*(11), 1341–1357.

Diekmann, A., Jann, B., Przepiorka, W., & Wherli, S. (2014). Reputation formation and the evolution of cooperation in anonymous online markets. *American Sociological Review, 79*, 65–85.

Dowling, P. (1999). Completing the puzzle: Issues in the development of the field of international human resource management. *Management International Review, 39*(3), 27–43.

Duijn, P., Kashirin, V., & Sloot, P. (2014). The relative ineffectiveness of criminal network disruption. *Scientific Reports, 4*, 4238–4251.

Duxbury, S., & Haynie, D. (2018). Building them up, breaking them down: Topology, vendor selection patterns, and a digital drug market's robustness to disruption. *Social Networks, 52*, 238–250.

Duxbury, S., & Haynie, D. (2019). Criminal network security: An agent-based approach to evaluating network resilience. *Criminology, 57*(2), 314–342.

Duxbury, S., & Haynie, D. (2020). The responsiveness of criminal networks to intentional attacks: Disrupting darknet drug trade. *PLoS One, 15*(9), 1–20.

Eck, J., & Liu, L. (2008). *Artificial crime analysis systems: Using computer simulations and geographic information systems*. IGI Global.

Eilstrup-Sangiovanni, M., & Jones, C. (2008). Assessing the dangers of illicit networks: Why Al-Qaida may be less threatening than many think. *International Security, 33*(2), 7–44.

Epstein, J. M., & Axtell, R. (1996). *Growing artificial societies: Social science from the bottom up*. The MIT Press.

Forrester, J. W. (1971). *World dynamics*. MIT Press.

Frias-Martinez, E., Williamson, G., & Frias-Martinez, V. (2011). An agent-based model of epidemic spread using human mobility and social network information. In *Proceedings of the 2011 IEEE 3rd International. Conference on Privacy, Security, Risk and Trust/IEEE 3rd International. Conference on Social Computing* (pp. 57–64).

Gilbert, N. (2008). *Agent-based models* (Vol. 153). Sage.

Gilbert, N., & Terna, P. (1999). *How to build and use agent-based models in social science*. Discussion paper. http://web.econ.unito.it/terna/deposito/gil_ter.pdf.

Gilbert, N., & Troitzsch, K. (2005). *Simulation for the social scientist*. Open University Press.

Granovetter, M. (1978). Networks of collective action: A perspective on community influence systems. *American Journal of Sociology, 83*(6), 1538–1542.

Groff, E. (2007). Simulation for theory testing and experimentation: An example using routine activity theory and street robbery. *Journal of Quantitative Criminology, 23*(2), 75–103.

Groff, E., & Birks, J. (2008). Simulating X look at the possibilities: A look at the possibilities. *Policing, 2*(2), 122–145.

Groff, E., Johnson, S., & Thornton, A. (2019). State of the art in agent-based modeling of urban crime: An overview. *Journal of Quantitative Criminology, 35*, 155–193.

Hanneman, R. A., Collins, R., & Mordt, G. (1995). Discovering theory dynamics by computer simulation: Experiments on state legitimacy and imperialist capitalism. *Sociological Methodology, 25*, 1–46.

Hardy, R., & Norgaard, J. (2016). Reputation in the Internet black market: An empirical and theoretical analysis of the Deep Web. *Journal of Institutional Economics, 12*(3), 515–539.

Herley, C., & Florêncio, D. (2009). Nobody sells gold for the price of silver: Dishonesty, uncertainty and the underground economy. *Economics of Information Security and Privacy*, 33–53.

Holland, J., & Miller, J. (1991). Artificial adaptive agents in economic theory. *American Economic Review, 81*(2), 365–370.

Holt, T., Strumsky, D., Smirnova, O., & Kilger, M. (2012). Examining the social networks of malware writers and hackers. *International Journal of Cyber Criminology, 6*(1), 891.

Janetos, N., & Tilly, J. (2017). *Reputation dynamics in a market for illicit drugs*. https://jtilly.io/reputation-dynamics.pdf

Janssen, M. (2005). Agent-based modelling. *International Society for Ecological Economics*, 1–9.

Keegan, B., Ahmed, M., Williams, D., Srivastava, J., & Contractor, N. (2010). Dark gold: Statistical properties of clandestine networks in massively multiplayer online games. In *Proceedings of 2010 IEEE Second International Conference on Social Computing (SocialCom)* (pp. 201–208).

Kennedy, D. (2008). *Deterrence and crime prevention: Reconsidering the prospect of sanction*. Routledge.

Kenney, M. (2007). The architecture of drug trafficking: Network forms of organisation in the Colombian cocaine trade. *Global Crime, 8*(3), 233–259.

Krebs, V. (2001). Mapping networks of terrorist cells. *Connections, 24*(3), 43–52.

Macy, M., & Willer, R. (2002). From factors to actors: computational sociology and agent-based modeling. *Annual Review of Sociology, 28*, 143–166.

Malleson, N., Evans, A., Heppenstall, A., & See, L. (2014). Optimising an agent-based model to explore the behaviour of simulated burglars. *Intelligent Systems Reference Library, 52*, 179–204.

Malm, A., & Bichler, G. (2011). Networks of collaborating criminals: Assessing the structural vulnerability of drug markets. *Journal of Research in Crime and Delinquency, 48*(2), 271–297.

Martin, J. (2014). *Drugs on the dark net*. Palgrave Macmillan.

McGloin, J. M. (2005). Policy intervention and the considerations of a network analysis of street gangs. *Criminology & Public Policy, 4*, 607–636.

McGloin, J. M., & Rowan, Z. (2015). A threshold model of collective crime. *Criminology, 53*, 484–512.

Meadows, D. L., Behrens, W. W., III, Meadows, D. H., Naill, R. F., Randers, J., & Zahn, E. K. O. (1974). *The dynamics of growth in a finite world*. MIT Press.

Miller, J. H., & Page, S. E. (2007). *Complex adaptive systems: An introduction to computational models of social life*. Princeton University Press.

Morselli, C. (2009). *Inside criminal networks*. Springer.

Morselli, C., Giguere, C., & Petit, K. (2007). The efficiency/security trade-off in criminal networks. *Social Networks, 29*(1), 143–153.

Namatame, A., & Chen, S. (2016). *Agent-based modelling and network dynamics*. Oxford University Press.

Natarajan, M. (2006). Understanding the structure of a large heroin distribution network: A quantitative analysis of qualitative data. *Journal of Quantitative Criminology, 22*(2), 171–192.

Newman, M. E. J. (2002). Assortative mixing in networks. *Physical Review Letters, 89*, 2087–3001.

Newman, M. E. J. (2003). The structure and function of complex networks. *SIAM Review, 45*, 167–256.

Newman, M. (2006). Modularity and community structure in networks. *Proceedings of the National Academy of Sciences, 103*(23), 8577–8582.

O'Sullivan, D. (2004). Complexity science and human geography. *Transactions of the Institute of British Geographers, 29*(3), 282–295.

O'Sullivan, D., & Haklay, M. (2000). Agent-based models and individualism: Is the world agent-based? *Environment and Planning A: Economy and Space, 32*(8), 1409–1425.

Papachristos, A. V. (2009). Murder by structure: Dominance relations and the social structure of gang homicide. *American Journal of Sociology, 115*, 74–128.

Papachristos, A. V. (2011). The coming of a networked criminology. *Advances in Criminological Theory, 17*, 101–140.

Papachristos, A. V. (2014). The network structure of crime. *Sociology Compass, 8*, 347–357.

Przepiorka, W., Norbutas, L., & Corten, R. (2017). Order without law: Reputation promotes cooperation in a crypto market for illegal drugs. *European Sociological Review, 33*(6), 752–764.

Qin, J., Xu, J., Hu, D., Sageman, M., & Chen, H. (2005). Analyzing terrorist networks: A case study of the global Salafi Jihad network. In *3rd IEEE Conference on Intelligence and Security Informatics, Atlanta, Georgia, USA, 18 May 2005–19 May 2005* (pp. 287–304). Springer.

Raab, J., & Milward, B. (2003). Dark networks as problems. *Journal of Public Administration Research and Theory, 13*(4), 413–439.

Resnick, P., & Zeckhauser, R. (2002). Trust among strangers in internet transactions: Empirical analysis of eBay's reputation system. In M. R. Baye (Ed.), *The economics of the Internet and e-commerce* (pp. 127–157). Elsevier.

Schelling, T. (1971). Dynamic models of segregation. *Journal of Mathematical Sociology, 1*, 143–186.

Schwartz, D., & Rouselle, D. (2008). Targeting criminal networks: Using social network analysis to develop enforcement and intelligence priorities. *Journal of Intelligence and Analysis, 18*(1), 18–44.

Shamil, M., Legese, N., & Tadiwos, Y. (2021). Assessment of knowledge, attitude, practice and associated factors towards post-exposure prophylaxis for HIV/AIDS among health professionals in health centers found in Harari Region, Eastern Ethiopia. *PubMed, 13*, 41–51.

Shaw, C. R., & McKay, H. D. (1942). *Juvenile delinquency and urban areas.* University of Chicago Press.

Shortis, P., Aldridge, J., & Barratt, M. J. (2020). Drug crypto market futures: Structure, function and evolution in response to law enforcement actions. In D. R. Bewley-Taylor (Ed.), *Research handbook on international drug policy* (pp. 355–379). Edward Elgar Publishing Ltd.

Simon, H. (1952). A behavioural model of rational choice. *The Quarterly Journal of Economics, 69*(1), 99–118.

Soska, K., & Christin, N. (2015). *Measuring the longitudinal evolution of the online anonymous marketplace ecosystem.* Paper presented at the 24th USENIX Security Symposium, Washington, D.C.

Sparrow, M. K. (1991). Network vulnerabilities and strategic intelligence in law enforcement. *Journal of Intelligence and Counterintelligence, 5*(3), 255–274.

Stephen, A., & Toubia, O. (2009). Explaining the power-law degree distribution in a social commerce network. *Social Networks, 31*(4), 262–270.

Thomaz, F., Salge, C., Karahanna, E., & Hulland, J. (2020). Learning from the dark web: leveraging conversational agents in the era of hyper-privacy to enhance marketing. *Journal of the Academy of Marketing Science, 48*(1), 43–63.

Tsvetovat, M., & Carley, K. (2003). *Bouncing Back: Recovery mechanisms of covert networks.* NAACSOS Conference.

Van Buskirk, J., Bruno, R., Dobbins, T., Breen, C., Burns, L., Naicker, S., & Roxburgh, A. (2014). The recovery of online drug markets following law enforcement and other disruptions. *Drug and Alcohol Dependence, 173*, 159–162.

Van Der Heide, B., Johnson, B. K., & Vang, M. H. (2013). The effects of product photographs and reputation systems on consumer behavior and product cost on eBay. *Computers in Human Behavior, 29*(3), 570–576.

Varese, F. (2010). General introduction: What is organized crime? In F. Varese (Ed.), *Organized crime: Critical concepts in criminology* (pp. 1–35). Routledge.

Wall, D. S. (2001). Maintaining order and law on the internet. In D. S. Wall (Ed.), *Crime and the Internet* (pp. 167–183). Routledge.

Wang, N., Liu, L., & Eck, J. E. (2014). Analyzing crime displacement with a simulation approach. *Environment and Planning B: Planning and Design, 41*(2), 359–374.

Warr, M. (2002). *Companions in crime: The social aspects of criminal conduct.* Cambridge University Press.

Weisburd, D., Braga, A. A., Groff, E. R., & Wooditch, A. (2017). Can hot spots policing reduce crime in urban areas? An agent-based simulation. *Criminology, 55*(1), 137–173.

Westlake, B., Bouchard, M., & Frank, R. (2011). Finding the key players in online child exploitation networks. *Policy & Internet, 3*(2), 1–32.

Wood, G. (2017). The structure and vulnerability of a drug trafficking collaboration network. *Social Network, 48*, 1–9.

Xu, S., & Chen, T. (2003). Robust filtering for uncertain stochastic time-delay systems. *Asian Journal of Control, 5*(3), 364–373.

Zhu, H., & Wang, F. (2021). An An agent-based model for simulating urban crime with improved daily routines. *Computers, Environment and Urban Systems, 89*, 1–8.

Chapter 6
Cryptomarkets, Trust, and Enforcement: What Have We Learned?

Introduction

The digital age has undeniably streamlined many aspects of everyday life, including access to information, communication and transportation. Crime has evolved, too, with routine criminality increasingly moving online in the form of fraud, bullying and harassment in lieu of street crime (Buil-Gil et al., 2021; Caneppele & Aebi, 2019; Hamid & Ariza, 2022; Lewis et al., 2019). Organised crime has similarly substantially shifted operations to the cyber domain (e.g. Kruisbergen et al., 2019; Wang et al., 2021). Cryptomarkets represent both a unique permutation within the domains of organised crime and cybercrime and an amalgamation of the two fields. Illicit transactional networks on the dark web present new and unique challenges for law enforcement, forcing a paradigm shift as law enforcement institutions advance into the digital age.

The application of social network analysis and agent-based modelling makes apparent that these methods offer unique insights into the functional mechanisms of illicit transactional networks in both online and terrestrial settings. Moreover, the methods presented in this book provide plausible opportunities and actionable approaches for researchers and police practitioners wanting to examine and disrupt the macro-level structure of illicit transactional networks. This recognises that nascent increases in the number and sophistication of cybercriminals require a commensurate increase in the technical and logistical sophistication of law enforcement interventions. Although this book's material might be interesting from a technical and even a theoretical standpoint, the findings must be leveraged in some capacity to inform and improve targeted interventions in cryptomarkets by law enforcement. To this end, understanding which strategies work and which do not hinges on not only a more fluid comprehension of the phenomenon of interest but also an approach guided by an evidence-based calculus and high-yield computer simulations. This chapter examines what has been learned thus far and what other things might be learned by expanding cryptomarket research.

Implications for Dark Web Interventions

Given its size and relative influence, Abraxas is by no stretch of the imagination representative of all cryptomarkets. However, it is a platform that features all of the characteristics and qualities of a standard dark web market. Consequently, while the results and conclusions drawn from this book are not perfectly generalisable to all cryptomarkets, they should serve to instruct law enforcement activity on the dark web. This book examined how sequential node deletion may affect a cryptomarket's ease of operation. To achieve this, computer simulations incorporating network adaption and preferential selection were leveraged to better understand which strategic intervention(s) were most effective at disrupting the structural integrity of Abraxas' network structure.

This particular research is important for cryptomarket disruption strategies because it demonstrates that the behaviour of an illicit trade network can be modelled (Duxbury & Haynie, 2019) and subsequently vivisected using an evidence-based calculus. Moreover, it provides insight into how law enforcement might approach curtailing criminal activity on cryptomarkets. Because cryptomarket takedowns and the opportunistic arrest of vendors are not particularly effective long-term disruption strategies, a carefully calibrated intervention that considers network dynamics (e.g. preferential selection) is warranted.

These findings make clear that a "power law dynamics" of Abraxas render the market susceptible to targeted attacks: A small proportion of vendors is disproportionately more active compared to most vendors on the network. As such, law enforcement agencies need not target the entirety of the transactional network but instead focus on the most influential vendors, that is, those involved in most market activity. This fits an evidence-based policing calculus that aims to do more with less. In this case, a cryptomarket's ease of operation may be effectively disrupted should law enforcement officials focus on several powerful vendors. There are also clear benefits to country and product-based isolation and disruption topics. Chap. 4's analyses demonstrate that buyers, pursuant to preferential attachment and geographical constraints, prefer to purchase specific products from specific vendors located in a specific nation. Naturally, law enforcement might remove key export countries by targeting national or supranational vendors residing within those specific nations. Furthermore, the sale of certain goods and services might be eliminated from a cryptomarket by targeting vendors who specialise in the distribution of those products.

The available evidence makes apparent that law enforcement interventions in cryptomarkets have been ineffective and perhaps counterproductive. In the aftermath of market closures, sales volumes generally return to comparable pre-closure levels, with new markets emerging to take the place of those shut down. In fact, as discussed in Chap. 3, the FBI's efforts to shut down the original Silk Road utterly fragmented the composition of the cryptomarket ecosystem. Indeed, a once consolidated market dominated by the Silk Road devolved into a hypercompetitive affair between various small- and mid-sized cryptomarkets vying for volatile market shares. These new cryptomarkets included Agora, Silk Road 2.0, Black Market Reloaded, Sheep Marketplace and Pandora. These forms of mobility and durability equate to a difficult-to-exterminate illicit entity. Although it is perhaps reprehensible to allow the unabated operation of organised crime, it is arguably far worse for law enforcement to destroy a criminal monopoly.

It is imminently clear that large-scale market closures are not the way forward, suggesting that a broad-based focus on the trust dynamics within transactional cryptomarket networks may represent a viable alternative. Based on the findings in Chapters 4 and 5, a carefully calibrated network-based approach targeting trusted, high-earning vendors may yield the most disruptive impact. Importantly, these findings also indicate that a strategy that randomly targets actors in a cryptomarket is not advisable. Although controversial, a vendor-centric targeting strategy that exploits trust dynamics in the transactional network but leaves the market's transactional structure intact might offer maximal disruptive impact without displacing actors to either or both new and rival cryptomarkets. This strategy resembles approaches to wild animal population control that keep those populations at a manageable level to prevent harm to humans. Similarly, here, cryptomarkets are permitted to function but at a heavily reduced capacity.

Based on the findings, trust in Abraxas is predicated on a Pareto distribution where a small number of trusted vendors reap the rewards of their reputation. As such, reputations serve as a tool for identifying the quality of merchandise and, to an extent, counteract uncertainty in a highly volatile environment. Importantly, trust plays a key role in determining Abraxas' transactional network, with the market's global network structure a product of initial and repeated transactions between buyers and vendors. Each vendor and their respective buyers constitute an individual community within Abraxas. These communities were also location- and product-specific, suggesting the importance of geographic distance and niche markets for moulding the network structure. This can be exploited by law enforcement.

Although trust between buyers and vendors fundamentally determines the structure of a transactional network, it can also be exploited to undo this structure. That is, trust operates as a double-edged sword, enabling buyers to identify top vendors and law enforcement to identify high-priority targets. This reveals a theoretical game problem within cryptomarkets. When buyers attempt to mitigate risk by trading with the most trustworthy vendors, this creates easily exploitable vulnerabilities in the market's network structure, a vitally important lesson that law enforcement must learn and leverage.

From these findings, the removal of vendors with the highest cumulative reputation scores (i.e. the most trusted vendors) yielded the largest disruptive impact on Abraxas. Importantly, actors with the highest cumulative reputation are also the actors with the most trade partners, products sold and revenue generated. Based on these findings, a targeting strategy that sequentially removes these prolific actors would likely result in a fragmentation cascade. Bereft of their primary vendor, buyers would presumably take their chances with a vendor they have little experience with or leave the market entirely. The scale and profitability of a cryptomarket might be curtailed by such a strategic intervention.

As Duxbury and Haynie (2020) note, "When networks are attacked, actors grow more cautious about forging ties, connecting less frequently and only to trustworthy alters". In short, the entire premise of such a targeted intervention in a cryptomarket would be to rattle the trust and confidence of those operating on the market. Eliminating the most trustworthy operators dissipates the overall level of trust within the market. That is, in both abstract and practical terms, the objective is not to target vendors but to target trust.

In general, the scale-free properties of both Abraxas and the cryptomarket examined by Duxbury and Haynie (2017) suggest that these network topologies are premised on preferential attachment. Accordingly, law enforcement organisations should avoid launching large-scale attacks targeting the entirety of the vendor cohort. Instead, maximal gains can be achieved by focusing on the powerful few vendors who account for the majority of sales made, buyers transacted with and revenue generated. Evidence-based policing is premised upon doing more with less, and this seemingly represents a sensible option for law enforcement organisations working with scarce resources.

However, it is important to note that a high-level metagame is embedded within this strategy. As discussed in Chap. 5, a metagame assumes that underlying rules within a game mean that understanding and abiding by them confers strategic dominance over those who understand and abide by baseline rules. These findings suggest that a disruptive impact on cryptomarkets can be maximised if certain actors are first removed in order to establish higher-impact removals. Examining the disruption impact made evident that the nodes that produced the greatest impact were often those that were not first removed (i.e. those with the highest value according to the parameters of a specific targeting strategy). In fact, the nodes demonstrating the greatest disruptive impact were often those outside of the first ten nodes deleted.

For law enforcement agencies, initial arrests or apprehensions of cryptomarket vendors should be used to set up future arrests or apprehensions that have a greater capacity to disrupt the criminal network. This specific strategic approach is perhaps antithetical to standard law enforcement practices, which generally tend towards more direct approaches such as leadership decapitation and opportunistic removals. In general, metagame dynamics must be consciously considered by law enforcement organisations contending with both online and offline criminal organisations. The possibilities of negative side effects or a move backfiring completely must be carefully considered before launching an operation. Part of this involves law enforcement also contemplating the strategic value of an intervention at the macro-level, that is, the ways that disrupting the activity of one criminal entity might affect the entire criminal ecosystem within which that entity operates. This was demonstrably not considered by law enforcement agencies that shut down cryptomarkets in 2011, 2014 and 2017. Based on the findings in Chap. 5, the optimal metagame strategy involves curtailing existing cryptomarkets via the targeted removal of vendors rather than the complete shutdown of these markets. Ultimately, targeting key actors within a cryptomarkets serves to control the spread of a market instead of completely eliminating it. Outright market seizure or elimination compounds the problem, creating larger and more sophisticated markets that will demand more resources to adequately manage.

Furthermore, it remains unclear whether prior interventions against cryptomarkets were simply ineffective or whether the cryptomarket environment is antifragile, growing more robust with each major shock endured. If the latter supposition is correct, it would make little sense for law enforcement to pursue operations that seek to dismantle these markets in their entirety (i.e. market seizure). Instead, law enforcement resources would be better spent on targeted (or pinprick) interventions that curtail the growth of these markets by removing prolific actors that drive market activity. Indeed, the embeddedness of cryptomarkets may mean that these illicit entities are incapable of being eradicated in their entirety. Nevertheless, such a strategy would also rely on entropy within the cryptomarket environment. Because markets are generally operational for several months (Christin, 2013) and are subject to closure due to the duplicity of the actors therein, law enforcement may seek to play to this dynamic when targeting prolific actors in large markets. This might involve leaving small and uninfluential markets to their own devices while targeting actors generating the most active vendors on the largest markets. This strategy equates to catching the biggest fish in the largest pond while leaving smaller fish to die as smaller ponds dry up.

This concept of "leaving cryptomarkets to their own devices" is particularly controversial because it implies that law enforcement organisations are simply allowing criminal groups to operate unimpeded. However, this notion is incorrect. Because resources are limited in policing contexts, not all crime and criminals can or should be policed equally. Indeed, criminals and crime events are not equal in terms of either the damage they cause or the resources required to adequately police them. This explains strategies designed to inhibit offline crime, such as hotspot policing and targeted foot patrols. These particular approaches prioritise the areas most afflicted by crime, allocating resources to the locales that need them most. A similar logic can be applied to the cryptomarket intervention strategy proposed here. The overarching goal is to optimise the resources expended. In other words, this strategy intends to get the most bang for one's buck, targeting areas of the dark web environment where the largest possible impact can be made without compounding the problem further.

Bastions of Responsible Use

Given the aforementioned issues and questionable benefits of cryptomarket interventions, it is an open question whether law enforcement should target these markets at all. Furthermore, an extensive and long-running debate questions the harm

reduction capabilities of enforcing drug trafficking laws. Given the negative externalities created by police crackdowns on drug markets, law enforcement strategies
may aim not to eradicate drug markets but to instead reduce the potential harm
caused by the sale and consumption of illicit substances. Cryptomarkets fit neatly
within this discussion: In many ways, they represent a more viable and preferable
alternative to terrestrial markets and street dealing.

Notably, cryptomarkets serve to mitigate the negative externalities endemic to
terrestrial drug markets, especially physical violence, which is difficult to actuate on
cryptomarkets given the immateriality of the context. The anonymity and geographical dispersion afforded to cryptomarkets means that participants simply cannot
harm other actors, with the dematerialisation of voluntary economic transactions
rendering violence on cryptomarkets improbable. This has been documented in several studies (Aldridge & Décary-Hétu, 2014; Morselli et al., 2017; Van Hout &
Bingham, 2013a). One study found that cryptomarket vendors were less likely than
"street" dealers to experience violence because they mostly sold to middle-class
university students characteristically averse to violence (Mohamed & Fritsvold,
2011). Elsewhere, Barratt et al. (2016a) surveyed 3794 respondents from 57 countries on drug use and found that 1.3% and 1% of cryptomarket users had experienced "threats to personal safety" and "physical violence" compared to 14% and
6% of those who purchased from friends, 24% and 10% of those who purchased
from known dealers and 35% and 15% of those who purchased from strangers. In
general, buyers reported safer and more convenient transactions given the complete
circumvention of face-to-face meetings with potentially dangerous dealers (Barratt
et al., 2016b; Van Hout & Bingham, 2013a, b).

For Martin (2014), "cryptomarkets are displacing potentially violent drug market
norms in favour of more cordial relationships between market participants", calling
this the "gentrification hypothesis", which predicts that the safety and anonymity of
illicit online transactions precludes the use of and necessity for violence.
Cryptomarket vendors compete on the basis of reputation, relying on the quality of
their products and marketing campaigns. As Martin indicates, cryptomarket vendors
are encouraged to create a "socially constructive public image that is both free from
violence and more attuned to the perceived priorities of their customer base" (2014,
40). Creating rapport and behaving in a trustworthy manner carry more currency on
cryptomarkets than violence (even if it were an available option).

The importance of vendor reputations is entwined with the quality of the goods
and services offered on cryptomarkets. As such, consumer feedback mechanisms
serve to reward the accountability of vendors, likely increasing the quality of products on cryptomarkets compared to offline markets. According to Horton-Eddison
et al. (2021, 6), "this is important because some drug harms arise from uncertain
content and strength, thereby creating the risk of unwanted effects or overdose".
Furthermore, vendors often provide warning labels that inform buyers of the potential dangers of specific products. This allows buyers to make safer purchases, some-
thing that is less possible in the context of terrestrial markets where street dealers
are less forthcoming about their wares. Cryptomarkets may also opt to remove or

ban products that are harmful to users, with prominent examples including fentanyl, contract killings, child pornography and assault weapons.

According to Horton-Eddison et al. (2021, 7), "cryptomarket discussion forums have [also] provided a rich source of drug safety information (e.g., quality, purity, adulterants, dosing), enabling buyers and vendors alike to share information about product and batch content, and about buying and selling more safely". This information is often absent from Clearnet forums, much less offline markets. Although the information provided on cryptomarket forums is not guaranteed to be accurate, the adoption and spread of best practices on these platforms are often fostered by qualified drug harm reduction professionals, as exemplified by the case of Dr. Fernando Caudevilla, who provided expert harm reduction advice to buyers and vendors operating on the Silk Road and other dark web markets.

Although outright support for cryptomarkets by state actors is unfeasible, an argument can be made about the merits of toleration. To this end, state actors may choose to allow these platforms to operate because of their potential to offset the violence and customer harm endemic to terrestrial markets. This may involve converting illegal markets into licit markets, as demonstrated by the cases of Portugal and certain states in the United States, where specific drug markets have been legalised.

Future Research

Cryptomarkets represent a fascinating area of study for researchers interested in the intersection of cybercrime and network science. Indeed, these platforms present a novel opportunity for researchers to test the accuracy of key practical, technical and theoretical precepts. However, the dearth of research on the network structure and resilience of cryptomarkets mean more research is required in these areas. Accordingly, future research should continue to examine these topics by testing their generalisability on other markets. Several different methodological approaches might be pursued by these prospective studies. Recognising the likelihood that this book's results might have been slightly or entirely different had different techniques been used, researchers should endeavour to push the methodological boundaries of cryptomarket research with the aim of developing more efficient strategies and tactics for intervention and disruption.

Beyond these broad concerns, several specific areas require further research. According to Barratt and Aldridge (2016, 9), "we do not yet have good evidence to indicate what proportion of the population may be sourcing drugs from cryptomarkets, and whether their numbers may be increasing". Given the increasing technological sophistication of younger generations, it is also an open question whether cryptomarkets are primarily frequented by those defined as Millennials and Gen Z. Furthermore, it remains unclear why these individuals choose to purchase drugs and other illegals goods and services on the dark web rather than or in tandem with terrestrial markets.

This demands that cryptomarket scholars respond to several pressing questions: What is the role of cryptomarkets in facilitating new trends in drug use? What role, if any, have cryptomarkets played in the proliferation of fentanyl and other synthetic opioids? What is the demographic profile of those who set up and operate cryptomarkets?

Although administrators such as Ross Ulbricht have been arrested, it is unclear who exactly establishes cryptomarkets and, more importantly, what their motivations are. At the macro-level, it is worth trying to understand how migration from terrestrial markets to cryptomarket affects the incidence of violence and the well-being of cryptomarket participants. While Chap. 2's literature review makes clear that cryptomarkets reduce violence, it is unclear to what extent. This has political implications because the widespread use of cryptomarkets may encourage calls for further drug legalisation, introducing further questions: How have cryptomarkets innovated in response to law enforcement interventions? How fast were these adaptations made and how effective have they been? This particular set of questions concerns the innovative nature of cryptomarkets, and pursuing answers may help law enforcement to understand the potential outcomes of future interventions.

Although these represent some of the more pressing questions demanding the attention of cryptomarket researchers, this is not an exhaustive list, with further questions abounding. Nevertheless, it is undeniable that cryptomarkets call for inquiry from criminologists, with the increasing technologisation of crime representing a phenomenon with serious implications for the future of illicit trade.

Conclusion

Cryptomarkets represent a relatively new criminal phenomenon that offers a glimpse into the future of illicit e-commerce and criminal networks. The functional dynamics of trust and reputation within these ecosystems serve to mimic the same mechanisms in licit markets. This makes it fascinating to see criminal entities engage in corporate mimicry, adopting the mindset and practices of licit organisations. Furthermore, cryptomarkets represent the bleeding edge of organised crime by leveraging encryption and cryptographic technologies such as TOR and cryptocurrencies. This raises questions about the increasing professionalisation and upskilling of the criminal class, which affects the volume and quality of crimes and has direct consequences for the law enforcement agencies that must contend with this growing threat.

Nevertheless, law enforcement has long demonstrated an affinity for adapting to and overcoming new challenges, from both a conceptual and a technological standpoint, developing new strategies and tactics for countering the efforts of criminals. This book has sought to outline various methodological practices that offer some operational upside for law enforcement wanting to combat cryptomarkets, recognising that prior interventions have been ineffective and even counterproductive. Importantly, while these methods, findings and consequent conclusions offer some path forward for law enforcement, this is entirely contingent on whether they have been tried and tested in the field. To some extent, the concepts and methods mentioned in this book are just that. Without a rigorous empirical testing regime, these objects of inquiry will remain in a limbo state, in both theoretical and practical terms. In short, it is intended that these concepts and methods are seriously considered and their potential to offer some respite against the ever-encroaching dangers of the dark web tested.

References

Aldridge, J., & D. Décary-Hétu (2014). *Not an 'eBay for drugs': the cryptomarket 'Silk Road' as a paradigm shifting criminal innovation.* Available at SSRN.

Barratt, M., & Aldridge, J. (2016). Everything you always wanted to know about drug cryptomarkets* (*but were afraid to ask). *International Journal of Drug Policy, 35,* 1–6.

Barratt, M., Ferris, J., & Winstock, A. (2016a). Safer scoring? Cryptomarkets, social supply and drug market violence. *International Journal of Drug Policy, 35,* 24–31.

Barratt, M., Lenton, S., Maddox, A., & Allen, M. (2016b). "What if you live on top of a bakery and you like cakes?" – Drug use and harm trajectories before, during and after the emergence of Silk Road. *International Journal of Drug Policy, 35,* 50–57.

Buil-Gil, D., Zeng, Y., & Kemp, S. (2021). Offline crime bounces back to pre-COVID levels, cyber stays high: interrupted time-series analysis in Northern Ireland. *Crime Science, 10*(26), 1–16.

Caneppele, S., & Aebi, M. F. (2019). Crime drop or police recording flop? The relationship between the decrease of offline crime and the increase of online and hybrid crimes. *Policing: A Journal of Policy and Practice, 13*(1), 66–79.

Christin, N. (2013). Traveling the Silk Road: A measurement analysis of a large anonymous online marketplace. In *Proceedings of the 22nd International Conference on World Wide Web, International World Wide Web Conferences Steering Committee* (pp. 213–224).

Duxbury, S., & Haynie, D. (2017). The network structure of opioid distribution on a darknet cryptomarket. *Journal of Quantitative Criminology, 34*(4), 921–941.

Duxbury, S., & Haynie, D. (2019). Criminal network security: An agent-based approach to evaluating network resilience. *Criminology, 57*(2), 314–342.

Duxbury, S., & Haynie, D. (2020). The responsiveness of criminal networks to intentional attacks: Disrupting darknet drug trade. *Plus One, 15*(9), 1–20.

Hamid, N., & Ariza, C. (2022). *Offline versus online radicalisation: Which is the bigger threat?* Global Network on Extremism and Technology. Available at https://gnet-research.org/2022/02/21/offline-versus-online-radicalisation-which-is-the-bigger-threat/

Horton-Eddison, M., Shortis, P., Aldridge, J., & Caudevilla, F. (2021). Drug cryptomarkets in the 2020s: Policy, enforcement, harm, and resilience. *Global Drug Policy Observatory, 16,* 1–12.

Kruisbergen, E. W., Leukfeldt, E. R., Kleemans, E. R., & Roks, R. A. (2019). Money talks money laundering choices of organized crime offenders in a digital age. *Journal of Crime and Justice, 42*(5), 569–581.

Lewis, R., Rowe, M., & Wiper, C. (2019). *Online/offline continuities: Exploring misogyny and hate in online abuse of feminists.* Online othering: Exploring digital violence and discrimination on the web, 121–143.

Martin, J. (2014). *Drugs on the dark net.* Palgrave Macmillan.

Mohamed, R., & Fritsvold, E. (2011). Is the college campus a safe haven for drug dealers?: Dorm room dealers: Drugs and the privileges of race and class. *Symbolic Interaction, 34*(2), 309–311.

Morselli, C., Décary-Hétu, D., Paquet-Clouston, M., & Aldridge, J. (2017). Conflict management in illicit drug cryptomarkets. *International Criminal Justice Review, 27*(4), 237–254.

Van Hout, M., & Bingham, T. (2013a). 'Surfing the Silk Road': A study of users' experiences. *International Journal of Drug Policy, 24*, 524–529.

Van Hout, M., & Bingham, T. (2013b). 'Silk Road' The virtual drug marketplace: A single case study of user experiences. *International Journal of Drug Policy, 24*(5), 155–165.

Wang, P., Su, M., & Wang, J. (2021). Organized crime in cyberspace: How traditional organized criminal groups exploit the online peer-to-peer lending market in China. *The British Journal of Criminology, 61*(2), 303–324.

Index

The manufacturer's authorised representative in the EU is Springer
Nature Customer Service Centre GmbH, Europaplatz 3, 69115 Heidelberg,
Germany. If you have any concerns regarding our products, please
contact ProductSafety@springernature.com

Printed and bound by CPI Group (UK) Ltd, Croydon, CR0 4YY
27/04/2026
02097573-0003